PC Magazine Guide to Client/Server Databases

PC Magazine Guide to
Client/Server Databases

Joe Salemi

Ziff-Davis Press
Emeryville, California

Development Editor	Denise Penrose
Copy Editor	Kate Hoffman
Technical Reviewers	Mel Raff and Brian Butler
Project Coordinator	Sheila McGill
Proofreader	Cort Day
Cover Design	Tom Morgan/Blue Design, San Francisco
Book Design	Paper Crane Graphics, Berkeley
Screen Graphics Editor	Dan Brodnitz
Technical Illustration	Cherie Plumlee Computer Graphics & Illustration
Word Processing	Howard Blechman and Cat Haglund
Page Layout	Tony Jonick and Anna L. Marks
Indexer	Valerie Haynes Perry

This book was produced on a Macintosh IIfx, with the following applications: FrameMaker®, Microsoft® Word, MacLink®Plus, Aldus® FreeHand™, Adobe Photoshop™, and Collage Plus™.

Ziff-Davis Press
5903 Christie Avenue
Emeryville, CA 94608

ISBN 1-56276-070-X

Manufactured in the United States of America
10 9 8 7 6 5 4 3 2

To Nancy, who always believed I could do it, even when I didn't believe it myself.

■ Contents at a Glance

■ Table of Contents

Chapter 7: Client/Server Databases for Mainframes   153

■ Acknowledgments

This book is the culmination of years of experience in networks and databases, followed by months of slaving away at the PC writing and rewriting the pages you now hold in your hand. But it isn't just the product of one person—a lot of folks contributed to its contents and ideas, both before and during the process of writing it. I would be remiss if I didn't acknowledge their contributions.

First and foremost, I want to thank my wife Nancy, who was the first person besides me to read the manuscript. She used her experience as an "average PC user" to make sure that what I wrote was understandable, and always encouraged me to continue when the task seemed impossible. I also want to thank Max, my four-legged friend who was smart enough to know when I needed a break by interrupting my work for a pet or a walk.

My experience in LANs and databases covers a number of years in a number of jobs, and along the way, I met some folks who taught me things I could have never learned on my own. My thanks to Joel Brown, who first introduced me to local area networks, running databases on a network, and SQL, and to Bernie Wass and Walt Mehlferber, who helped me understand the concepts of wide area networking and interconnecting PCs with the larger systems.

I have nothing but gratitude for the folks at *PC Magazine:* Charles Petzold, who convinced me to try my hand at writing for the magazine; Trudy Neuhaus and Robin Raskin, who recognized my writing abilities before I did and turned a rank beginner into a contributing editor; Frank Derfler, who helped me become a part of *PC Magazine*'s connectivity team; and Angela Gunn, whose tireless assistance and research for many *PC Magazine* reviews provided a wealth of background information for this book.

The staff and editors at Ziff-Davis Press have been tremendously helpful in turning the raw manuscript into the product you now hold. Thanks to Cindy Hudson and Cheryl Holzaepfel for agreeing that this book was a good idea in the first place, and for helping me shape its overall form; to Mel Raff and Brian Butler, for making sure no technical errors crept in; to Kate Hoffman, for making sure the prose was tight and somewhat resembled standard English; and to Denise Penrose, whose editing made sure the whole thing was consistent and made sense, and who provided many valuable suggestions about the book's structure. I also want to thank Sheila McGill for guiding the edited manuscript through the production process, and all the graphic artists who turned my crude drawings into the wonderful figures in these pages.

Don't let anybody kid you—writing a book is a long, involved process, and just plain hard work. My eternal gratitude goes to the gang at Murphy's Pub in Alexandria, Virginia, for reminding me that there *is* life away from the computer, and for helping me retain my sense of humor.

Finally, I want to thank both the city of New Orleans and the state of Colorado for providing a refuge when I just needed to get away for a while and recharge my batteries.

Note: The original manuscript for this book was printed on recycled paper. Support the environment—it's the only one we have.

■ Introduction

In the early 1990s, computer industry luminaries such as Bill Gates, chairman and founder of Microsoft, and Steve Jobs, chairman and founder of NeXT Computers and cofounder of Apple, predicted that Client/Server computing would be the "hot" technology of the 1990s. This book is certainly proof that I agree with that sentiment. PCs and PC-based LANs have matured and become stable technologies for important business applications, and Client/Server computing is the next logical step for harnessing the increasing power of these desktop systems and networks.

Like many people, you may be exploring the capabilities of Client/Server systems, trying to determine if this technology can benefit your business. Along the way, you'll face a bewildering array of vendor claims and counterclaims, traditional versus advanced hardware technologies, and products that are marketed too well or barely marketed at all. The Client/Server market is a mine field for the unwary, and unfortunately no single source of information describes the technology itself and the variety of products available—until now.

■ Who Is This Book For?

This book is designed as a guide for navigating through the Client/Server market. It's written for the business managers, information system managers, technical support personnel, and application developers whose bosses complained, "OK, now that we've spent all this money on LANs—what the heck do we do with them?" While the casual PC or database user may benefit from the information presented here, the very nature of the technology assumes that those who are considering a move toward the Client/Server architecture are already familiar with some of the basic concepts of database design and computer networking.

■ A Quick Tour of the Contents

You may be tempted to skip over the first three chapters and dive into the chapters that cover specific products. But I urge you not to. These first chapters cover concepts essential to a complete understanding of the capabilities and features of systems addressed throughout the book.

Chapter 1 presents a broad overview of the current database technology, including the different types, models, architectures, and programming languages available. Chapter 2 begins the discussion of the Client/Server technology and covers the foundation of the architecture, the types of systems it runs on, and the networking and communications needed to create a Client/Server system. Chapter 3 explains and shows you how to use the Decision Tree that's bound into the back of this book. The Decision Tree is a map designed to guide you through the basic questions that will help you identify which systems and products may meet your needs and which direction to move in next.

Chapters 4 through 7 describe the products available for each of the four major Client/Server platforms: PCs, RISC and UNIX systems, minicomputers, and mainframes. Each chapter opens with an overview of the products and the platform, discussing their advantages and disadvantages, things to consider before deciding to base your system on the platform, and some advice and tips that I and my colleagues have gathered from years of experience. The balance of each chapter examines the particular products that run on the platform, including information about their features, hardware and software requirements, native languages, and the front-ends provided. Each section closes with a discussion of the product's advantages, disadvantages, my recommendations, and a chart that summarizes its primary features. Bear in mind that the Client/Server market is rapidly evolving; many of the features listed (especially prices) will change over time.

Chapter 8 provides an overview of some of the client (front-end) applications available for accessing data stored in a Client/Server database, with emphasis on PC-based clients. It describes how front-ends work, identifies the different types available, and offers tips on choosing the right one for your needs. The chapter closes with a chart that links front-end applications with the particular databases they support.

Chapter 9 considers the future of database technologies. The opinions in this chapter are my own; however, I hope you'll find them useful as a starting point for your own explorations of where the technology is going and how it will affect your long-term plans.

The remainder of the book contains a glossary of the terms used throughout the book and three appendices. Appendix A brings together the quick summary charts of all the products in Chapters 4 through 7 to make it easy to compare the many products and platforms described in these chapters. In Appendix B, you'll find the names, addresses, and phone numbers for all the vendors covered in the book, along with their products. The Client/Server field combines several different technologies, and no one book can cover all of them, so Appendix C offers some suggestions for further reading about databases, SQL, and networks.

It's my sincere hope that you will find this book a useful guide to Client/Server databases. Use it as a reference point and foundation for your own explorations of this exciting and revolutionary technology.

- *What Is a DBMS?*

- *DBMS Models*

- *DBMS System Architectures*

- *Database Application Programming Languages*

An Overview of Database Management Systems

COMPUTERS ARE DESIGNED TO MANIPULATE INFORMATION IN THE form of data—but to a computer, data is nothing more than random bits of electricity. We give structure and meaning to the data we put into our computers through the use of data files, which contain numbers, text, or both. These data files are accessed by familiar applications such as spreadsheets, word processing programs, and databases.

A *database system* gives us a way of gathering together specific pieces or lists of information that are relevant to us in our jobs or our lives. It also provides a way to store and maintain that information in a central place. The first commercial computers were really nothing more than dedicated database machines used to gather, sort, and report on census information. To this day, one of the most common reasons for purchasing a computer is to run a database system.

A database system consists of two parts: the *Database Management System* (DBMS), which is the program that organizes and maintains these lists of information, and the *database application*, a program that lets us retrieve, view, and update the information stored by the DBMS. Databases are everywhere: a company's personnel system (the application) written in dBASE (the DBMS) on a PC; an inventory system (application) of the parts in a warehouse maintained in Rdb/VMS (DBMS) on a DEC VAX; or patient records (application) stored in DB2 (DBMS) on an IBM mainframe.

It's common for both the DBMS and the database application to reside and execute on the same computer; in many cases the two are combined in the same program. Most of the database systems available today are designed this way. However, a lot of attention is now focused on one of the latest stages in the evolution of DBMS technology—*Client/Server* (C/S) database technology.

A Client/Server database increases database processing power by separating the DBMS from the database application. The application runs on one or more user workstations (which are usually PCs) and communicates over a network with one or more DBMSs running on other computers. C/S Database Systems make the best use of today's powerful computers, and they can also be very complex. In order to fully understand how they function, and the advantages and disadvantages of the many different types available, we will first explore the historical evolution of methods of storing, accessing, and manipulating data. Along the way, we'll encounter many terms that are either specific to the world of databases or used in ways that conflict with how they're used elsewhere.

This chapter covers the basic terms used to describe what a database is, the different methods of storing the data, and the many ways of accessing and manipulating the data. I'll be defining these terms as we go along, and they'll also be covered in the glossary. Later chapters will cover the theory and practice of Client/Server databases, what's needed to set one up, and the specific C/S systems available.

◼ What Is a DBMS?

The data stored in a database can be thought of as a *population* of information. When used this way, population doesn't just describe a group of people that live in the same geographical area; it means any group or class of items or objects that we can define. When we create a database, the population we're interested in is the specific one we need to keep track of, which becomes the foundation of the database. For example, the populations of the previously mentioned database examples are the employees of the Acme Submarine Company, the parts in the company's warehouse, or the patients in FeelGood Hospital.

As Figure 1.1 demonstrates, the population of Acme Submarine's personnel database is the company's employees; each *record* in the database stores the information about one member of this population. The *fields* in each record store important details about that member. In Figure 1.1, a single record contains four fields of information (First Name, Last Name, Social Security Number, and Salary) for each member of the population.

Figure 1.1

The elements of a database

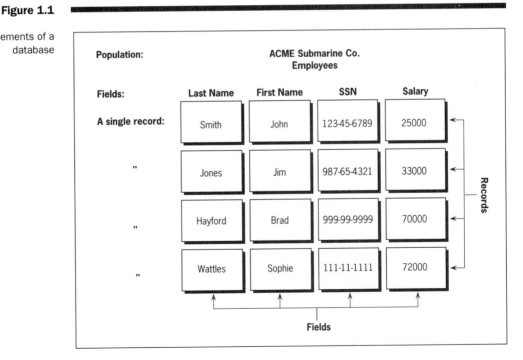

In order to store the population of data on a disk the DBMS has to provide some type of data definition services to define the records and fields in the database. It also needs an internal mechanism that maintains the data on disk and knows where each particular element resides.

Of course, we want to do more than just store data; we also need a way to enter or insert data into the database, sort it, retrieve all or portions of it, and maintain it by adding, updating or deleting records from the database. The DBMS is responsible for providing some or all of these data manipulation services to the user.

We also need a way to display the data, either on a terminal or PC screen, or as a printed report. The DBMS may provide these display services, or they may be provided by the database application. If the DBMS doesn't provide any of these services, it's commonly referred to as a *database engine*.

However, just having the data on disk and getting it back when we want it isn't any good if we can't trust that the data is accurate. The DBMS has to provide some type of *data integrity* services to ensure that the data isn't corrupted through outside means, such as disk crashes or power outages. It also has the more difficult job of protecting the database against unintentional changes caused by users or applications. These services are particularly important for *multiuser databases*, in which one or more users can be updating the same data at the same time. The DBMS has to make sure that only one of the changes actually takes place, and it should notify other users about the change made.

A database can store any type of information that the user wants, but to be useful, the data has to be stored according to its *domain*. A domain is the category and type of data elements allowed in a particular field—for example, a set of alphabetical (text) characters, all the words in the English language, or only integers. A domain is usually represented as a set and can also be restricted to only a certain portion of a set, such as positive integers between 1 and 20. Various programming techniques can even use *data lookups* from another database or file to restrict a field's domain to something as precise as only the street names within a particular city. Table 1.1 outlines some possible domains of the fields in the sample employee database.

Responsibility for ensuring that the data entered fits the field's domain is a data integrity service that can be left entirely up to the DBMS or can be split between the user application and the DBMS. Overall, providing this service is the most important job a DBMS can have; the more responsibility it has for providing it, the better the data integrity of the whole database system.

To pull it all together, a Database Management System (DBMS) provides the following services:

- *Data definition* provides a method of defining and storing a data population.

- *Data maintenance* maintains the population using a record for each item in the population, with fields containing particular information that describes that item.

- *Data manipulation* provides services that let the user insert, update, delete, and sort data in the database.

- *Data display* optionally provides some method of displaying the data for the user.

- *Data integrity* provides one or more methods of ensuring that the data is accurate.

Table 1.1

The Domains in the Sample Employee Database

FIELD NAME	DOMAIN
Last Name	[A...Z,a...z,-] Upper- and lowercase letters, and the hyphen; or, all names containing only these elements.
First Name	[A...Z,a...z] Upper- and lowercase letters only; or, all names containing only these elements.
Middle Initial	[A...Z,.] Uppercase letters and the period.
SS Number	[0...9,-] Integers and the hyphen; or numbers in the "999-99-9999" format.
Salary	["0.00"..."99,999.99"] Positive decimal numbers between 0 and 99,999.99.

■ DBMS Models

The Database Management Systems available today can be grouped into four different types, or as they're commonly called, models: the File Management System, Hierarchical Database System, Network Database System, and Relational Database Model. Each database model is a conceptual description of how the database works. Specifically, it describes how the data is presented to the user and programmer for access.

A database model also describes the relationships between different items; for example, in the sample employee database each item of information, such as salary or Social Security number, is related to the particular employee that the whole record describes. That particular employee's record may also be related to other items in the database, such as the employee's supervisor or department. Note that the relations between the different data items are separate and distinct from the Relational Database Model described later in this chapter—this is one of those circumstances where meaning depends on context.

With the one exception addressed below, the database models don't describe how data is stored on disk. These details are worked out by the designers of the DBMS. However, in some circumstances, a model may indirectly place constraints on how the data is stored if the DBMS is to meet all the requirements that comprise that particular model. These constraints (where applicable) are covered in the descriptions of the models that follow.

It's interesting to note that historically, the Relational model was the first description of a database model to precede development of such a DBMS; the other three models were defined after the fact to describe database systems that had already been in use for several years. The actual evolution of these database systems followed the path from File Management to Hierarchical to Network to Relational.

File Management Systems

The File Management System (FMS) is the easiest database model to understand, and it is the only one that describes how the data is stored on disk. In the FMS model, each field or data item is stored sequentially on disk in one large file. As with a word processing program, in order to find a particular element (word), the application starts at the beginning and checks each item until it finds a match.

The File Management System was the first method used to store data in a computerized database, and simplicity is its only advantage. Today, about the only DBMS products built on this model are the low-end, "flat-file" databases, such as Borland's *Reflex*. Figure 1.2 demonstrates how the sample employee database would look if it were stored on disk in an FMS database.

When you look at Figure 1.2, the disadvantages of the FMS become clear. First, there's no indication of the relationship between the various items other than the storage sequence. The programmer, and sometimes the user, has to know exactly how the data is stored in the file in order to manipulate it.

This complicates the task of data access by requiring knowledge of how the computer's operating system physically stores the data on disk. There's too much room for error when these details have to be handled by each application that accesses the database.

Second, the FMS creates problems with data integrity; all field values have to be checked by the application program prior to being stored on disk. The same database can be accessed by different applications, and each one can allow slightly different values for each field. The different applications have to be manually coordinated to ensure that they're defining each field's domain in the same way.

Figure 1.2

The File Management
System model

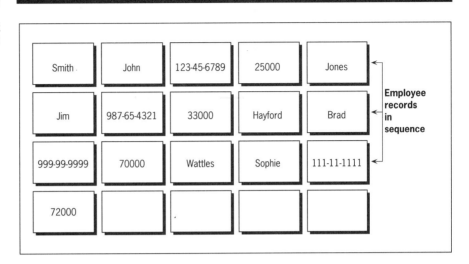

Third, there's no way to find a particular employee's record quickly; every search starts from the beginning of the file, examining each and every record. At best the DBMS can keep a *pointer* (a logical or physical indicator on the disk) to the last data item retrieved, so that searches for more occurrences of the same data type don't have to start again from the beginning of the file.

In addition, the only way to sort the data is by reading the entire file and rewriting it in the new order. This can be solved through the use of an *index file*—a subset of the data file based on one or more fields—that contains pointers to each record in the database. Index files can also quicken searches; however, they add a level of complexity to the database and must be constantly updated as the database changes.

Finally, the biggest disadvantage of the FMS is that it doesn't allow easy changes to the database structure. For example, adding the department name to each employee's record would require the DBMS to read each record, write it to a temporary file, and add the new information after the last field of each record. After scanning the whole file and writing the new one, it would delete the original file and rename the temporary file. This whole procedure occurs even if the programmer simply wants to change the size of a field to store more data. The system overhead involved in making structural changes is enormous, opening many opportunities for errors which might corrupt the entire database.

The need for a better way to describe *one-to-many relationships* among different records, as well as an easier and faster way to conduct searches, led to the development of the next database model, the Hierarchical Database System.

Hierarchical Database Systems

The next logical development in database models is the Hierarchical Database System (HDS). In this model, data is organized in a tree structure that originates from a *root*. Each class of data is located at different levels along a particular branch that stems from the root. The data structure at each class level is called a *node*; if no further branches follow, the last node in the series is considered a *leaf*.

The diagram of an HDS structure presented in Figure 1.3 resembles something that's familiar to just about all of us—the ubiquitous organization chart. In database terms, the tree structure of the HDS defines the *"parent-child"* and *"sibling"* relationships between the various items in our database, and it clearly shows the advantages over the File Management System model for defining one-to-many relationships. It also demonstrates how the hierarchical structure makes it easier, and faster, to search for data; for example, if a user wants to find the information that's in field 1B1, the DBMS doesn't have to search the entire file to find the data it wants. It examines the request, breaks it down into its components, and follows the B branch down to 1B, and then down one more level to the 1B1 field. As in the FMS, an index can be used to speed up searches even further, though in the case of a Hierarchical DBMS, the index would be on a particular class (level) of data instead.

Figure 1.3

The Hierarchical
Database System model

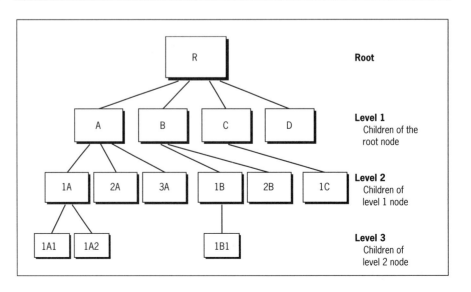

In an HDS, there's always one and only one *root node*, which is usually "owned" by the system or DBMS. Pointers from the root lead down to the level 1 nodes (the children of the root node), where the real database begins. The level 1 nodes represent a particular class of data—in our sample database, that class could be the departments in the Acme Submarine Company (Figure 1.4). Each level 1 node can have one or more level 2 children, which would represent the employees assigned to each department (identified by a unique identifier, such as their SSN). The children of the employee identifier class would then consist of the fields that contain the information about individual employees. In Figure 1.4, the structure of the level 3 nodes differs slightly from Figure 1.3 in order to show the sibling relationship between the different fields. The path between level 3 fields consists of a chain of pointers from one leaf node to the next; for example, from last name to first name to salary. Any or all of the different levels in an HDS can be clearly diagrammed with such a path. Also note that in this model, each child can have pointers to numerous siblings, but only one pointer to the parent, preserving the one-to-many relationship in a single direction.

Figure 1.4

A sample employee database in the HDS model

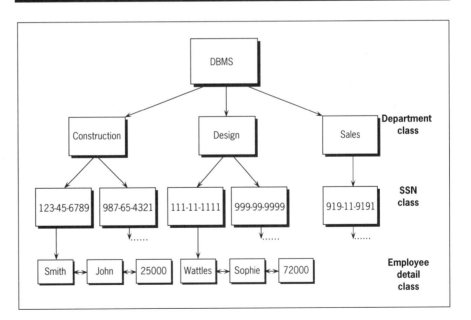

The physical structure of the data on the disk doesn't matter under the HDS model; the DBMS can (and usually does) store the data as a linked list of fields, with pointers that go from parent to child and from sibling to sibling, ending in a null or *terminal pointer* at the last leaf. It quickly becomes obvious that this design makes it easy to add new fields at any level, as the DBMS only has to change the terminal pointer to point to the next sibling node in the list. On the other hand, the HDS diagram doesn't quite show which fields comprise a particular record. For convenience, we can define a record as a parent and all its children; in the sample database, each employee's record starts at the SSN class level and includes all the leaves that describe that employee. However, we can also start the record at the department class level and define a record as all the information about the employees in that department. While this model provides a great deal of flexibility, it's not without its drawbacks.

The first problem arises from the initial structure of the database, which is arbitrary and must be defined by the programmer when the database is created. From that point on, the parent-child relationship can't be changed without redesigning the whole structure. Continuing with our example, suppose that Acme decides to open a branch office and moves the sales division to it. The database must now have another level between the root and the department class that contains the office identifiers. In order to make this change, the programmer must first create an entirely new structure to identify the new parent-child relationships, and then copy the data over from the original database to the proper locations in the new one.

Alternatively, the programmer could also simply add another field to each of the employees' records to identify their office assignments. However, adding an office field duplicates data, which wastes disk space. It also results in slowing a search for all the employees assigned to a particular office, since every branch has to be searched to the last leaf to check for the office identifiers.

Another problem created by the rigidity of the HDS structure is that it's not easy to change the definition of the class levels. Suppose the company decides to use employee numbers instead of Social Security numbers to identify each employee; the programmer would have to recreate the structure with the new employee number class replacing the SSN class, and then move the SSN information to the employee detail level.

The most significant drawback to the Hierarchical Database System model is that it provides no easy method of defining cross or many-to-many relationships. An example of a *cross-relationship* is when an employee is also a manager; in order to identify which employees report to which supervisors, the database would have to incorporate another level between the department name and the Social Security numbers to contain an identifier for every manager. Since each manager is also an employee under that department, this would create the slightly illogical situation in which a parent-child relationship exists between a manager and herself. Taking another approach, each employee's record could contain a field that identifies that employee's manager—but this method is inefficient, due to the duplication and slow search problems mentioned earlier.

The *many-to-many relationship* problem would also arise in an inventory database that (for example) tracked the parts of Acme's submarines and the suppliers of those parts. It's entirely possible that more than one vendor sells the same part and that the same vendor also sells different classes of parts. Under the Hierarchical model, the common solution to this problem is the highly inefficient one of storing multiple copies of the same data at multiple levels.

Another approach to solving the many-to-many relationship problem is adding secondary parent-child and sibling pointers to the hierarchical structure. This method creates numerous circular relationships; as these relationships become more complex, the database architecture gradually evolves into the next model.

Network Database Systems

Though the concepts behind the Network Database System model originated in the 1960s, the first written specifications were released in 1971 by the Conference on Data System Languages (CODASYL). DBMSs based on the Network model are still sometimes referred to as CODASYL databases. Note, however, that the name "network" has nothing to do with the physical medium that the database actually runs on—the Network model conceptually describes databases in which many-to-many (multiple parent-child) relationships exist. The relationships between the different data items are commonly referred to as "sets" to distinguish them from the strictly parent-child relationships defined by the Hierarchical model.

A Network Database System (NDS) relies on either straight-line or cyclical pointers to map out the relationships between the different data items. Take the example of Acme Submarine Company's inventory database; in many cases, Acme deals with multiple vendors that sell the same product. Figure 1.5 illustrates a simple straight-line form of an NDS inventory, showing the various relationships between parts and suppliers. An Acme manager can find out who sells propellers by having the DBMS search the parts set and then following the pointers back to the two vendors that supply them. Conversely, if this manager wants to know what Acme buys from Santa Fe Office Supplies, the DBMS can search the vendor set and follow the pointers from Santa Fe to the two items that they sell. This approach is very flexible, as the DBMS can also treat the combination of a particular vendor and the parts the vendor sells as a purchase set, as shown in Figure 1.5 by the circle around Mason's Metal Works and the rivets and propellers they sell.

The Network model can be used to describe even more complex relationships, as shown in Figure 1.6. Suppose an Acme manager wants to know not only who sells a particular part, but what they charge for it. Through the addition of a set called "prices," the DBMS can now trace a cyclical pattern from vendor to part to price. Again, the search can start at any of the defined sets. The Acme manager can decide that they need more rivets, and then can follow the pointers around to the vendor and to the price the vendor charges (or conversely, to the price and then the vendor who sells it at that price).

Figure 1.5

A simple Network
Database System model

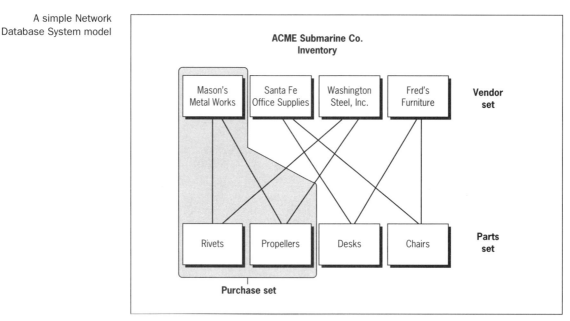

The flexibility of the Network Database System model in showing many-to-many relationships is its greatest strength, though that flexibility comes at a price. The interrelationships between the different sets can become extremely complex and difficult to map out. (Imagine Figure 1.6 with a hundred vendors, thousands of different parts, and multiple price ranges based on the quantity purchased.) This can become a severe problem, as most NDS databases require the programmer to write the application code that traces out the different data paths. Like Hierarchical databases, Network databases can be very fast, especially through the use of index pointers that lead directly to the first item in a set being searched. The NDS also goes a long way toward eliminating duplicated data.

However, the Network model also suffers from the same structural problems mentioned in the description of the HDS. The initial design of the database is arbitrary. Once it's set up, any changes to the different sets require the programmer to create an entirely new structure. The NDS does make it simpler to add new data items to the database or to change existing ones.

The programmer only has to define a new set and adjust the various pointers to put the new set in the proper relationship with the rest of the data.

Figure 1.6

A complex Network
Database System model

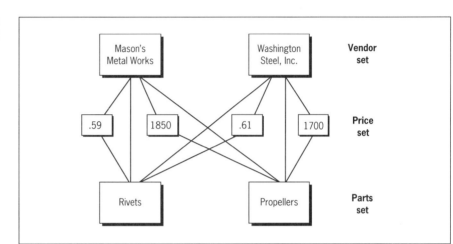

You'll have noticed by now that the descriptions of the previous three database models have constantly referred to the "relationship" between the different data items in the database. Thinking about the relationships between data led one IBM scientist to create an entirely different model for database design, the Relational Database Model.

Relational Database Models

In 1969, Dr. E. F. Codd published the first paper to define a model for databases based on the mathematical concept of relational sets. The Relational Database Model (RDM) has been constantly refined since then, most notably in Dr. Codd's 1985 paper that laid out the "12 Rules" for relational databases, and in his 1990 book that defines Version 2 (RV/2) of the Relational model through 333 rules that are subsets and expansions of the original 12.

The Relational model abandons the concept of parent-child relationships between different data items. Instead, the data is organized in logical mathematical sets in a tabular structure. In a RDM, each data field becomes a column in a table, and each record becomes a row in the table. Figure 1.7 shows the Acme inventory database arranged in relational form. Notice that the different sets under the complex Network model here become different tables that identify the particular data items by the column names in the first row. All the vendors are grouped in one table, the parts and prices in other tables. Different relationships between the various tables are defined through the use of the mathematical set functions, such as JOIN and UNION.

Figure 1.7

The Relational Database Model

VENDORS

V#	Vendor_Name	Contact
M1	Mason's Metal Works	Nigel Mason
S1	Santa Fe Office Supplies	Mike Michaels
W1	Washington Steel Inc.	Jane Austin
F1	Fred's Furniture	Fred Johnson

PARTS

P#	Part_Description	V#
1001	Rivets	M1
5204	Desks	S1
3333	Propellers	W1
3333	Propellers	M1
5210	Chairs	F1
5204	Desks	F1
1001	Rivets	W1
5210	Chairs	S1

PRICES

P#	V#	Price	Min_Quan
1001	M1	0.59	10
1001	M1	0.61	1
3333	W1	1700.00	1
3333	M1	1850.00	1
1001	W1	0.61	1

You'll notice that each table has one or more columns with the same name as that in another table. It's these common column names that are used to relate the different tables; however, the column names don't have to be identical in the Relational model, so long as the data in the common columns is of the same type and in the same domain.

In order to find a particular part from a particular vendor, the DBMS searches the PARTS table for the part name, finds the vendor number in the V# column and relates it to the similar data in the V# column in the VENDORS table to find the vendor's name and contact person. To find the price of the item, the P# and V# columns in the PARTS table are related to the same-named columns in the PRICES table. These separate relationships can also be combined: A user can ask the DBMS to display the vendor, part name, price, and minimum quantity at that price, and the DBMS will look up both relations described previously and display the information.

The Relational model has a number of clear advantages over the Hierarchical and Network models, the most important of which is its complete flexibility in describing the relationships between the various data items. The programmer defines the database by creating the tables and deciding which columns the tables will be related on. From that point on, users can query the database on any of the individual columns in a table or on the relationships between the different tables. Changing the structure of the database is as simple as adding or deleting columns from a table, which doesn't affect the other tables in any way. New tables can be created from scratch or as projections (subsets) of existing tables, and old tables can be removed at will. Not having to rebuild the entire database structure to make changes also represents an increase in the preservation of data integrity.

The major decision for a Relational database designer is the table definitions. The process of breaking down the data to be stored into subsets for the tables is called *normalization*. While the concepts behind normalization are beyond the scope of this book, in simple terms the RDM defines four levels of normalization, in which each level reduces the complexity of the structure of the previous level and also reduces the amount of duplicated data in the database. For an example of normalization, look at the PARTS table in Figure 1.7. You'll notice that even though the P# and Part Description columns contain some duplicated information, each row of data is unique because the values in the V# column are different for each row. This table can be taken to the next level of normalization by splitting up the V# column into multiple columns, as shown in Figure 1.8. This reduces the amount of space required to store the parts information even further (though it slightly increases the amount of storage needed for the PRICES table, as the V# column has to be replaced with V1 and V2). It's important to note that these changes in no way affect the data or structure of the VENDORS table.

Figure 1.8

The PARTS table after further normalization

PARTS			
P#	Part_Description	V1	V2
1001	Rivets	M1	W1
5204	Desks	S1	F1
3333	Propellers	W1	M1
5210	Chairs	F1	S1

In a properly designed Relational DBMS, the information on the structures that comprise the database is held in a separate set of tables, commonly called the *system tables* or *database dictionary*. This information consists of data elements such as the names of the database's tables, the names of the columns in those tables, and the type of data stored in each column. The DBMS treats these system tables just like any other data tables, so the programmer can query them to find out the names of the tables in a database or the names of the columns in each table.

The primary goal of the Relational Database Model is to preserve data integrity. To be considered truly relational, a DBMS must completely prevent access to the data by any means other than queries handled by the DBMS itself. While the Relational model (like the Hierarchical and Network models) says nothing about how the data is stored on the disk, the preservation of data integrity implies that the data must be stored in a format that prevents it from being accessed from outside the DBMS that created it.

The Relational model also requires that the data be accessed through programs that don't rely on the position of the data in the database. This is in direct contrast to the other database models, where the program has to follow a series of pointers to the data it seeks. A program querying a Relational database simply asks for the data it seeks; the DBMS performs the necessary searches and provides the information. The details on how the search is done are specific to the DBMS and vary from product to product. Searches can be sped up by creating an index on one or more columns in a table; however, the index is again under the control and use of the DBMS. The programmer simply asks the DBMS to create the index, and the index will be maintained and used automatically from that point on.

The emphasis on data integrity makes the Relational model ideal for transaction processing systems, and thus for Client/Server databases. In the other database models, changes have to be made directly to the data itself, which can cause conflicts when multiple users are updating the same records. A Relational DBMS treats every change (or group of changes) to the data as a transaction, which it executes on a temporary copy of the table being altered. Changes don't become permanent until the user or application commits the change to the database itself. Under this system, the DBMS itself controls conflicting changes to the data and can arbitrate between them. The disadvantage comes in the form of increased system and computational overhead; a trade-off is made between speedy access to the data and assurance that the data is accurate.

Until recently, the extra overhead involved in running a Relational DBMS meant such databases were only run on the largest mainframe and minicomputers. This lead to the phenomena of a number of DBMS packages (particularly those designed for PCs) implementing only portions of the Relational model. These databases, now known as semirelational databases, trade off portions of the model for increased speed or better data access by the programmer. It's only since 1987, with the increase in PCs based on the powerful Intel 80386 and 80486 CPUs, that DBMSs which more closely adhere to the Relational model have moved down to microcomputers. This move of relational databases to microcomputers has led to the development of Client/Server systems, which are the subject of the rest of this book.

■ DBMS System Architectures

The type of computer systems that databases run on can be broken down into four broad categories or platforms: centralized, PC, Client/Server, and distributed. The four differ the most in where the actual data processing occurs. The architecture of the DBMS itself doesn't necessarily determine the type of computer system that the database has to run on, though certain architectures are more suited (or more common) to some platforms than others.

Centralized Platforms

In a centralized system, all programs run on a main "host" computer, including the DBMS, the applications that access the database, and the communications facilities that send and receive data from the users' terminals.

The users access the database through either locally connected or dial-up (remote) terminals, as shown in Figure 1.9. The terminals are generally "dumb," having little or no processing power of their own, and consist of only a screen, keyboard, and hardware to communicate with the host. The advent of microprocessors has led to the development of more intelligent terminals in recent years, where the terminal shares some of the responsibility for handling screen drawing and user input. While mainframe and minicomputer systems are the primary platform for large corporate database systems, PC-based systems can also communicate with centralized systems through hardware/software combinations that emulate (imitate) the terminal types used with a particular host.

All the data processing in a centralized system takes place on the host computer, and the DBMS must be running before any database applications can access the database. When a user first turns on a terminal, he usually sees a log-in screen; the user enters a log-on ID and password to gain access to the host's applications. When the database application starts up, it sends the appropriate screen information "down the wire" to the user's terminal and responds with different actions based on the user's subsequent keystrokes. The application and the DBMS, both running on the same host, communicate through shared memory areas or application task areas that are managed by the host's operating system. The DBMS is responsible for moving the data to and from the disk storage systems, using the services provided by the operating system. Figure 1.10 represents one possible way these applications interact: The applications communicate with the users at the terminals and with the DBMS; the DBMS communicates with the storage devices (which may be, but aren't limited to, hard disks) and with the applications.

Figure 1.9

A typical centralized
database system

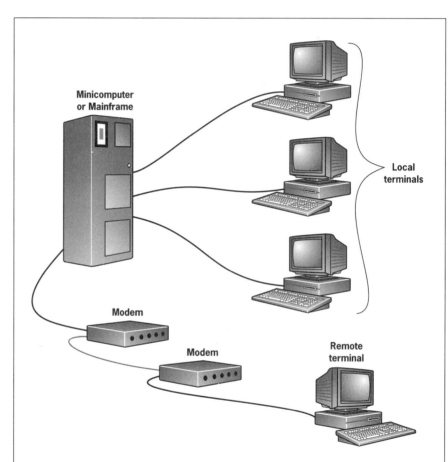

The DBMS that runs on the host system can be based on any of the four models, though the Hierarchical and Relational models are the most common. On mainframes, the DBMS is usually based on IBM's IMS, a Hierarchical database. In recent years, however, more and more mainframes are running DBMSs based on the Relational model, most notably IBM's DB2.

Minicomputers are the traditional home of DBMSs based on the Network model, databases such as the early DBMS-10 from Digital Equipment Corporation (DEC), the Image/1000 and Image/3000 from Hewlett-Packard

(HP), and the UNIFY DBMS from Unify Corporation. Since the early 1980s, a number of companies have produced Relational databases that run on minicomputers (under either UNIX or DEC's VAX/VMS), databases such as INGRES from Ingres Corporation, Rdb/VMS from DEC, and ORACLE from Oracle Corporation.

Figure 1.10

Database processing on a centralized system

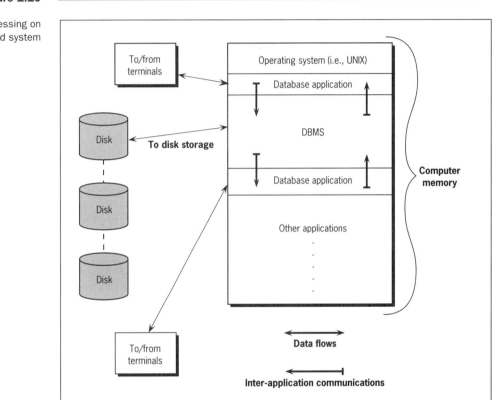

The principal advantages of a centralized system are centralized security and the ability to handle enormous amounts of data on storage devices. Centralized systems can also support numerous simultaneous users; it's not uncommon for a database on an IBM mainframe to support over 1,000 users at once. The disadvantages are generally related to the costs of purchasing and maintaining these systems. Large mainframe and large minicomputer systems require specialized support facilities, such as the fairly common data center with raised floors, water-cooling systems, and very large climate-control systems. A highly trained staff of operators and system programmers is usually necessary to keep the system up and running, which adds considerable personnel costs. Finally, the purchase price of hardware for large centralized systems often runs well into the millions of dollars, and maintenance costs run high as well.

In recent years, companies have increasingly opted for department-sized minicomputers, such as DEC's MicroVAX and IBM'S AS/400, which don't cost as much to purchase or support as centralized systems, and generally don't require a special environment to run in. These systems are best suited for smaller companies with fewer users (not more than 200) or for database applications that are of interest to only one particular department in a large company (that is, a minicomputer that runs engineering applications may only be of interest to a design department). These smaller computers may also be networked to other minicomputers and mainframes, so that all the computers can share data. These "distributed" systems will be covered later in this chapter.

Personal Computer Systems

Personal computers (PCs) first emerged in the late 1970s and began a revolution in how we view and use computers. One of the earliest successful operating systems for PCs was Digital Research's CP/M (Control Program for Microcomputers). The first successful PC-based DBMS, Ashton-Tate's dBASE II, ran under CP/M. When IBM released the first MS-DOS–based PC in 1981, Ashton-Tate ported dBASE over to the new operating system. dBASE has since spawned newer versions, compatibles and look-alikes, and competing DBMSs that have proven to the data processing community that PCs can perform many of the same tasks that the large systems do.

When a DBMS is run on a PC, the PC acts as both the host computer and the terminal. Unlike the larger systems, the DBMS functions and the database application functions are combined into one application. Database applications on a PC handle the user input, screen output, and access to the data on the disk. Combining these different functions into one unit gives the DBMS a great deal of power, flexibility, and speed, though usually at the cost of decreased data security and integrity.

PCs originated as stand-alone systems; however, in recent years many have been connected to Local Area Networks (LANs). In a LAN, the data and usually the user applications reside on the File Server, a PC running a special Network Operating System (NOS) such as Novell's NetWare or Microsoft's LAN Manager. The File Server manages the LAN users' shared access to data on its hard disks and frequently provides access to other shared resources, such as printers.

While a LAN enables users of PC-based databases to share common data files, it doesn't significantly change how the DBMS works; all the actual data processing is still performed on the PC running the database application. The

File Server only searches its disks for the data needed by the user and sends that data across the network cable to the user's PC. The data is then processed by the DBMS running on the PC, and any changes to the database require the PC to send the whole data file back to the File Server to be stored again on disk. This exchange is shown in Figure 1.11. Though multiuser access to shared data is a plus, the most significant disadvantage of a LAN-based DBMS is that regardless of how fast or powerful the File Server is, its performance is limited by the power of the PC running the actual DBMS. When multiple users are accessing the database, the same data files have to be sent from the File Server to every PC accessing them; this increased traffic can cause the network to slow down.

Figure 1.11

A database on a
PC-based LAN

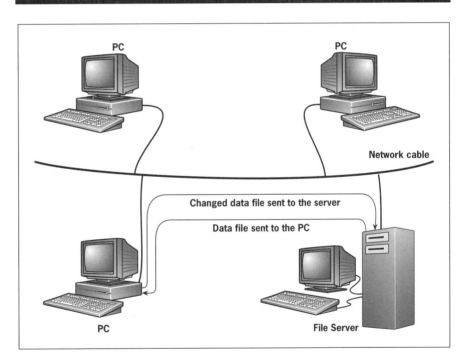

The only enhancement needed by a multiuser DBMS over a single-user one is the ability to handle simultaneous changes to the data by multiple users. This is usually accomplished by some type of locking scheme, in which the record or data file that a user is updating or changing is locked to prevent other users from also changing it. Most LAN-based DBMSs available today are simply multiuser versions of common stand-alone database systems, though the types of locking schemes vary widely and can significantly affect the performance of a multiuser database.

The majority of PC-based DBMSs are designed on the Relational model, though the fact that the DBMS isn't separated from the database application means that many (if not most) of the relational principles aren't implemented. The most notable missing components are those that address data integrity. Most PC databases allow direct access to the data files outside of the DBMS that created them. This creates a situation in which changes can be made to the data files that violate the rules by which the database application ensures data integrity. Such a violation can even cause the data file to be unreadable by the DBMS. For this reason, PC databases based on the Relational model are more accurately described as semirelational. Some of the more common semirelational PC databases available today include Microrim's R:Base, Borland's dBASE IV (Borland acquired Ashton-Tate in late 1991) and its many "clones" such as Micrsoft's FoxPro, Borland's Paradox, DataEase International's DataEase, and Revelation Technologies's Advanced Revelation.

As mentioned previously, the more limited flat-file PC databases are commonly based on the File Management System model. There are also PC-based DBMSs that derive from the Network model, such as Data Access Corporation's DataFlex and Raima Corporation's db_Vista III.

Most PC-based multiuser database systems handle the same number of users as the smaller centralized systems. However, the problems of handling multiple simultaneous transactions and increased network traffic, and the limits to the processing power of the PCs running the DBMS cause increasing complexity and performance degradation as the number of users multiplies. The solution that was developed for these limitations is the Client/Server Database System.

Client/Server Databases

In its simplest form, a Client/Server (C/S) database splits the database processing between two systems: the client PC which runs the database application, and the database server which runs all or part of the actual DBMS. The LAN File Server continues to provide shared resources, such as disk space for applications, and printers. The database server can run on the same PC as the File Server, or (as is more common) on its own PC. The database application on the client PC, referred to as the *front-end system*, handles all the screen and user input/output processing. The *back-end system* on the database server handles data processing and disk access. For example, a user on the front-end creates a request (query) for data from the database server, and the front-end application sends the request across the network to the server. The database server performs the actual search and sends back only the data that answers the user's query, as shown in Figure 1.12.

Figure 1.12

A Client/Server system

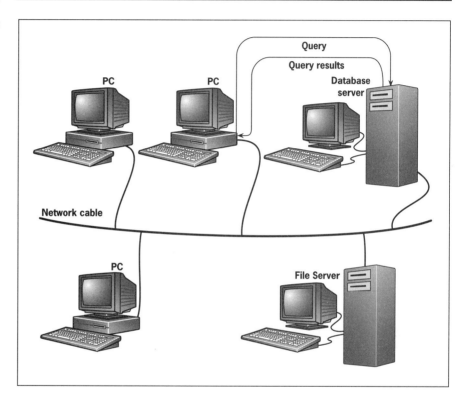

The immediate advantage of a C/S system is obvious; splitting the processing between two systems reduces the amount of data traffic on the network cable. Chapter 2 will discuss the other advantages (and disadvantages) of Client/Server systems and will describe the system architecture in more detail. Typical platforms for C/S systems will also be discussed.

In one of the typically confusing cases of different meanings for the same term that we sometimes encounter in the computer field, the definition of Client/Server is apparently reversed on UNIX-based systems running the graphical interface X-Windows. The split in processing is the same as on a PC-based C/S system; however, the front-end is called the server under X-Windows, as it provides the display and user interface services. The back-end system, on which the DBMS runs, is referred to as the client of the services provided by the front-end system.

The number of C/S systems is growing rapidly—new ones are being designed and released almost monthly. While the client systems generally run on PCs, the database server can run on anything from another PC to a mainframe. Chapters 4 through 7 will cover the various Client/Server DBMSs available today. More and more front-end applications are coming out as well, including those that extend the reach of the traditional PC-based DBMSs to database servers. Chapter 8 will give an overview of representative front-end systems.

The greatest disadvantage of the database systems described so far is that they require the data to be stored on a single system. This can be a problem for large companies, which may have to support database users scattered over a wide geographical area or which need to share portions of their departmental databases with other departments or a central host. Some way of distributing the data among the various hosts or sites is needed, which has led to the development of distributed processing systems.

Distributed Processing Systems

A simple form of distributed processing has existed for several years. In this limited form, data is shared among various host systems via updates sent either through direct connections (on the same network) or through remote connections via phone or dedicated data lines. An application which runs on one or more of the hosts extracts the portion of data that's been changed during a programmer-defined period, and then transmits the data to either a centralized host or other hosts in the distributed circuit. The other databases are then updated so that all the systems are in sync with each other. This type of distributed processing usually occurs between departmental computers or LANs and host systems; the data goes to a large central minicomputer or mainframe host after the close of the business day.

While this system is ideal for sharing portions of data among different hosts, it doesn't address the issue of users' access to data not stored in their local host. Users must change their connections to the different hosts to access different databases, remembering which database is where. Combining data from databases that exist on different hosts also presents some serious challenges for both users and programmers. There's also the issue of duplicated data; although disk storage systems have declined in price over the years, providing numerous disk systems to store the same data can be expensive. Keeping all the duplicate sets of data in sync adds additional complexities to the system.

The solution to these problems is emerging in the technology of "seamless" data access called *distributed processing*. Under a distributed processing system, a user requests data from the local host; if the local host makes the determination that it doesn't have the data, it goes out over the network to get it from the system that does. It then passes the data back to the user without the user ever knowing that the data was retrieved from a different system, except, perhaps, for a slight delay in getting the data. Figure 1.13 illustrates one form of a distributed processing system. First, the user creates and sends a data query to the local database server. The database server then sends the request for data it doesn't have over the network to the mainframe (possibly through a gateway or bridge system that joins the two networks together). It gets back a response answering the query. The local database server then combines those results with the data found on its own disks and sends everything back to the user.

Figure 1.13

A distributed processing system

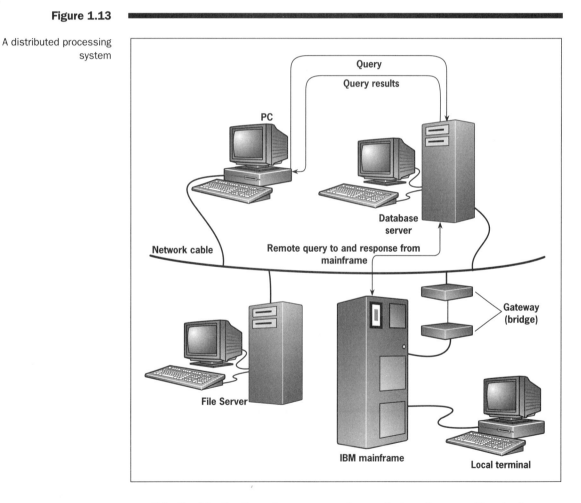

Ideally, this distributed system can also work the other way: Terminal users connected directly to the mainframe can access data that exists on remote database servers. The design and implementation of distributed processing systems is a very new field; many pieces aren't in place yet, and existing solutions are not always compatible with each other. I'll mention some of the existing solutions when I cover Client/Server DBMSs in later chapters, and I will discuss the future of distributed processing in Chapter 9.

■ Database Application Programming Languages

A sophisticated DBMS doesn't do anyone a bit of good if the users don't have a way of accessing the data. I've mentioned database applications throughout this chapter; now it's time to explore exactly what a database application is and how it communicates with the DBMS.

A database application is simply a computer program that allows users to enter, change, delete, and report on the data in a database. Applications, traditionally written by programmers, are written in one or more general or specialized programming languages. However, there has been a trend in recent years toward user-oriented database access tools that simplify the process of using a DBMS and eliminate the need for custom programming.

While the topic of actually programming a database is well beyond the scope of this book, an understanding of some of the languages and mechanics behind the programming will make it easier to understand the topics that will be covered in upcoming chapters. Appendix C lists other books that cover programming databases in more detail if you want to pursue this topic further.

The languages used to create database applications can be grouped into three broad categories: procedural languages, SQL (and SQL-like) languages, and all other languages.

Procedural Languages

The vast majority of programming languages can be described as "procedural." When the programmer creates a database application in one of these languages, he or she has to write the application's code as a series of procedures. Each procedure does the work of one portion of the application, such as a procedure to query the database or a procedure to update data in the database. The different procedures are then tied together through other user-interface procedures (for example, a menu system) and run at the appropriate points in the application.

The standard computer programming languages, such as Pascal, COBOL, BASIC, and C, are procedural languages. These languages can be used to create database applications through the use of an *Application Programming Interface* (API), which consists of a standard set of functions (or calls) that extend the language to give it access to the data on the DBMS.

The API functions are usually contained in "libraries" that are included in the application when it's compiled. Most DBMS vendors have these libraries available as part of the DBMS package or as an extra-cost option. Some DBMS file types (such as the .DBF files used by dBASE) are so common, or the structure of the file so well documented, that it's possible to create database applications to access the data without having to use an API library. All these high-level languages, which can also be used to create nondatabase applications, are generally referred to as "third generation languages" (3GLs).

Some procedural programming languages are specific to one particular DBMS. These languages are commonly referred to as "fourth generation languages" (4GLs) to distinguish them from the general-use 3GLs. The most common example of a database-specific procedural language is the dBASE language, available in different products from a number of vendors. Other examples of database-specific languages are PAL (Paradox Application Language) used by Paradox, and the R/BASIC language used by Advanced Revelation.

Structured Query Language (SQL)

The Structured Query Language (SQL) was initially designed as a database language to explicitly access DBMSs based on the Relational model. The initial version of the language first appeared as SEQUEL in the mid-1970s and was developed by IBM as the standard language for accessing an early Relational database that ran on IBM mainframes. By the late '70s, the name had been shortened to SQL, though there are those that still pronounce it "sequel" out of habit.

SQL is more properly described as a sublanguage, since it doesn't contain any facilities for screen handling or user input/output. Its main purpose is to provide a standard method for accessing databases, regardless of the language the rest of the database application is written in. It's designed for interactive queries of a database (and referred to as dynamic SQL) or as part of an application written in one of the procedural languages (and referred to as embedded SQL).

Since it was originally created, SQL has been revised several times. In the early '80s, an attempt was made by the American National Standards Institute (ANSI) to standardize the SQL language, which led to the release of the ANSI-86 SQL specifications and later on to the ANSI-89 SQL specifications. IBM has been at the forefront of expanding the SQL language, working particularly to extend the capabilities of their DB2 relational mainframe database. For this reason it's become common to see the SQL implementations from other DBMS vendors described as "ANSI SQL with DB2 extensions." Attempts are underway to incorporate many of these extensions into the SQL2 specifications, which are due out from ANSI sometime in the next few years, though such releases are difficult to predict. However, don't assume that one vendor's SQL implementation can talk to another's. Every DBMS vendor adds their own extensions to the SQL standard, and these extensions can make the various SQL versions incompatible with each other.

It's important to note that while SQL is primarily used with databases based on the Relational model, no hard-and-fast rule says that a database that "understands" SQL has to be relational, or for that matter, that a Relational database has to understand SQL. The Relational model doesn't address the subject of languages, other than that the language used to access the DBMS has to preserve data integrity. There are numerous DBMSs that use SQL on the market, yet they are only semirelational or based on one of the other database models.

When you're evaluating a DBMS for use in your business, don't assume that it's a Relational database just because it understands SQL; make sure that the underlying database is actually based on the Relational model, if that's what you want. This is an important issue that will be addressed throughout the rest of this book, particularly in the chapters that cover specific C/S databases.

Other Languages

Into this group fall the languages that don't neatly fit into the previous two categories. The most common of these other languages are the *Object Oriented Programming* (OOP) languages such as Modula-2 or C++. OOP languages represent an entirely different approach to programming, where actions are defined as taking place on "objects," instead of as a series of procedures. The use of OOP languages for database applications is in its infancy, but I'll cover them more fully in Chapter 9.

Another type of language that's used with databases is a *macro* (or script) language. Macro languages aren't full programming languages; they're actually a list of the keystrokes that a user manually enters into an application to automate certain tasks. Highly specific to a particular application, macro languages are commonly found in the low-end DBMS packages or in the front-ends for database servers.

A language specifically designed for accessing relational databases, QUEL was developed by Ingres Corporation for their VAX-based INGRES Relational database. Unfortunately, QUEL didn't catch on with other Relational DBMS vendors and has been superseded by SQL as the de facto standard relational language.

Finally, there's *Query-By-Example* (QBE). QBE is not strictly a language; it's an interface that presents the user with one or more blank tables that correspond to the tables in the database. The user then picks and chooses the columns to be included in the query through keystrokes, and defines any search conditions for the query by filling the conditions into the appropriate columns. The DBMS then translates the QBE into the actions necessary to fulfill the user's request.

Figure 1.14 represents a possible QBE screen for the Acme Submarine Company's inventory database. The column names of the PARTS table appear in the first row of the QBE table; then the user is directed to choose the columns that are to appear in the query answer (the check-marks in row 2) and the search conditions (the =1001 in row 3). This QBE screen would then produce a smaller table that shows the part number and description of the part that matches P# 1001. Currently, the most popular example of a QBE interface is found in Borland's Paradox DBMS. Some vendors are also starting to include QBE screens in their front-end applications for accessing C/S databases.

Figure 1.14

A sample Query-By-Example screen

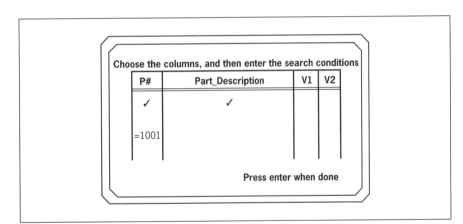

- *Capabilities*
- *Platforms*
- *Communications*

Client/Server Database Technology

Now that we've covered the basics of a DBMS, it's time to examine the specifics of Client/Server technology. This chapter will cover the reasons for selecting a C/S system, and the hardware and software you need to run one. We'll also cover the network technologies used to connect the various systems.

If you want to start a heated debate, ask your colleagues to define Client/Server computing and to identify Client/Server products. Of course, any local area network could be considered a Client/Server system, since the workstations (clients) request services such as data, program files, or printing from the server. However, "Client/Server" is now generally accepted to mean any system that splits its data processing between two distinct components.

By this definition, C/S systems aren't limited to database applications: Any application that has a user interface portion ("front-end") that runs locally on the client and a processing portion that runs on the server ("back-end") is a form of C/S computing. Examples of non-database C/S applications include such products as Lotus's groupware product Notes, Novell's MHS (Message Handling Service) EMail system, and 3Com's 3+Mail. Products such as these have a relatively easy-to-use front-end that lets the user enter, read, and reply to electronic mail. The back-end application that runs on the server handles the storage and routing of the EMail until it reaches its final destination.

Currently the primary focus is on database applications. The reason for this is simple: Many corporations and businesses are reducing their computing costs by "downsizing" their databases to smaller, more manageable platforms. The idea behind downsizing is simple—moving corporate databases away from large and expensive centralized systems to smaller, less expensive systems that don't have as extensive support and maintenance requirements. Client/Server databases that run on the smaller systems are the primary means of handling the large amounts of data that these larger systems typically store and manipulate. The split in processing power that is the foundation of C/S computing makes it possible for the smaller systems to handle this data. We'll be covering the relative costs of the various systems in the discussions that follow.

Note that there's no such thing as a stand-alone C/S system. Vendors may provide single-user versions of their C/S software for developers, but a true Client/Server system needs some type of network with one or more interconnected workstations and servers. The workstations also have to have some type of CPU (central processing unit); diskless PCs would qualify as workstations, but dumb terminals need not apply for the job.

There's some debate about which software vendor first used the term to describe their product, though the honors generally fall to Microsoft, who co-wrote their SQL Server with Sybase for the OS/2 PC operating system. After Microsoft started using the term, other DBMS vendors such as Oracle and Ingres said, "Oh yes, we do that too," and the term Client/Server is now used to describe a whole class of products and applications.

◼ Capabilities

How Client/Server systems are implemented depends on the platforms the front- and back-ends run on, and the degree to which the processing is split between the two. As yet, there's no standard way of classifying the different levels or implementations of C/S systems, so for the purpose of making comparisons between the different software and hardware platforms described later in this book, I'm proposing a classification system (Table 2.1). The C/S systems are ranked in class order; the most complete implementation is Class 1, the least complete is Class 5. While many products don't fit one category exactly (they may have elements of more than one class), it's easier to compare specific products as well as implementation solutions using a common ranking system.

The systems described later in this book can be categorized as Class 2, 3, or 4. Class 1 systems pretty much don't exist yet or exist only in limited form through a combination of the services provided by Class 2 and Class 3 systems. Class 5 systems have become virtually nonexistent, since these vendors decided to provide wide front-end access to their DBMSs in order to remain competitive. Note that the Class 2 through 4 systems don't rule out using a proprietary server (proprietary means that the DBMS software will only run on hardware provided by the same vendor), as long as the user and/or applications developer has a choice of front-ends to access it.

Advantages of Client/Server Databases

The primary advantages of a Client/Server system arise from splitting the processing between the client system and the database server. Since the bulk of the database processing is done on the back-end, the speed of the DBMS isn't tied to the speed of the workstation. As a result, the workstation need only be able to run the front-end software, effectively extending the life of many older or smaller PCs which don't have the horsepower needed to run a complex DBMS.

This division of work also reduces the load on the network connecting the workstations. Instead of sending the entire database file back and forth on the wire, the network traffic is reduced to queries to and responses from the database server. Some database servers can even store and run procedures and queries on the server itself, further reducing the traffic. On a large network with many workstations, this reduction in network traffic can more than offset the added cost of switching to a C/S system.

Another benefit of separating the client from the server is workstation independence; users aren't limited to one type of system or platform. In a C/S system, the workstations can be IBM-compatible PCs, Macintoshes, UNIX

Table 2.1

Ranking of Client/Server
Systems and Platforms

RANK	DESCRIPTION	COMMENTS
Class 1: Full Distributed Processing	• Data resides on multiple systems and/or platforms. • User access is transparent: Users connect to one server, which accesses the other systems. • Server performs all DBMS functions and processing. • Users cannot access the data from outside the DBMS running on the server. • Multiple front-ends provide query, data modification, and reporting services.	Very limited implementation to date.
Class 2: Full Client/Server	• Data resides on one or more servers. • User or application makes explicit connections to each server. • Server performs all DBMS processing. • Users can only access the data via the DBMS running on the server. • Multiple front-ends provide query, data modification, and reporting services.	Most common type of C/S system today.
Class 3: Gated Client/ Server	• Gateway systems and applications create a bridge between the user's front-end application and the DBMS running on the non-C/S system. • Gateway systems translate queries, data modifications, etc. into procedures and calls the database system can process. • The gateway supports multiple front-ends.	Commonly used between PC-based systems and DBMSs running on a mainframe or minicomputer, or as a link between a Class 2 system and a mainframe or mini.
Class 4: Limited Client/ Server	• Server provides some DBMS functions, usually just data storage and indexing functions. • Server doesn't always prevent users from accessing the data from outside the DBMS running on the server. • Most processing takes place on client system. • Multiple front-ends are supported, though not as many as in a Class 2 system.	Systems of this type add server functionality to standard PC-based databases, using common file formats such as dBASE's .DBF.
Class 5: Proprietary Client/Server	• Requires a proprietary hardware platform and operating system. • Data can only be accessed through front-end software provided by the vendor of the DBMS.	Common in the early '80s; recently evolved into more open systems.

workstations, or a combination of these, and can run multiple operating systems, such MS/PC-DOS, MS Windows, IBM OS/2, or Apple's System 7. A corollary to this is application independence; the workstations aren't required to use the same DBMS application software. Users can continue to use familiar software to access the database, and developers can design front-ends for a specific workstation or for particular users.

Another major advantage of a Client/Server system is the preservation of data integrity. Today, most database servers run a DBMS based on the Relational model, and users are prevented from accessing the data from outside the DBMS (Class 4 and some Class 3 systems are the exception to this). In addition, the DBMS can provide services that protect the data, such as encrypted file storage (the data is encrypted to prevent it from being viewed outside the DBMS); real-time backups to tape, which occur while the database is being accessed; disk mirroring, in which the data is automatically written to a duplicate database on another partition of the same hard disk; and disk duplexing, in which the data is automatically written to a duplicate database on a different hard disk. The DBMS can also provide transaction processing, which tracks changes to the database and helps correct errors in the database in case the server crashes.

Transaction processing is a method by which the DBMS keeps a running log of all the modifications made to the database over a period of time. It's primarily used for databases that are constantly being modified, such as an order-processing system, to ensure that the data modifications are properly recorded in the database. The log is used to restore the database (as much as possible) to a previous error-free state in the event the system crashes while modifications are being made. These capabilities make Client/Server systems ideal for large multiuser databases, particularly those which allow multiple simultaneous modifications to the data. The DBMS is responsible for handling the locks necessary to prevent multiple changes to the same record or field, and can provide better multiuser access through judicious use of those locks, for example, locking only a record or a field for update, instead of the whole file. Conflicts and deadlocks between users modifying the same record are significantly reduced when they're handled by a central DBMS.

Disadvantages of Client/Server Databases

The major disadvantage of Client/Server systems is the increased cost of administrative and support personnel who maintain the database server. On a small network (generally under 20 users), the network administrator can usually maintain the database server and user access to it, and support the front-end applications. However, as the number of users rises or as the database itself grows, a database administrator may be needed just to run the DBMS and support the front-ends. Training can also add to the start-up costs, since the DBMS may run on an operating system unfamiliar to support personnel.

There's also an increase in hardware costs. While many C/S databases run under the common operating systems (NetWare, OS/2, or UNIX), and most vendors claim that the DBMS can run on the same hardware side-by-side with the File Server software, the database server should run on its own dedicated machine to ensure performance and data integrity. This usually means purchasing a high-powered system with a large amount of RAM and hard disk space (at least 10 to 12Mb RAM and a 300Mb hard disk), as well as additional support equipment such as an uninterruptable power supply (UPS) to protect the server from power outages.

The overall cost of the software is usually higher than traditional PC-based multiuser DBMSs (though equivalent to or lower than the cost of most minicomputer and mainframe-based central systems). The cost-per-server for a C/S database can range from under $1,000 for five users to tens-of-thousands of dollars for unlimited users. Add to that the separate cost of the front-end applications or development tools, as well as the personnel costs for training programmers in the new system, and the difference in price over a traditional PC-based DBMS can be substantial.

There's also the issue of complexity. With so many parts comprising the entire C/S system, Murphy's Law can (and usually does) kick in—the more pieces that compose the system, the more pieces that can fail. It's also harder to track down problems when the system crashes. And it can initially take longer to get all the components set up and working together. All this is compounded by the general lack of experience and expertise of potential support personnel and programmers, due to the relative newness of the technology. As C/S systems become more common, this last problem should abate.

The C/S advantage of application independence also has a downside. Having multiple front-ends to the database increases the amount of programming support needed, because more and varied program code must be developed and maintained. Making a change to the structure of the database also has a ripple effect throughout the different front-ends. It becomes a longer and more complex process to make the necessary changes to the different front-end applications, and it's also harder to keep all of them in sync without seriously disrupting the users' access to the database.

Currently, there's also little support for interconnectivity between different Client/Server DBMS systems. Most back-end systems can only share data with similar systems, and nearly all the available front-ends support only a select set of the many back-ends. Setting up a C/S system can lock you into using the front-ends from only a few vendors and can limit the number of tools available for developing custom front-end applications. You may also find it tedious or nearly impossible to import existing databases into the

C/S DBMS, and it's sometimes difficult to link a new C/S system with existing DBMSs. Hopefully, these problems will decrease as Client/Server databases become more widespread and as the vendors of front- and back-ends provide more support for accessing other systems.

■ Platforms

The platform is the hardware and software combination that the Client/Server DBMS runs on. There are four categories of platforms: PCs, UNIX (usually RISC) workstations, minicomputers, and mainframes. While the most common platform for C/S computing is a PC, all four have their advantages and disadvantages. I will cover these when I address the specific products that run on those platforms.

While hardware systems vary widely in features and capabilities, certain common features are needed for the operating system software. The operating system (OS) is the primary software that acts as an interface between the hardware and the applications that run on that hardware. Applications are usually written to run under a particular OS. Some common examples of OS software are MS/PC-DOS, OS/2, the many UNIX variants, DEC's VMS, and the MVS/XA that runs on IBM mainframes.

The primary OS feature needed for a C/S DBMS is *multitasking*—running numerous applications concurrently. Multitasking allows the DBMS software to properly handle the different user queries and requests without their interfering with each other by splitting (time-slicing) the CPU's processing time between the different tasks or processes. Multitasking operating systems can be *preemptive* or *nonpreemptive*. In a preemptive system, the OS controls the amount of CPU time for each task. Conversely, the application controls the CPU time in a nonpreemptive system, and only relinquishes it to other tasks when it's finished running its own tasks. Preemptive systems have a natural advantage for C/S databases, as they prevent any one task from dominating the entire system.

The operating system can also be *multiuser* (can support simultaneous users doing different tasks), particularly when dumb terminals are used to access the DBMS. A multiuser OS offers no particular advantage or disadvantage for a C/S DBMS.

Multithreading is a recent addition to commonly available preemptive multitasking OS software, though the concept dates back to the early '70s. This capability lets an application multitask within itself; for example, a multithreaded single-user DBMS can start a new thread (process or task) of execution to do a complex report in the background while the user is querying the system in the foreground. Multithreading has significant implications for the designing of complex Client/Server DBMSs, as it gives the application greater control over when a new task is started or stopped. The application can be designed with built-in intelligence to identify which process or task has a higher priority and should be given more CPU time than other tasks. For example, the DBMS can give slightly higher priority to data modifications over data queries, reducing the performance penalty that the more complex task incurs without significantly affecting the query speed.

No one platform suits every need or is right for every situation. How can you choose the right one for you? First examine your current DBMS systems, project their growth, and estimate how many users will access them at the same time. After reading this book, choose a couple of alternative platforms and DBMS systems, and talk to the vendors. To help you in this process, I've included a Decision Tree at the back of this book, which will be explained in detail in Chapter 3.

Personal Computers

Only in recent years have IBM-compatible PCs become an acceptable platform for Client/Server databases. The advent of high-powered 32-bit 80386 and 80486 systems, hard disks in the gigabyte (G, or one billion bytes) range, and stable multitasking operating systems make these PCs able competitors to the RISC workstations and minicomputers that have been the traditional platforms for resource-intensive DBMSs.

Hardware

While a PC based on a 80386 CPU can perform adequately as a database server, for sheer power and future growth potential, the best system to start with is one based on a 33Mhz 80486. Many of the newer PCs come with the CPU on a replaceable card, which makes it easier to upgrade the power of the system to a faster 486 or even an 80586 as they become available in 1993.

Your next decision will be how much RAM (random access memory) to acquire for the system. The bare minimum is 8Mb, and most of the PC-based DBMS vendors recommend at least 12Mb for adequate performance. Depending on the number of simultaneous users and the DBMS, I'd recommend 12 to 16Mb of RAM as the best starting point. Remember too, that many of the inexpensive 486 systems limit you to 16Mb of 32-bit memory. While this is fine for high-end workstation use, you definitely want the capability for at least 32Mb of RAM for a database server. Even if you don't need that much memory immediately, it pays in the long run to have the room to expand.

Also be aware that some systems limit the amount of RAM that can be put on the motherboard and require additional RAM to be put on a proprietary 32-bit add-in card. Avoid them. Instead, buy a system that lets you expand to the full 32Mb of RAM right on the motherboard, so you're not locked into one vendor when it's time to upgrade your servers.

Probably the most critical component for database performance is the hard disk subsystem, since the bulk of the DBMS's activities involve reading data from or writing data to it. Benchmark tests have shown that the best choice for speed and expandability is a hard disk based on the small computer system interface (SCSI) standard. A single SCSI board can support up to seven attached drives, each as large as 1.2G, giving you tremendous room to expand. The SCSI standard has its flaws, but most hard disk vendors make sure their drives are compatible with a wide variety of SCSI cards, again preventing your being locked into one vendor.

An interesting alternative to SCSI boards is the Disk Drive Array designed by Compaq for their SystemPro line of high-performance servers. The Drive Array lets you link a number of smaller drives together into what appears to the system to be one large hard disk. It also provides for increased data security, as the drives can be set up to automatically mirror data between themselves and to switch to the backup disk when the primary fails, all without administrator intervention.

Finally, the last decision you should make is what type of internal bus (data connection system for add-on cards) the server should have. The Industry Standard Architecture (ISA) bus is based on the original 16-bit bus that IBM designed for its PC-AT systems. As 32-bit processors became more common, the PC vendors saw the need for a 32-bit data bus—unfortunately, they couldn't agree on a standard. IBM proposed the Micro Channel architecture (MCA) standard and implemented it in their line of PS/2 computers. However, the otherwise technically excellent MCA bus had two problems to overcome: It wasn't backwards-compatible with ISA cards, and IBM originally demanded a large licensing fee from other PC vendors. Although they've since lowered the fees, the MCA bus hasn't spread much beyond IBM systems.

Compaq and a number of other PC vendors banded together and proposed an alternative 32-bit bus standard—Extended Industry Standard Architecture (EISA). The design of the EISA bus lets users continue to use ISA add-on cards, while supporting 32-bit EISA cards when needed. The number of PC vendors providing EISA systems has grown over the years, giving users a wide choice of systems.

Your decision of which bus standard to use should be based on factors besides speed, such as the availability of fast-disk subsystems and vendor support. Regardless of which standard you choose, go with a 32-bit bus for your database server. A full 32-bit bus will speed up both disk processing and network access when 32-bit interface cards are used, eliminating the most serious bottlenecks a server faces.

Multiprocessor (MPU) systems, an emerging technology in the PC world, may have a significant impact on the performance and capabilities of Client/Server databases in the future. However, at this time few MPU systems are available, and little or no support for them exists among the various C/S products. It's a technology to watch for future developments.

Operating System Software

The first PC-based C/S databases were announced shortly after IBM and Microsoft announced their new protected-mode operating system (OS), called OS/2, in early 1987. OS/2 was the first full 16-bit preemptive multitasking, multithreaded OS designed expressly for PCs based on the 80286 (and higher) CPU. Though limited to accessing 16Mb of real RAM, OS/2 version 1.x provides superior capabilities over DOS for the resource-intensive database server software; its multitasking lets multiple services run on the same system, including both the LAN software and the DBMS. Multithreading means applications multitask within themselves, making it easy for software to support numerous users simultaneously running multiple tasks. Finally, it has native support for up to 512Mb of virtual memory (VM), which means that if an application runs out of RAM, the OS can swap portions of unused or idle data to the disk to free up working space. Vendors of UNIX-based DBMSs rushed to port their software to the new platform.

Novell countered the release of OS/2 with a 32-bit version of their network operating system (NOS), NetWare 3.0 (since upgraded to NetWare 3.11, with 3.2 due sometime in 1993). NetWare 3.11 provides access to up to 4G of RAM, though current hardware limitations usually restrict this to 32Mb RAM. It also has the ability to run applications on the File Server as NetWare Loadable Modules (NLMs) and provides nonpreemptive multitasking capabilities; however, it can only access the actual RAM present in the system. Early implementations of NetWare 3.x had problems running NLMs, but Novell quickly fixed this. With the release of 3.11 in 1991, a number of DBMS vendors created NLM versions of their OS/2 or UNIX software.

In April of 1992, IBM released their 32-bit version of OS/2, which ups the ante in the database server OS race. OS/2 2.0 increased the amount of real RAM support to 32Mb and continued support for virtual memory, multitasking, and multithreading. OS/2 2.0 is currently brand new, and only a few DBMS vendors have announced support for it yet, but this will probably change quite soon.

Finally, some versions of UNIX run on 80386 and 80486 systems, and can be used as the OS for PC-based Client/Server databases. However, running UNIX on PCs isn't that common, and it's generally better to go with a hardware platform specifically designed for it if you must run C/S software that only comes in UNIX versions.

Some Client/Server DBMS vendors provide MS/PC-DOS versions of their software, but other than for application development purposes, I don't recommend using them. There's a lot of system overhead involved in providing all the services of a C/S DBMS, and DOS, which is limited to 640k of RAM, just isn't up to the task.

Which operating system is right for you? Currently, the number of C/S DBMS systems available for OS/2 or NetWare is about equal, with some systems able to run under either OS. However, some only run under one or the other OS. Unless the DBMS you choose is one of these single-OS versions, either software platform is acceptable for use on a dedicated database server, as platforms based on OS/2 can still be used on a NetWare LAN. There are numerous arguments between supporters of OS/2 or NetWare over the amount of protection they provide in preventing errant applications from crashing the whole server—NetWare sacrifices some protection for speed, and OS/2 sacrifices speed for protection. Since increased data protection is a primary reason for moving to a C/S system in the first place, it makes sense to go with an OS/2-based platform. However, Novell's NetWare 3.2 is supposed to address the current limited protection by giving the administrators a choice of sacrificing some speed for increased protection.

In late 1992 or early 1993, Microsoft promises to release Windows/NT, a 32-bit, preemptive, multitasking, and multithreaded operating system. Windows/NT is being developed to run on multiple hardware systems, including both PCs based on the 80386/486 CPUs and a number of RISC CPUs. It has the potential to be the unifying OS between these disparate systems, and many DBMS vendors have committed to porting their software over to it when it's released. I'll be discussing the future of Windows/NT and other operating system advancements, and how they affect C/S computing, more fully in Chapter 9.

RISC and Other UNIX Workstations

Workstations based on Reduced Instruction Set Computing (RISC) processors are primarily used for scientific or engineering applications, since the RISC CPUs are generally faster and more powerful than the top-of-the-line Intel 80486. A RISC CPU gets its enhanced performance by reducing the amount of microcode in the chip itself; less code means the CPU can perform its internal operations faster. There are numerous RISC chips available today, such as the Sun SPARC, DEC's Alpha, the MIPS line of third-party CPUs, and the Motorola 88000 series. Most RISC chips are proprietary to a single vendor's hardware, but all share similar performance capabilities. Since the usual operating system for a RISC workstation is UNIX, this platform has recently come into use as a database server.

The line between a high-powered RISC or other UNIX workstation and a full minicomputer can become very fuzzy. To make things simple, workstations include any desktop single-user UNIX-based multitasking system that can be used as a server through a network connection. In contrast, minicomputers are multiuser systems that support both network connections and directly connected terminals.

Hardware

Most workstations resemble and operate like PCs—they sit on the desktop or alongside the desk in a tower-type case, and have a directly attached keyboard, mouse, and screen (usually high-resolution color). Common entry-level workstations come with 8Mb of RAM and a hard disk of 100Mb to 300Mb. Workstations are commonly used for scientific or engineering applications.

This configuration may be fine for a user's system, but, similar to PCs, a database server should have more RAM. A good working minimum is 16Mb of RAM (depending on the DBMS software), including support for at least 32Mb for later expansion. Of course a larger hard disk is needed as well, as the UNIX operating system can easily take up close to 100Mb of disk space all by itself.

Most of the smaller hard-disk subsystems ("smaller" meaning below 300Mb in the UNIX world) are SCSI-based. For larger disk subsystems, the vendors use a proprietary disk interface for higher performance, which can add considerable cost to the workstation.

Having to rely solely on a single system vendor for most of your expansion equipment (RAM or disk drives) is the price you pay for getting the extra power of a RISC workstation. RISC systems aren't as widespread as PCs, so the large market for third-party add-ons doesn't yet exist. While entry-level workstations only cost a little more than a high-powered PC, expanding the system to server capabilities can increase the cost two to four times over an equivalent PC in the long run.

A number of well-known RISC vendors and systems are available today. The ones most commonly used for database servers are the Sun SPARCstation series, the IBM RS/6000 series, the workstations offered by Apollo (a subsidiary of Hewlett-Packard), and Digital Equipment Corporation's DECstation. Though not as widespread, the NeXT workstations, based on the non-RISC Motorola 68040 CPU, can also be used as database servers.

The increasing interest in Client/Server computing has led some workstation vendors to create high-powered RISC systems designed explicitly as database servers. These approach the traditional minicomputers in capabilities and power. The best examples of this type of RISC system are Sun's 470 and IBM's RS/6000 Server.

Operating System Software

All the RISC workstations used for Client/Server DBMSs use a variant of UNIX as their operating system. While at first glance this may seem ideal, the truth of the situation is that each vendor's UNIX system software differs slightly from other vendors' software, so they're not 100 percent compatible. This prevents software vendors from selling one version of their application software that can run on any UNIX system, and it is the primary reason that UNIX workstations haven't become more common on the desktop. The software vendors must tailor their application's source code to each UNIX variant that they want to support.

The bottom line is that even though most of the top Client/Server DBMSs started out on UNIX, a particular C/S DBMS may not be available in a version that runs on every workstation. If you decide to use a workstation as a database server, first choose the DBMS you want to run, and then find out which UNIX versions it runs under. You can then explore the hardware options from that vendor, as well as the DBMS's performance on that particular system.

UNIX is a multitasking operating system, originally developed on a DEC minicomputer at AT&T's Bell Laboratories in the early 1970s. It is well suited for multiuser applications. It includes support for virtual memory, but generally doesn't support multithreading—the Mach variant of UNIX used by NeXT is the only multithreaded version to date, though other vendors have promised it in upcoming versions. Most UNIX systems are based on one of two variations: UNIX System V (the current version of the AT&T original) and Berkeley UNIX, a variant of AT&T's UNIX developed at UC's Berkeley campus.

Criticized as a "techie" operating system, UNIX can be difficult for many computer users to understand. This criticism is not without merit and should be factored into your decision process. In addition to the extra cost of the RISC workstation platform, it can also be difficult to find support personnel who are familiar with the operating system. Some of these objections have been met in recent years through the increased use of a graphical user interface (GUI) on UNIX systems. Two of the most common UNIX GUIs are Sun's Open Look (co-developed with AT&T), and the Open Systems Foundation's Motif (OSF is a consortium of UNIX vendors, most notably DEC, IBM, and HP/Apollo). These GUIs add a degree of user-friendliness to UNIX and make it somewhat easier to use and support. Sun includes Open Look in its Solaris operating system, and IBM and DEC include Motif in their UNIX variants (AIX and ULTRIX, respectively).

Minicomputers

Minicomputers and mainframes are the traditional workhorses when it comes to database applications, and minicomputers are generally optimized for multiuser applications. In recent years, various methods of connecting a mini to a PC-based LAN have been developed, and it's now possible to use a minicomputer as both a File Server and a database server. Mini-based DBMSs that provide either Class 2 or Class 3 C/S services will be covered in Chapter 6.

Many businesses already have one or more minicomputers. A Client/Server DBMS can enhance the mini's capabilities by extending data access to the many PCs and LANs in the company. A C/S system also reduces the workload on the minicomputer by moving part of the processing to the front-end system, which lets the mini support more users without expanding or enhancing the hardware. The initial costs involved in purchasing and setting up a C/S DBMS can often be more than offset by the savings in not having to purchase additional hardware.

Hardware

Minicomputers are usually based on proprietary CPUs that are generally more powerful than those in the previous systems and on proprietary expansion equipment. They range in size from small tower-type systems to boxes that resemble overgrown refrigerators. Minis usually have a number of serial ports for connecting dumb terminals and commonly include network cards. They support much more RAM (typically 128 to 256Mb) than is common on PCs or workstations, which makes them better suited for applications that allow hundreds of users simultaneous access.

The high-end minicomputers also support multiple CPUs in the same box, which adds both processing power and system redundancy in case of failure.

Minis also support high-speed hard disk systems that can range into the hundreds and thousands of gigabytes, which makes them well-suited for company-sized databases. The disk systems usually support fault tolerance—a method of controlling and correcting errors caused by hardware problems—as an option through disk mirroring and/or duplexing, which provide more data redundancy and integrity.

Most minicomputers can be *clustered*, which means that machines are linked together through high-speed connections, and all the machines in the cluster share the same disks. Clustering lets users expand the capabilities of the computer (that is, number of users supported) without having to purchase more disk drives or move data between different machines.

Minicomputers suffer from the same problem as RISC workstations, namely, the general lack of third-party expansion products. In most cases, purchasing a minicomputer locks you into buying all future equipment from the same vendor, at proportionally higher costs over third-party hardware.

The more common minicomputers are made by Digital Equipment Corporation (DEC), IBM, and Hewlett-Packard (HP). DEC's line ranges from the tower-sized MicroVAX that supports less than 100 users to the VAX 6000 that approaches mainframes in size and capabilities. IBM's primary minicomputer is the AS/400 line, which comes in a number of sizes and capabilities; all of them include hardware support for the database applications that the AS/400 is primarily designed for. HP's HP3000 series comes in both proprietary CPU and RISC CPU models.

An interesting variation on the minicomputer theme is the Teradata systems. Especially designed to be Relational database servers, these minicomputers contain much of the code that supports the DBMS in ROM for speed. They support from three to 1024 CPUs (80386 or 80486), up to 8G of main memory, and come with fault tolerant disk systems as standard equipment.

Operating System Software

Just about all minicomputers use a proprietary operating system with UNIX as an optional OS. DEC systems are based on VAX/VMS, and IBM's systems on the AS/400 Operating System. HP has both the older MPE operating system, and the new MPE/XL OS, which is designed for RISC-based systems.

DEC's ULTRIX also runs on the entire VAX line, and IBM's AIX runs on all the AS/400s. HP's version of UNIX is HP-UX, a variation on AT&T's UNIX. The Teradata machines run either UNIX or MS-DOS. While C/S DBMSs are available for all these operating systems, running UNIX on a minicomputer has the advantage of giving you a wider choice in applications software and DBMSs, and generally a larger pool of support personnel to choose from. I recommend using UNIX if you're going to run your DBMS on a mini, unless you also need to run applications that are specific to the vendor's proprietary operating system.

Versions of NetWare are also available for VMS and UNIX systems, and LAN Manager/X is available for UNIX systems. Both let you use a minicomputer as a File Server on a PC-based LAN through a familiar network operating system (NOS) interface. However, the degree of integration between the LAN software and the native minicomputer system varies, and the LAN NOS may run only as an application on the minicomputer host without giving you access to other applications running on the same machine. Before you decide to use a mini as a LAN server, make sure that the particular minicomputer's operating system supports access to the applications you need through the NOS.

Some minicomputer operating systems still don't support Class 2 Client/ Server applications and require some type of gateway system to provide PC access to the DBMS running on the mini. The gateway can either be an additional hardware/software combination or can be a software application that runs on the mini and interfaces between the PC-based front-ends and the DBMS on the host. You should check to see which type of access your DBMS software supports, as a gateway system can add considerable hardware, software, and support costs, as well as additional complexity in the overall network. As C/S applications become more common, most mini-based DBMS vendors are adding direct Client/Server support to their software, so this is less of a complication than it once was.

Mainframes

The mainframe is the most powerful general-purpose computer available; it supports multiple high-speed processors, enormous amounts of hard disk space, and hundreds to thousands of simultaneous users. Mainframes offer the most security of any available systems, both in terms of data security and hardware redundancy.

Mainframes are also the most expensive computers available, in terms of hardware, software, support environments, and personnel. Unlike the smaller computer systems, a mainframe requires a controlled environment, including a constant temperature, raised floors, and even special cooling equipment (the larger mainframes are still water-cooled). Because of this, mainframes are usually found in company-owned data centers, which can be located in either a section of a company's office building or a completely separate building.

Today's mainframes can support hundreds and even thousands of users accessing multiple applications through terminals or network connections. While still used as the primary system for central database applications in many large companies—IBM recently started calling mainframes the "data warehouses" for large businesses—the rapid spread of PCs and workstations has led to a slow evolution in the role of the mainframe as host for Client/ Server DBMSs.

It was in the mainframe world that the term *mission critical* first came to be used, referring to database applications that are so critical to a business's operations that the business could collapse if the data wasn't available. For this reason, the mainframe is still looked upon as the most important system for central data storage for large corporations—even with moves toward downsizing corporate databases to minicomputers and PC-based LANs, mainframes will be around for years to come, fulfilling their role as "data warehouses" for businesses.

Hardware

Unlike most other computers, a mainframe is not contained in a single box—it usually consists of a number of different *subsystems* that handle different tasks, all linked together through high-speed copper wire and/or fiber-optic cables. Typical subsystems include the CPUs, RAM modules, communications systems, and disk and tape drives.

The computer is accessed through terminals or PCs with terminal emulators, which are connected to *terminal controllers* (specialized subsystems that handle the terminal's communications network connections). They are then connected to the mainframe. Dial-in access is accomplished through a *front-end processor* (FEP)—a hardware subsystem not to be confused with the front-end applications used to access a C/S database. This processor handles the communications between the remote terminals and the central host. Network connections are also accomplished through add-in controllers that go into the front-end processor.

The mainframe's processing power and speed comes from proprietary multiple CPUs, high-speed disk drives, and high-speed communications paths between all the different elements that make up the system. Fault tolerant disk subsystems and redundant processing systems and data paths are also typical features. Mainframes generally have over 256Mb of RAM; the top-end machines can support gigabytes of RAM. The disk drive subsystems are measured in the hundreds of gigabytes, and it's not uncommon for a mainframe to have disks that hold more than a *terabyte* (1 trillion bytes) of data.

The most common mainframes are those put out by IBM. They range in size from the 4381s, which are not much larger than some of the bigger minicomputers and support only a few hundred users, to the room-filling 390 series that can support thousands of users. IBM-compatible mainframes are also available, such as those from Ahmdal and Fujitsu.

The machines in DEC's top-of-the-line VAX 9000 series also qualify as mainframes, based on size and the number of users supported. They also have most of the same hardware support requirements as other mainframe systems.

IBM and DEC mainframes have existed long enough for the development of a stable third-party hardware industry that provides "plug-compatible" disk and tape drives, front-end processors, terminal controllers, and terminals that can be added to the system via common adapters. While most of the third-party hardware is cheaper than equivalent parts from IBM and DEC, the overall cost of mainframe equipment is usually measured in the hundreds of thousands to millions of dollars.

The top-end mainframes in speed and processing power (and cost) are the super computers, such as those by Cray and Control Data Corporation. These computers are usually used for specialized applications such as weather forecasting, where billions of calculations per second are necessary. Super computers, rarely used for database systems, are not a factor in the Client/Server world at this time (or in the foreseeable future).

Operating System Software

Mainframe operating systems are very modularized, with different subsystems handling CPU assignments, communications with the disk and tape storage systems, and user interactions with the computer.

IBM mainframes were the host to the original developments in multitasking and multiuser operating system software, and today they run the most sophisticated operating systems available. IBM's mainframes run one of two proprietary multitasking, multiuser operating systems: VM (usually on the low to midrange systems) and various versions of MVS (such as MVS/XA and MVS/ESA) on the midrange and high-end systems. IBM also provides a version of AIX that lets users run UNIX applications on the mainframe. The underlying IBM operating system software is only a part of the whole—all it provides are the system services. Other system-level software from IBM or third-party vendors provides the interface between the users and the applications on the mainframe. Specialized security software governs user access and data security.

DEC's mainframes primarily run on the same VAX/VMS operating system as their minicomputers and can be clustered with the minicomputers as a company's data processing needs grow. DEC's UNIX-variant ULTRIX is also an option on the 9000 series.

The interrelationships between the various system-level software applications and user applications add to the mainframe system an enormous cost in support personnel. It's not uncommon for a corporation with a mainframe to have an entire Information Systems (IS) or Management Information Services (MIS) department consisting of system programmers, communications network specialists, and system operators to keep the whole system up and running. Program analysts and applications programmers are also necessary to create the applications for the ultimate end-users of the mainframe, since most mainframe applications are custom-written.

It's these large personnel and maintenance costs that have led to the concept of and trend toward downsizing mainframe systems to minicomputers and PCs, as the smaller systems have increased in power and features. Client/Server systems are approaching the power and capabilities of many mainframe applications while using more "off-the-shelf" software that doesn't require such large support staffs.

However, the smaller systems cannot yet completely replace mainframes as the systems of choice for large corporate-wide databases. Because of this, a number of Class 3 C/S hardware and/or software systems have become available; they provide Client/Server-type access to databases residing on an IBM mainframe. DEC mainframes have more native support for C/S applications, as DBMSs that run under the VAX/VMS OS run on the entire line of VAXes.

The trend today is toward integrating existing mainframes into new corporate-wide Client/Server systems rather than toward installing new mainframes, and it's in this light that I'll be discussing mainframe DBMSs later in this book.

■ Communications

A Client/Server Database System depends on splitting the processing between an intelligent front-end system (usually an IBM PC compatible, a Macintosh, or a RISC workstation) and the database server. Networks allow communication between these two parts of the overall system. While the topic of computer networks is beyond the scope of this book, this section covers some basic concepts necessary for understanding Client/Server communication. (Appendix C provides references for a more thorough understanding of networks.)

Network Hardware and Software

The client systems communicate with the server through a network that consists of a combination of hardware and software. The hardware which connects the PC to the network's wiring consists of a network interface card (NIC) that's added to the PC, workstation, and server (in some cases, the NIC is built right into the system).

A network of PCs, workstations, and servers is referred to as a local area network (LAN) if all the systems are in the same building. When a LAN extends across buildings (either in the same location or across the country), the entire network is referred to as a wide area network (WAN).

Three LAN topologies (cabling schemes) are in common use today: Ethernet, ARCnet, and Token Ring. Unless some type of bridging system is used, all the PCs and servers on the network have to have NICs that support the same topology. An Ethernet system commonly runs at 10 megabits/second (Mbps) and uses either coaxial cable in a bus (daisy-chain) configuration (see Figure 2.1) or twisted-pair (TP) cable in a hub-and-star configuration from one or more central concentrators (see Figure 2.2).

Token Ring, a token-passing network that uses twisted-pair wiring in a ring configuration, runs at 4 or 16Mbps (see Figure 2.3). Note that most Token Ring networks resemble star-and-hub Ethernet in real life, as the ring actually exists in the central wiring closet between the various multiple access units (MAUs).

Figure 2.1

Ethernet bus network

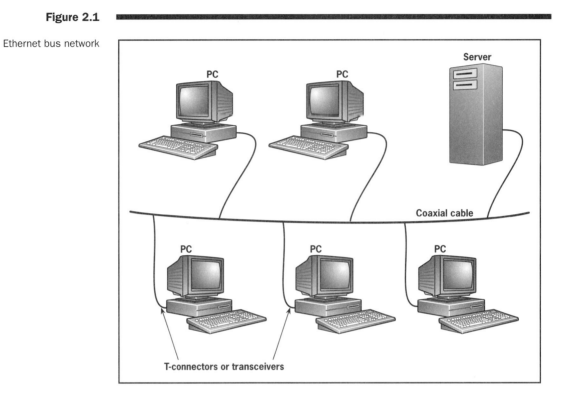

Figure 2.2

Twisted-pair Ethernet network

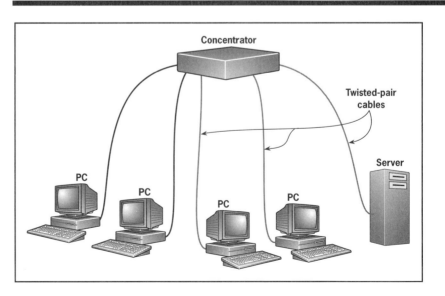

Figure 2.3

Token Ring network

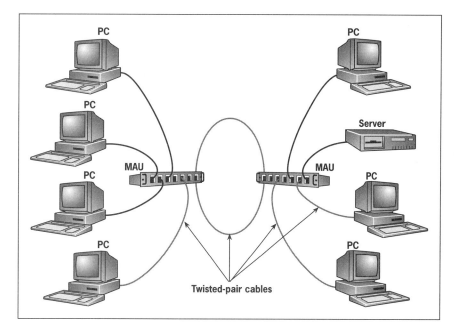

ARCnet, a 2Mbps token-bus network, uses a series of active and passive hubs connected with coaxial cable (shown in Figure 2.4). Passive hubs connect to the PCs, and active hubs connect the passive hubs to other passive hubs and PCs. A 20Mbps version of ARCnet has been announced, but is not yet available.

Due to the speed limitations of copper-based cable (20Mbps or less), high-speed fiber-optic (light-based) cabling schemes have increasingly come into use. Fiber-optic cabling is generally more expensive to install and support than copper cable, but is resistant to outside interference, so it's most commonly used for connecting LANs on different floors to a building-wide backbone or as a high-speed link between different LANs across a site. Widely scattered WANs can be linked through standard telephone lines via modems, though current technology limits these links to 38,400bps. Higher-speed (and higher-cost) WANs can be linked with special modem-like devices called Data Service Units (DSUs) through data-grade T-1 (1.54Mbps) phone lines provided by all the major telephone companies. Modems are also used for individual remote PCs to dial in and connect to the LAN to share data and services.

Once the PCs are connected to the network cabling, software drivers are installed to tell the PC how to communicate on the cable through the NIC. Other software drivers allow the PC's applications to access data and files on the LAN's File Server, send print jobs to shared printers on the server, or communicate with the database server.

Figure 2.4

ARCnet network

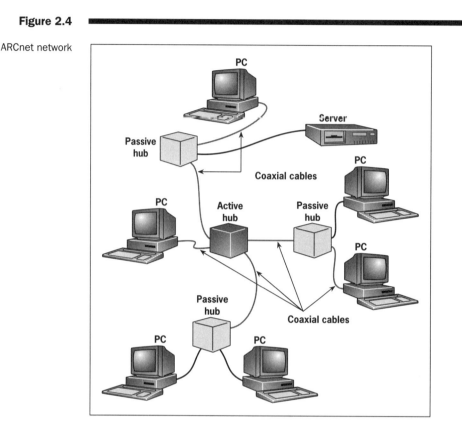

Network Protocols

A protocol is a standard method of communicating between two computer systems across a network. Many proprietary network protocols exist today, but only a few are relevant to designing a Client/Server Database System.

NetWare LANs use the Novell IPX/SPX protocol to provide communications between workstations and server(s). Microsoft's LAN Manager and IBM's LAN Server use variations of the NetBIOS protocol, and DEC-based LANs use the DECNet protocol. IBM mainframes primarily use System Network Architecture (SNA) to communicate with terminals and LAN Gateways, and IBM's LANs also support the Data Link Control (DLC) protocol for direct communications between the LAN PCs and the mainframe front-end processors.

The most common cross-platform protocol is the Transmission Control Protocol/Internet Protocol (TCP/IP). Originally developed as the UNIX networking protocol, TCP/IP is now available for almost every platform and operating system, and it is widely used for linking together PCs, workstations, minicomputers, and sometimes mainframes.

Though sufficient for basic LAN communications, these protocols generally don't provide sufficient capabilities for Client/Server applications, so a second protocol layer is required. One such C/S protocol, Named Pipes, is primarily used by database servers that run on OS/2. Other Client/Server DBMS vendors provide their own (usually proprietary) protocols for communications between the front-end applications and the database server. These protocols will be discussed in more detail in the descriptions of the particular database server software packages in Chapters 4 through 7.

- *Asking the Right Questions*
- *What Are the Next Steps?*

The Decision Tree

Choosing the right type of client/server system can be an intimidating process; there are a number of different ways to go, and a wrong choice early in the process can waste a lot of time and money over the long run.

No one Client/Server system is right for every situation. Your solution may be to replace existing systems with a single-vendor C/S DBMS, or you may need to keep the existing databases and integrate them with a new C/S system. Or, you may find you require multiple C/S databases on multiple platforms to fulfill different functions.

A fold-out Decision Tree is bound in the back cover of this book to guide you through the process of choosing the right Client/Server platform for your needs. This chapter explains how to use the Decision Tree, so you'll want to keep the tree handy while you're reading through it.

■ Asking the Right Questions

Before you take the first steps toward a Client/Server solution, you need a knowledgeable database expert to help you decide which system is right. This expert should also help design and install the system, and support it once it's up and running. If you don't have this expertise in-house, your best course of action is to hire a qualified consultant. Be careful, though, and check the consultant's credentials before hiring him—it's unfortunate but true that anyone with the slightest amount of computer knowledge can call themselves a consultant, and there's (as yet) no certification standard to rely on to prove any level of expertise. It's also a good idea to contact the consultant's previous clients and ask them if they were satisfied with his performance. A Client/Server Database System can be a long-term and expensive investment; you want to be quite certain that you've investigated your options fully before committing yourself and your company.

While the Decision Tree won't replace the services of an expert, it will help you to ask the right questions along the way. It will also make you aware of any issues you may have overlooked in your early investigations of Client/Server DBMSs.

Do You Need a Client/Server Database System?

First you should decide if you actually need a Client/Server system. Starting in the upper-left corner of the Decision Tree, you'll see that the first question addresses whether multiple users must have access to the database. If not, any of the stand-alone PC DBMSs would solve your problem without a Client/Server system.

If you do need multiuser access, the next question is how many simultaneous users must you accommodate? If the answer is less than 20, follow the tree to the right, where the next question asks if you have an existing LAN. If you do have a LAN, a multiuser PC-based DBMS would more than suffice. If you don't have a LAN, you might want to consider one of the smaller multiuser operating systems (such as one based on a multiuser DOS, multiuser OS/2, or UNIX) running on a high-powered PC or RISC workstation/minicomputer. Your existing PCs can act as terminals to the multiuser host, and future expansion can be via PCs or dumb terminals, depending on the needs of your end-users.

If you expect to have more than 20 simultaneous users, you must determine what type of access the users are going to have to the database. If the bulk of the access is for data lookups, and only a few users will be modifying data (insertions, deletions, and updates), a traditional multiuser DBMS should provide acceptable performance for up to 32 to 40 users. However, if most or all of the DBMS users have data modification rights (for example, in a transaction-processing system such as an inventory and order-taking database), you'll need the multiuser power and data integrity of a Client/Server database. Twenty simultaneous users is an admittedly arbitrary figure, though testing in the PC Magazine Labs has shown that the performance of traditional PC-based DBMSs can vary widely above that number.

How Can You Design Your Own C/S System?

Congratulations! If you've gotten to this point, you're on the road to designing and installing a Client/Server Database System. From here on, your decisions will primarily address whether or how to integrate existing DBMSs into the new C/S system.

Following the tree, you'll see that if you have an existing PC-based single or multiuser database, you should first determine how to upgrade it. If your database relies heavily on existing dBASE-type code (sometimes referred to as "xBASE") and you don't want to completely rewrite it, you can reap some of the benefits of a Client/Server system by moving your data to the File Server and using a Class 4 DBMS to provide data access to the users. This method is the easiest way to move an existing system to the C/S architecture, though it does not provide as much data integrity control as a full Client/Server system.

If you're willing to rewrite existing applications or don't have them to begin with, the next question is whether you already have RISC workstations in your organization. If you do, you might want to consider a full C/S DBMS that runs under UNIX on the workstation. This provides a high-power solution, although it does add some complexity to communications and operating systems. If you don't already have RISC systems or decide that you don't want the added complexity of having to support a new type of hardware platform on the server side, your choice is clear: You want one of the many PC-based Client/Server DBMSs that are available. A PC-based system can be easily integrated into existing LANs and doesn't add the complexity of a different hardware platform (though you may have to learn and use a new operating system for the database server).

Returning to the "Existing multiuser PC-based DBMS?" question in the tree reveals another path to take. If you already have a DBMS on a minicomputer or mainframe, you can either replace the existing system or integrate it into your Client/Server system. If you don't have an existing large system, you should follow the tree along the RISC path described in the previous paragraphs.

Should You "Downsize" from Your Existing Platform?

When you already have minicomputers and/or mainframes, your biggest decision is whether to downsize those systems to a PC-based Client/Server DBMS or to integrate them into the total C/S architecture. If you decide that downsizing is right for you, your choice is easy: Design and install a PC-based Client/Server DBMS and move your existing data to it.

However, you may not want to downsize your systems right away. The amount of data may be more than a PC-based system can handle, or you may have a large investment in custom-written applications which would take a long time to rewrite. In such cases, you must consider the different methods of providing Client/Server functionality on the existing systems.

Many large system DBMS vendors provide a Client/Server option for their software (usually gateway-type software that runs on top of the DBMS). If your vendor is one of these, one final question needs to be answered: Does the vendor's C/S software use the same protocols that the proposed front-end platforms support? If so, you can just install the vendor's gateway software, and you're ready to go. If not, you'll need the extra complexity of a hardware and software gateway that translates both the C/S and network protocols into something the systems on the other side of the gateway understand.

If the DBMS vendor doesn't provide a Client/Server option, your only choice is one of the third-party C/S gateways. These gateways can be either software only or hardware/software combinations that do all the translations necessary for the front-end systems to access the data on the host. While these gateways give you the ability to link multiple systems together, they also add a high level of complexity to both the DBMS software and the network itself; they're also generally more costly to implement and support.

■ What Are the Next Steps?

Now that you've looked over the Decision Tree and have an idea of which direction to go to move to a Client/Server DBMS, it's time to examine the choices available. The next four chapters will cover the various C/S DBMSs currently available for the different platforms described earlier in Chapter 2. Each chapter will have comparison charts of the features of each DBMS, and Appendix A will summarize all the charts for all the products. You'll find suggestions for further reading on the topics covered so far in Appendix C.

Chapter 8 covers a broad representative sampling of the many different types of front-end software available and what DBMSs they support. Appendix B gives a listing of contact points for all the vendors discussed in this book. Finally, Chapter 9 considers the current and future trends in the DBMS world that may influence your long-term plans.

- *Evaluating Client/Server Databases for PC Platforms*

- *Microsoft/Sybase SQL Server 4.2*

- *Gupta SQLBase 5.0*

- *IBM OS/2 ES Database Manager 2.0*

- *XDB-Server*

- *INGRES for OS/2*

- *NetWare SQL and Novell BTrieve*

- *ORACLE Server 6.0*

- *Class 3 C/S Databases for .DBF Files*

Client/Server Databases for PC Platforms

IN THE SPRING OF 1992, A REPORT ON THE CURRENT STATE OF CLIENT/ server computing was released by the Business Research Group (BRG), an industry research firm, and was reported on in the weekly computer newspapers. BRG's survey of existing users of C/S DBMSs found that an overwhelming 58 percent of the sites depended on 386- and 486-based PCs for their database servers. Mainframes came in a distant second, and minicomputers and RISC systems brought up the rear.

The choice of PCs as the prevalent platform-of-choice for Client/Server systems isn't as surprising as it may seem at first glance—C/S computing is the natural evolution of PC-based LANs beyond simply sharing files and printers. And the high-end PCs have become powerful enough to function as cost-effective alternatives to minicomputers and mainframes as database servers. As LANs become more and more widespread in businesses (and as PCs become more powerful), this trend will probably continue, and PCs will remain the dominant base for C/S systems.

■ Evaluating Client/Server Databases for PC Platforms

The Client/Server database field is rapidly evolving, with both enhancements to existing products and new products becoming available almost monthly. The product information in this chapter, as well as the next four chapters, is at most a snapshot of what's available in the market in the summer of 1992.

Before discussing the individual products, each chapter will cover the overall advantages and disadvantages of the particular platform. I'll also be pointing out any considerations or problems you should be aware of when considering this platform for your C/S system. Finally, I'll pass along advice and tips about C/S databases and particular platforms that I've learned through experience or in conversations with those who have successfully (or unsuccessfully) implemented their own C/S systems.

Use the information in these introductory sections and the details about the individual products as the basis for your own evaluation of which product and platform are right for your organization.

Advantages and Disadvantages

The clear advantages to PCs are that they are well known and widely available. LAN support staffs will require minimal additional hardware training (if any) to add a PC to the network as a database server. Depending on which LAN OS is used, support staff may not even need training on the operating system that the DBMS runs under. Widespread availability also ensures that it's easy to find and purchase the support hardware needed to maintain the integrity of the server, hardware such as tape drives for backups, and uninterruptible power supplies (UPSs) for protection against power outages.

There's also a wider choice of operating systems that can be used for the database server; unlike the larger systems, PC-based DBMSs aren't limited to running only on UNIX or on a proprietary OS. Client/Server databases can be run under NetWare 3.11, OS/2, or any of the various UNIX packages for 486 systems. Any of the major LAN operating systems and protocols can be used for communications between the clients and the servers. The rise in other 32-bit operating systems, such as OS/2 2.0 or Microsoft's Windows/NT (due to be released in early 1993), will only serve to increase the number (and power) of C/S software choices.

The dominance of PCs as the platform for C/S databases also leads to a self-perpetuating cycle in DBMS software development. The early PC-based C/S DBMSs were mostly ported down from minicomputer systems, so the products were already mature and didn't usually suffer from the problems associated with new software. As the size of the market increases (driven by enhancements to the current offerings), new DBMS vendors enter it, offering more powerful and feature-filled server software packages. This increased power and sophistication then leads more users to install C/S databases, increasing the market's size, and so the cycle continues to expand.

Since most PC C/S DBMSs are based on existing large-system database packages, you'll be able to draw on a large pool of experienced support personnel and DBMS programmers, which reduces the need for (and costs of) training existing staff in the new systems. Minicomputer and mainframe programmers can usually adapt to the different platform.

The downside is the increased cost of purchasing new high-powered PCs for use as dedicated database servers. There's also the cost of equipment duplication (that is, UPSs or tape drives), or of replacing existing equipment with higher-capacity versions to support the additional servers.

Personnel costs can also increase dramatically, especially if the existing large system staff can't be moved to the new platform. While a small C/S system can usually be supported by existing LAN personnel, increased size and complexity eventually leads to the need for a support staff for the DBMS alone. The Client/Server DBMS market is also evolving rapidly, and it will probably become necessary to provide for regularly scheduled training on the new features and capabilities of the software.

Existing databases may prove incompatible with the new system, making it difficult to integrate the new Client/Server system into the enterprise-wide data services. You may also have difficulties moving data from existing systems to the C/S DBMS designated as the replacement.

Finally, it's very easy to get caught up in the rush to Client/Server systems and to overestimate their current (and maybe even future) capabilities. Doing so can lead to major problems in both the MIS and financial areas; personnel costs can rise dramatically when staff spends more time getting the systems to work than in actually using them. Losing access to "mission-critical" data while the problems are resolved can have a ripple effect across the entire business organization, leading to major financial losses. A *mission-critical* application is one that is so important to the functioning of a business that, should the application fail, the business would suffer a serious disruption in its operations.

C/S systems aren't the be-all and end-all solution to data-management problems, and the decision to move to one should be based on extensive research and careful planning. There's no place for impulse buying or cost-cutting without careful study when designing a Client/Server DBMS system for business use.

Special Considerations

There are some important points to keep in mind when you're deciding whether or not to base your Client/Server database system on a PC server. Use the information in this section as the starting point for questions to ask the different DBMS vendors before making your purchase:

- **Hardware:** Is the server hardware already in place, or will it be purchased as part of the total system? Either way, make sure the hardware is compatible with the operating system the DBMS runs under. Client/Server vendors are usually happy to provide a list of PCs that have been tested for compatibility. It's a good idea to get a copy of the list before purchasing the hardware. The data that resides on the database server is too critical to your business to trust it to an off-brand, knocked-together PC.

  Find out if any other hardware is needed, such as tape drives for backups. Some DBMSs support backups to any tape drive on the network; others require that the tape drive be connected directly to the database server to get the full functionality of the built-in backup capabilities.

- **Compatibility with existing networks:** It may be easier in the long run to get a DBMS that runs under the operating system that your support staff already knows. Balance the features of the different DBMSs against the costs and complexities of having to learn (and support) a new operating system.

- **Support:** Support from the vendor is critical to successfully designing, developing, and running a Client/Server system. What kind of support plans does the vendor offer? Do they cover bug fixes and minor updates to the DBMS software, or is that an extra-cost option? Does the vendor provide on-site support or only telephone support? Or is support only provided through the dealer or VAR (value-added reseller) that you bought the software from? And what are the support hours? Does the vendor provide support 24 hours a day, seven days a week? Or is it limited to the vendor's business hours (which may not be the same as yours, due to time zone differences)? Depending on the size and complexity of your system, it can be very helpful to have a technical representative in your offices while the system is being set up and programmed.

If the vendor provides telephone support only, will a support technician be assigned to your account or will support be provided by whoever answers the phone? Having an assigned technician saves time and money in the long run. If you're dealing with someone familiar with your system, you won't have to describe it every time you call for support.

If support is only provided through the dealer or VAR, find out how the support staff is trained. It's also important to find out what kind of fall-back support is available if the dealer is unable to fix any problems you're having—or worse, if the dealer goes out of business in your area.

Finally, it would be a good idea to contact other customers of the vendor or dealer to find out about their experiences with the support provided. The best product in the world doesn't do you any good if you can't get proper support when you need it the most.

- **Training:** What type of training does the vendor provide for your in-house staff? Will they send a trainer to your site, or do you have to send your staff out to a training center? If you have to send the staff to a center, find out if the vendor has one near you; the costs for training obviously increase the farther away the training center is, due to transportation and housing needs.

- **Performance monitoring:** Does the DBMS have built-in performance monitoring functions? Or are third-party monitors available? A database monitor is the only way to detect whether a delay in response is due to a temporary increase in data requests or a permanent degradation in performance. Also make sure that the monitor provides some type of historical records, so you can check database performance over a period of days, weeks, or months.

- **Front-end software:** Client/Server DBMS vendors will also provide an up-to-date list of the front-ends that support their server. Get a copy of the list, and make sure the software you want to use for your application development is on it.

Advice and Tips

Every Client/Server system is unique; each has its own requirements, quirks, and special performance features. However, a few tricks, applicable to all of them, can make it easier to get and keep a Client/Server database up and running.

First, buy the fastest machine you can for the database server. It doesn't take long for the database to get large enough to start bogging down on a slower system. The disks can be the cause of the most serious performance bottleneck, so make sure the system's disks are high-performance. I'd recommend at least a 33MHz 80486 with fast-access (under 20ms) hard disks.

Next, get as much memory as the server system supports. Every user on the DBMS requires an area of memory on the server, so it makes sense from a performance standpoint to load up the server with as much memory as possible. When first starting out, add at least 4Mb to 8Mb of RAM beyond the minimum recommended by the vendor for best performance, and make sure you have room for future memory expansion.

Also make sure the hard-disk subsystem on the PC is expandable. SCSI drives are a good choice, as one SCSI card can support up to seven devices. Disk array systems, also expandable, are good alternatives. Disk throughput is also a factor; 32-bit disk controllers provide better data transfer-per-second rates than 16-bit controllers. Use a system that supports 32-bit cards whenever possible.

A Client/Server database is best run on its own dedicated system. While you can run just about all the PC-based DBMSs on the same system as the LAN file server, I recommend doing this only in the early design and development stages. As noted previously, it doesn't take long for a database to get large, and the contention between the database services and the file and print services can ultimately have a severe impact on performance. Data integrity may be jeopardized if you run a DBMS on the same server as other network services, because an errant application can bring down the server, possibly damaging the database. Running the DBMS on a dedicated server reduces the risk of this happening.

One final bit of advice—whenever you can, run the C/S DBMS under a LAN operating system that the DBMS has native support for. For example, while you can use an OS/2-based DBMS on a NetWare LAN, slight incompatibilities and/or differences are likely to arise in the functions if you run it on a LAN Manager or LAN Server network. I'll be pointing out these differences wherever necessary in the descriptions of the Client/Server DBMSs that follow.

■ Microsoft/Sybase SQL Server 4.2

Shortly after their announcement of OS/2 in April 1987, Microsoft announced that they were working with Sybase (a UNIX and VAX-based RDBMS vendor) to port the Sybase SQL Server to the new operating system. The 1.x versions of the Microsoft/Sybase SQL Server were actually subsets of the Sybase product, which contained most of the features of the UNIX version. However, the OS/2-based DBMS had a major impact on the PC community, as it was the first product from a major PC vendor to bring the concept of Client/Server databases to PC-based LANs. It soon became the top-selling C/S

DBMS for PC LANs; to date it has the widest support among third-party, front-end vendors.

In early 1992, Microsoft released SQL Server Version 4.2, which brought the DBMS up to full compatibility with the current Sybase product. The significant enhancements over the 1.x versions raised 4.2 to the level of an entirely new product.

In mid-1992, Sybase released a NetWare 3.11 NLM (NetWare Loadable Module) version of SQL Server 4.2, which is functionally compatible with the Microsoft version. Except where noted, the following discussion applies to both products.

Significant Features

SQL Server is a Class 2 DBMS whose traditional claim to fame has been its support for stored procedures on the database server. *Stored procedures* are SQL routines that are stored as part of the database itself; they are executed entirely on the server when called from a client. Because they move more of the processing to the server, stored procedures can have a significant, positive impact on database performance. Access to them is controlled through the DBMS's security features, adding a measure of additional data integrity by preventing unauthorized users from inadvertently changing the database. A number of stored procedures are included in the package to provide functions such as administering users, monitoring the server, and assisting in creating new databases.

Version 4.2 added support for remote stored procedures, which provide a form of distributed processing by letting a procedure on one database server call and execute stored procedures on another database server running any version of SQL Server.

SQL Server also supports a special type of stored procedure called a *trigger*, which is a procedure that is automatically executed when certain events (such as an INSERT, UPDATE, or DELETE) take place on the server. Triggers are particularly useful in creating and enforcing data and referential integrity rules (SQL statements which preserve the data and referential integrity requirements of the Relational model); because they're automatically activated, they can be used for a number of database checks and alerts. For example, a trigger can be set for a DELETE command on a particular table, which then automatically checks to make sure that the data being deleted is not linked to dependent data in another table. Or, one can be set to calculate the value of a column on an update and alert the user when the value reaches a certain threshold.

SQL Server supports groups of users for security and database access. Groups make database privilege administration easy, as privileges can be assigned on both a group and an individual level.

Version 4.2 has built-in, fault-tolerance features, such as real-time backups and disk mirroring, that increase the reliability of the database server. Under Microsoft's version, real-time, on-line backups to tape are performed using the included Systron Systos Plus tape backup software, which runs under OS/2 and supports a number of different tape drives. The NLM version can be backed up with any tape backup software that supports NetWare. Backups can be run while users are accessing the database server and can be scheduled to run automatically throughout the day.

Database disk devices, which contain either the data itself or the transaction recovery logs (log files maintained by the DBMS that keep track of all database transactions), can optionally be automatically mirrored. Mirroring constantly creates an exact duplicate of the primary files on a backup disk, and the DBMS will automatically switch to the mirrored drive if an error occurs on the primary one. Mirroring slows down performance somewhat; however, the increased data integrity and security may be worth the penalty in system overhead.

The maximum number of database devices per server is 256, and, for additional performance, you can store the transaction logs on a device other than the one where the actual databases are stored. A database can span multiple disks, so databases can store up to the maximum OS/2 disk size of 2G or the NetWare 3.11 purported maximum of 32T (terabytes), minus disk space for the log files (although 4G is the current realistic limit).

Microsoft provides a service known as Open Database Connectivity (ODBC), an API and programming library that lets SQL Server clients connect to any other SQL Server, regardless of platform. Their Open Database Services option provides vendors with the ability to create gateways between SQL Server clients and other non-Microsoft/Sybase database servers. Microsoft hopes that ODBC will become a standard for interconnecting database servers, and a number of DBMS vendors have announced support for it in future versions of their software.

Hardware and Software Requirements

The Microsoft SQL Server requires at least a 80286-based system running OS/2 1.3 or higher, though a 80386 or better is strongly recommended. The minimum memory needed is 8Mb, though again at least 12Mb is recommended; minimum disk space needed is 20Mb. SQL Server ships with a server-adapted version of OS/2 1.3 that is certified for well over 100 different PC systems. Microsoft's SQL Server uses Named Pipes as its communication protocol, so it works with any NOS that supports Named Pipes, such as LAN Manager, Novell's NetWare, or IBM's LAN Server. Microsoft has also announced a version that will use the native NetWare IPX/SPX protocol, due to be released in late 1992.

The Sybase SQL Server NLM requires at least a 80386 running NetWare 3.11. Sybase recommends 12Mb of RAM as the minimum, and it also needs about 20Mb disk space. The Sybase version uses the NetWare IPX/SPX transport protocol as its communications protocol, so it only supports NetWare LANs at this time.

Native SQL Language

TRANSACT-SQL, the native language used by SQL Server, provides complete ANSI SQL level 1 (1986) compatibility, with some elements of the level 2 (1989) standard. The enhancements provided by TRANSACT-SQL over the standard SQL language are particularly aimed at programming and using stored procedures and triggers. A number of math, financial, and statistical functions are also provided for use in data analysis.

Version 4.2 supports the concept of scrollable cursors, an SQL construct that treats the result of a query as a set that the client application can scroll through backward and forward; however, it implements them on the client end through the use of a data buffer with pointers. (Scrollable cursors are discussed in further detail in "Gupta SQLBase 5.0" later in this chapter.) While this method is better than not having scrollable cursors at all, it doesn't provide the data manipulation benefits of implementing them on the server itself.

TRANSACT-SQL statements are optimized using cost-based algorithms; a cost-based optimizer determines the best and fastest way to execute the SQL statements based on the structure, size, and indexing of the tables in the database, in order to reduce the transaction's "cost" in time and CPU cycles.

TRANSACT-SQL has no statements that provide database and referential integrity. Referential integrity, one of the key aspects of the Relational model that deals with overall database integrity, ensures consistency between tables when the values in one table are dependent on parent values in another table. DI and RI are provided through the use of programmed stored procedures and triggers to ensure that the database tables are consistent. While this is again better than not providing RI at all, the better method is to include it as part of the DBMS.

Front-ends Provided

Microsoft's SQL Server includes a Windows 3.x-based SQL Administrator tool that lets the database administrator (DBA) easily administrate one or more SQL Servers through Window's usual icons, drop-down menus, pick-lists, and dialog boxes. The SQL Administrator program also provides the DBA with a real-time monitor of server performance, as well as a way to preserve a history log of performance for analysis and comparison when tuning the server. Figure 4.1 shows an SQL Query Window used for performance monitoring.

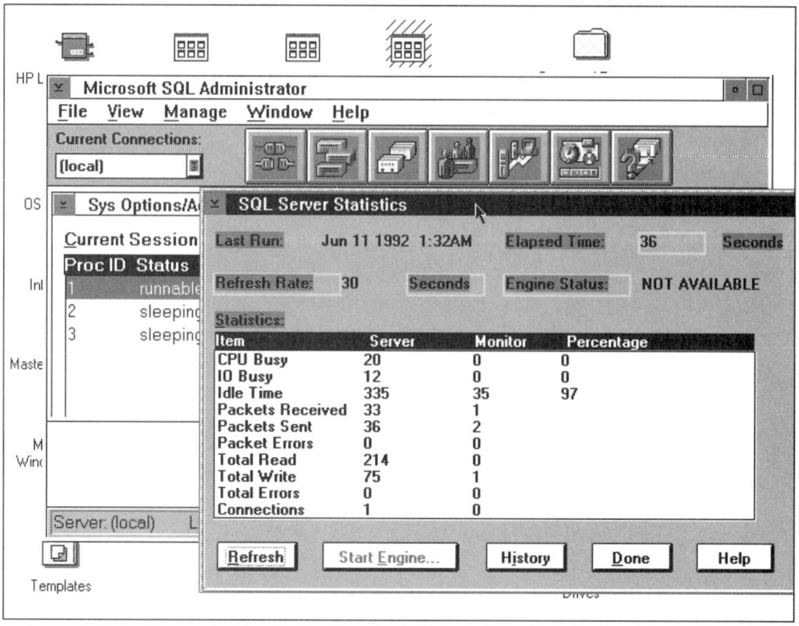

Figure 4.1

Microsoft's Windows-
based SQL Administrator
provides real-time
database performance
monitoring.

Both Microsoft and Sybase provide two character-mode utilities that provide administration and interactive SQL query capabilities. ISQL (Interactive SQL) is a command-line tool that lets the user access or administrate the databases through directly entered TRANSACT-SQL statements. System Administration Facility (SAF) is a character-based graphics mode interface that provides fairly easy menu access to administrative facilities, as well as a method of scrolling back and forth through the query results. Figure 4.2 shows some of the on-line help available from SAF.

Microsoft also offers a line of programmer's toolkits that can be used to create custom client applications for SQL Server. Versions are available for Visual BASIC, C, and COBOL. A single-user SQL Server Developer's System is available for those who want to create SQL Server clients without the expense of a full system.

Advantages and Disadvantages

The most significant advantage of the Microsoft/Sybase SQL Server DBMS is the wide variety of third-party client support available. While researching a story in the spring of 1992 on SQL databases and front-ends, *PC Magazine*'s research staff found that SQL Server was supported by the majority of the over 400 front-ends available at the time. Every type of front-end software is available, from those designed strictly for application development to add-in SQL Server access modules for standard PC-based DBMSs such as Paradox and dBASE. There are even access modules that let the users query the database from the leading spreadsheet programs (such as Lotus 1-2-3 and Microsoft Excel).

Figure 4.2

The character-based Microsoft/Sybase System Administrator Facility (SAF) runs on a number of client platforms.

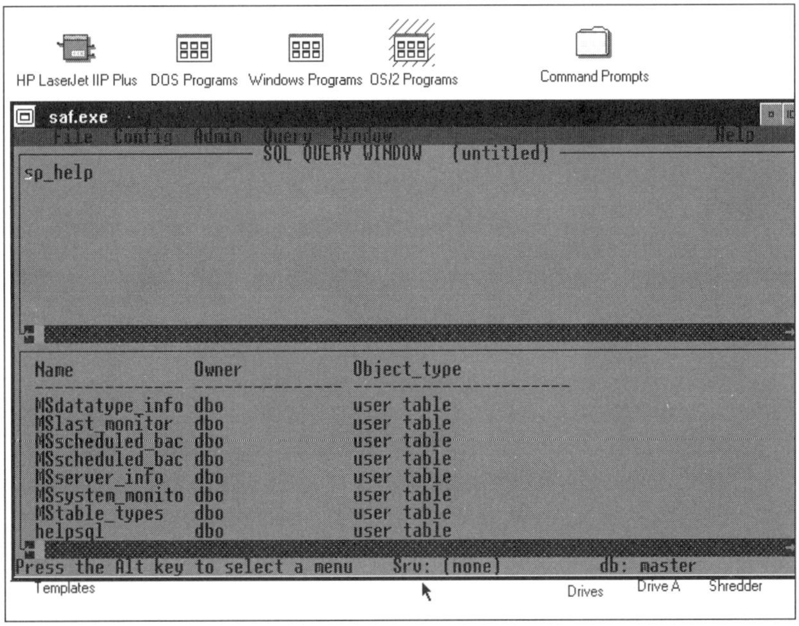

Microsoft's other advantage is also in part a serious disadvantage—it runs on OS/2. On the plus side, an OS/2-based database server is network independent and can be used with any of the popular NOSs. In addition, OS/2's preemptive multiprocessing and built-in multithreading make it an ideal platform for mission-critical databases. However, Microsoft's SQL Server is still based on OS/2 1.x code, so it's still a 16-bit system and suffers from the performance limitations imposed by the older operating system. Microsoft hasn't committed to a 32-bit version of SQL Server based on OS/2 2.0. Instead, the first 32-bit version will probably be based on Microsoft's Windows/NT, due out in late 1992 or early 1993. Sybase has indicated that they will probably be doing the OS/2 2.0 32-bit version, but only when SQL Server 5.0 is released sometime in 1993.

Sybase's NLM version is faster than Microsoft's version, largely because it's a full 32-bit application and because NetWare is not preemptive, providing the DBMS with complete access to the host systems' resources. The NLM is also 100 percent compatible with client front-ends designed for the Microsoft version. On the other hand, it's much more expensive than Microsoft's version and supports an equal number of users.

Unfortunately, the overall question of the safety of NLMs (which I briefly mentioned in Chapter 2) for mission-critical applications is still being debated in the industry and has not yet been put to rest by definitive testing. In my opinion, until the problem of NLM safety is either resolved or dismissed as a real issue, alternatives to an NLM version should be used whenever they exist.

The Microsoft version of SQL Server has a proven track record and wide support, and it is my preference of the two. Only time and further testing will tell if the Sybase version will prove a viable alternative.

Table 4.1

Microsoft/Sybase SQL
Server Quick Summary

PRODUCT INFORMATION	
Name	Microsoft/Sybase SQL Server 4.2
Vendor	OS/2: Microsoft Corporation (MS)
	NLM: Sybase, Inc. (SB)
Price	1 user: $1,495 (MS), $1,995 (SB)
	10 users: $2,995 (MS), $8,995 (SB, 16 users max.)
	25 users: $15,995 (SB, 32 users max.)
	Unlimited: $7,995 (MS), $29,995 (SB)
	(Sybase charges an additional $290 per workstation for software, but offers a 25 percent discount when more than one copy is purchased.)
OPERATING SYSTEMS	
On Database Server	OS/2 1.21 or higher (MS); NetWare 3.11 (SB)
On LAN Server	MS LAN Manager, IBM LAN Server, Novell NetWare, or any other network that supports Named Pipes (MS); Novell NetWare 3.11 (SB)
On Workstations	DOS 3.x or higher, Windows 3.x, or OS/2 1.21 or higher (both)

Table 4.1

(continued)

MINIMUM REQUIREMENTS	
RAM on Server	8Mb (MS), 12Mb (SB)
RAM on Workstation	512k (DOS), 6Mb (OS/2) (both)
Disk Space on Server	20Mb (both)
UTILITIES PROVIDED	
Administration Utility	Yes (both)
Interactive User Utility	Yes (both)
Operating Systems/ Environments Supported	DOS 3.1 or higher, OS/2 1.21 or higher, or Windows 3.x (MS); DOS 3.1 or higher, OS/2 1.21 or higher (SB)
NATIVE LANGUAGES	
ANSI SQL	Level 1 (both)
DB2 SQL Extensions	No (both)
Other SQL Extensions	Yes (both)
Non-SQL Language	No (both)
MAXIMUMS	
Database Size	2G (MS); 32T (SB)
Column Size	Normally 1,962 bytes; "image" and "text" data types store 2G through pointers to external data (both)
Row Size	1,962 bytes (both)
# of Columns in Row	255 columns (both)
# of Rows per Table	Limited by disk space (both)
# of Rows per Database	Limited by disk space (both)
# of Tables per Database	2 billion (both)
# of Views per Database	Unlimited (both)
# of Tables per View	Unlimited tables, but only 250 columns per view (both)

■ Gupta SQLBase 5.0

Even though it's third in market share behind Microsoft and Oracle, Gupta's SQLBase is unique among the different PC-based C/S DBMS in that it wasn't ported down from a large system. The initial version of SQLBase that shipped in 1986 was developed for and ran under PC/MS-DOS. Since then, versions have been released for OS/2 and NetWare 3.11. Gupta has also developed a variety of front-ends and connections to other DBMSs; their goal is to be a "one stop" source for Client/Server computing.

In many ways, SQLBase is the technological leader in the RDBMS market, and it provides many relational features that other RDBMS have yet to implement. The impetus behind these advanced features lies with Dr. Umang Gupta, the company's founder and president. Prior to starting Gupta, he was an executive with Oracle and formerly held sales and marketing positions in IBM. He brought his experience with a variety of database systems to his own products and is still very involved in the design and development of present and future products.

Significant Features

Gupta's Class 2 SQLBase comes in versions for all three primary PC-based operating systems: DOS, OS/2, and NetWare. A version that runs on SUN's version of UNIX is also available and will be discussed in Chapter 5.

SQLBase is also one of the few RDBMS that includes full support for the ANSI level 2 SQL standard with the Integrity Addendum. This means that SQLBase supports declarative referential integrity (RI), the preferred implementation. In SQLBase, RI is declared as part of the database definition, instead of being left up to stored procedures and triggers (as MS/Sybase and Ingres implement it) or entirely up to the front-end application programmer. SQLBase implements RI as part of the table definition through primary and foreign keys, and through SQL keywords that tell the DBMS what actions to take when a parent row is deleted. The full implications of implementing referential integrity is beyond the scope of this book; for more information, check both the current ANSI standard papers and the reference books listed in Appendix C.

Databases can be partitioned so that portions can reside on multiple disks or disk volumes. Depending on the platform, a SQLBase database can range up to 500G in size. For additional performance, the transaction logs can be stored on a different drive than the database files. SQLBase also supports on-line (real-time) backups using the tape backup system appropriate to the platform.

Various benchmarks performed by *PC Magazine* and others have shown SQLBase to be one of the fastest SQL Servers available today. One of the reasons is that Gupta supports *hashed clustered indices*, which change the physical location of the data to reduce the amount of disk I/O when multiple rows of data are retrieved. Another factor is *data compression*, a built-in option in which the server compresses the query responses prior to sending them back to the client, further reducing the traffic over the network cable.

SQLBase also supports precompiled (another way of saying preoptimized) SQL procedures that are stored on the server for faster execution. While not as integral to the database as the stored procedures used by SQL Server and thus not as high performance, precompiled SQL speeds up database operations by performing the optimization of the SQL statement once, instead of each time the statement is executed. Because they're stored alongside the database on the server, precompiled SQL also adds a measure of data consistency by letting different front-end applications use the exact same statements to access the database—an advantage shared with DBMSs that implement stored procedures.

Gupta's SQLBase is also one of only two RDBMSs that support true scrollable cursors. (NetWare SQL is the other.) Standard SQL queries return the results one row at a time, and it's up to the front-end application to devise a buffer to store the results so that the user can scroll (browse) forward through the query results. A scrollable cursor is an SQL construct that lets the DBMS return, simultaneously, multiple rows of data that can be scrolled in either direction. RDBMSs such as the Microsoft/Sybase SQL Server implement it through an automatic buffer (or pseudocursor) on the front-end that uses a pointer to track where the user is in the results set. If the user wants to scroll backward, the SQL request is first reexecuted on the server, and the response is restricted to the previously viewed rows. Gupta implements scrollable cursors on the server through the use of a temporary results table that the client application then views in either direction. Because the cursor is implemented on the server, the user can also manipulate the data to have the changes written back to the original database. However, implementing scrollable cursors this way adds a significant amount of overhead to server processing, so SQLBase makes them an option that can be turned on and off by the client application as needed.

In line with their stated goal of being a one-stop source for C/S solutions, Gupta provides an IBM DB2-compatible SQL syntax, so front-end applications can be created for SQLBase servers that can also directly access DB2 databases through a gateway system. This capability is aimed primarily at easing the transition for those looking to downsize their DB2 applications to a PC-based C/S platform. Gupta also markets a number of gateways/routers that let SQLBase users and developers access data on other DBMSs such as Oracle, SQL Server, and DB2 using SQLBase's standard SQL syntax. (A *router* is a hardware/software combination that links different networks that use the same protocol together.)

Hardware and Software Requirements

The DOS version of SQLBase requires at least a 286 with 2Mb of RAM, 10Mb of disk space, and PC/MS-DOS 3.1 or higher. The OS/2 version is still 16-bit and also requires at least a 286 running OS/2 1.0 or higher, with at least 4Mb of RAM and 10Mb of hard-disk space. A 32-bit OS/2 version is due to be released in early 1993. The NLM version requires a 386 or higher running NetWare 3.11, with 8Mb of RAM and 10Mb of disk space.

Gupta's SQLBase supports numerous network protocols, including IBM's Advanced Peer-to-Peer Communications (APPC), Named Pipes, NetBIOS, TCP/IP, and IPX/SPX. However, its own communication driver has one major problem—the amount of RAM it needs on top of the network protocols on the client workstation. While all the other C/S DBMSs keep their communications protocols under (in some cases, well under) 100k in size, SQLBase's takes a whopping 200k of RAM on the client.

Native SQL Language

As stated previously, SQLBase's native SQLTalk language is fully compatible with the ANSI level 2 with Integrity Enhancements standard. It also has a number of optional extensions that make it fully DB2-compatible.

Gupta has implemented a cost-based optimizer in SQLBase that is particularly designed for speeding up database queries when using precompiled SQL code. However, it's advisable to periodically recompile the stored code so that the optimizer can adjust the SQL statements to properly reflect the current state of the database.

Front-end Processors Provided

Gupta includes two front-end database administration utilities with SQL-Base: a character-mode utility and a Windows 3.x-based utility. SQLTalk/Character is the command-line interface that lets the DBA directly enter SQL statements at a command prompt. The rather primitive interface is similar to Microsoft/Sybase's ISQL. Gupta doesn't provide a character graphics-based administration tool like SQL Servers SAF. Due to the high RAM requirement of SQLBase's client-side communications drivers, there isn't always enough RAM to run SQLTalk/Character, so Gupta also provides a version that includes the appropriate drivers as part of the program to get around the limitation.

The preferred interface is SQLTalk/Windows, a Windows 3.x-based administration utility that uses Windows's memory management capabilities to circumvent the RAM limitations of the SQLBase communications drivers. While not as sophisticated as Microsoft's SQL Administrator, SQLTalk/Windows makes it much easier to administrate and query the database than with the character version. SQLTalk/Windows provides different windows for entering queries and viewing the results, and also has a number of pull-down menus with predefined choices for creating users, setting security levels, and switching between databases.

A C/API library is included in the standard SQLBase package for creating custom client applications in C. A COBOL API library is also available from Gupta.

Advantages and Disadvantages

SQLBase has two significant advantages: price and scalability, particularly on PC platforms. (*Scalability* is the ability to run on different platforms.) SQLBase is the least expensive of all the C/S RDBMSs, with the unlimited versions costing $2,995, $3,995, and $4,995 for DOS, OS/2, and NetWare respectively. Five-user versions for all three platforms cost a mere $995.

SQLBase's scalability is an important factor for those starting out with a small Client/Server system, because front-end applications designed for one server version are completely compatible with all the other versions. For example, your initial database design and development can take place with the DOS-based version, and the database can be moved up to the OS/2 or NLM version as needed.

SQLBase's compatibility with the DB2 SQL syntax and Gupta's various gateways/routers to other C/S RDBMSs make SQLBase capable of being a part of existing corporate-wide databases, either for integrating PC-based databases into the whole system or for gradually downsizing existing large databases to the smaller platforms.

The most notable disadvantage of SQLBase is its relative lack of support by third-party front-end applications, which is most likely attributable to the communication driver's high RAM requirements on the client side. However, Gupta markets a couple of Windows-based front-ends that are well designed and can access other DBMSs besides SQLBase. These products are discussed in Chapter 8.

While the NLM version of SQLBase was benchmarked as one of the fastest Client/Server RDBMS available as of the spring of 1992, I'd act with the same caution I suggested for the Sybase SQL Server NLM. I recommend that potential users of SQLBase look at the OS/2 version for mission-critical applications, especially since a 32-bit OS/2 2.0 version is under development for release in early 1993.

I hesitate to give Gupta's SQLBase a completely unqualified recommendation, though. While testing SQLBase in the PC Magazine Labs for the Fall

1992 review of SQL back-ends, I was dismayed to find that as a company, Gupta may put marketing ahead of letting their product's technical excellence speak for itself. Overall, my experience made me wonder if Gupta can adequately support their products when customers need that support. In later conversations with executives in the company, I was assured that they were going to reassess their marketing and technical support policies in light of what happened. Gupta has since reorganized their entire support operation.

So, while I have no qualms in recommending SQLBase as a technically advanced and sound product, I advise potential customers to do their own investigation of both the product and Gupta's technical support to be sure that the problems I encountered have been resolved.

Table 4.2

Gupta SQLBase Quick Summary

PRODUCT INFORMATION	
Name	SQLBase 5.0
Vendor	Gupta Technologies, Inc.
Price	5 users: $995 (all versions)
	Unlimited: $2,995 (DOS), $3,995 (OS/2), $4,995 (NLM)
OPERATING SYSTEMS	
On Database Server	DOS 3.1 or higher, OS/2 1.0 or higher, NetWare 3.11
On LAN Server	Microsoft LAN Manager, Novell NetWare 2.11 or higher, IBM LAN Server, or Banyan VINES
On Workstations	DOS 3.1 or higher, Windows 3.x
MINIMUM REQUIREMENTS	
RAM on Server	2Mb (DOS), 4Mb (OS/2), 8Mb (NLM)
RAM on Workstation	640k (DOS), 6Mb (OS/2)
Disk Space on Server	10Mb (all versions)
UTILITIES PROVIDED	
Administration Utility	Yes
Interactive User Utility	Yes

Table 4.2

(continued)

UTILITIES PROVIDED	
Operating Systems/ Environments Supported	DOS 3.1 or higher, Windows 3.x, or OS/2 1.0 or higher
NATIVE LANGUAGES	
ANSI SQL	Level 2 with Integrity Enhancement
DB2 SQL Extensions	Yes
Other SQL	Yes
Non-SQL Language	No
MAXIMUMS	
Database Size	500G
Column Size	Limited by disk space (LONG VARCHAR data type)
Row Size	Limited by disk space
# of Columns in Row	250 columns
# of Rows per Table	Limited by disk space
# of Rows per Database	Limited by disk space
# of Tables per Database	Limited by disk space
# of Views per Database	Unlimited
# of Tables per View	Unlimited

■ IBM OS/2 ES Database Manager 2.0

The original version of IBM's OS/2-based Database Manager, released as a part of the OS/2 1.1 Extended Edition (EE) version, was primarily designed as a local database manager; C/S capabilities weren't added until the release of Version 1.3.

With the release of OS/2 2.0, IBM unbundled the Extended Edition services from the base operating system and now markets the Database Manager as part of the OS/2 Extended Services 2.0 package.

Significant Features

IBM's Database Manager is a Class 2 system that runs on OS/2 1.31 or 2.0. Its most significant feature is its fairly close SQL compatibility with the mainframe-based DB2 and its ability to transparently connect and share data with a DB2 database through the additional Distributed Database Connection Services/2 (DDCS/2) package. Database Manager's DB2 compatibility is also its greatest strength; DB2 is IBM's premier RDBMS and any features implemented in it soon filter down to the OS/2-based product.

Database Manager also includes support for declarative referential integrity; like SQLBase, RI is implemented through primary and foreign keys and includes SQL statements that govern how deletions of parent data are handled when dependent data exists in other tables.

Database Manager supports IBM's Database Application Remote Interface (DARI), a method of moving large portions of the SQL statements to the server to be executed there. The SQL procedures are compiled into a Dynamic Link Library (DLL), an OS/2 and Windows feature that stores portions of an application in libraries that are linked to the application and used only when needed. IBM calls these programmer-created DLLs "stored procedures," but they're more like the precompiled SQL statements in SQLBase than the stored procedures implemented by the MS/Sybase SQL Server. The DLLs can be created using C, FORTRAN, or COBOL; once they're on the server, the routines in the library can be called by any front-end application. The routines are then executed on the server, reducing network traffic and boosting performance.

Hardware and Software Requirements

OS/2 ES Database Manager runs under either OS/2 1.31 or 2.0. An OS/2 1.31 system needs at least a 286, with 8Mb of RAM and 15Mb of hard-disk space. If you'd rather run it under OS/2 2.0, you need at least a 386 with 12Mb of RAM and the same amount of disk space.

Database Manager uses either NetBIOS or APPC for communications between the client and server, and will work with any network that supports either of those protocols. Client communications are provided through the Remote Data Services protocol that's part of the ES Communications Manager (included in the extended services package). In addition to the standard PC-LAN protocols, Remote Data Services lets clients communicate with the server over such wide-area protocols as X.25 and IBM's SDLC and 3174 Peer Communications. The latter two provide access to Database Manager from terminals connected to an IBM host network.

Native SQL Language

Database Manager's SQL is compatible with the ANSI level 2 with Integrity Enhancement standard—not surprising, since SQL was originally created by IBM, and IBM is one of the major players on the ANSI SQL Standards Committee. Virtually all of the DB2 extensions are included as well, providing Database Manager applications source-code compatibility with DB2 databases.

Front-end Processors Provided

Database Manager includes three OS/2-based front-ends, including the Command Line Interface (CLI), a Database Tools module, and the Query Manager. The CLI is a simple interactive SQL program that lets the DBA enter and execute SQL statements on a command line.

The Database Tools are a set of utilities specifically designed to assist the DBA in configuring and maintaining both the Database Manager and individual databases. The Configuration tool makes it easy to configure and tune the server, and the Recovery tool provides database recovery services for backing up and restoring a database. The Directory tool is used to create and catalog databases.

The Query Manager is an interactive SQL utility that provides character-based menus and panels to speed the process of creating and administrating databases. It's the primary administration utility for Database Manager.

A SQL precompiler is included to allow application programmers to embed SQL statements in programs written in C, COBOL, and FORTRAN. Dynamic SQL statements can also be embedded in programs created in IBM's REXX, a powerful batch language that runs on every IBM system from PCs based on OS/2 to the largest mainframes.

Advantages and Disadvantages

Database Manager's most significant advantage is its DB2 compatibility, especially when the DDCS/2 package is added to provide transparent access to IBM's DB2, SQL/DS, and SQL/400 databases. This compatibility makes Database Manager ideal for use in what are traditionally known as "IBM shops"—customers whose primary computer platform is an IBM mainframe. Database Manager can be used as a platform for either downsizing existing DB2 databases or as a way of enhancing existing systems by providing distributed database capabilities. Unfortunately, DDCS/2 only supports access to the large system databases through the Database Manager CLI or programmed applications.

Database Manager is still only a 16-bit application; a 32-bit version that's specific to OS/2 2.0 is due to be released sometime before the end of 1992. However, it's inexpensive compared to other RDBMS servers; the only version available supports unlimited users and sells for $1,995 (which includes the Communications Manager software).

IBM has not entirely moved away from its former position of supporting only its own software products on IBM systems, so setting up and using Database Manager on LANs other than IBM's LAN Server can be a difficult process. Also, Database Manager is a relative newcomer to the Client/Server database market, and it doesn't yet have wide support among third-party, front-end application vendors. IBM is very committed to seeing OS/2 2.0 become a success, though, and I expect that IBM will continue to pursue wider support for Database Manager, both on non-IBM networks and among the front-end vendors.

Table 4.3

IBM OS/2 ES Database Manager Quick Summary

PRODUCT INFORMATION	
Name	OS/2 Extended Services Database Manager
Vendor	IBM, Inc.
Price	Unlimited users: $1,995
OPERATING SYSTEMS	
On Database Server	OS/2 1.31 or higher
On LAN Server	Microsoft LAN Manager, Novell NetWare 3.11, IBM LAN Server, or any network that supports NetBIOS or APPC
On Workstations	DOS 3.1 or higher, Windows 3.x, or OS/2 1.21 or higher
MINIMUM REQUIREMENTS	
RAM on Server	OS/2 1.3: 8Mb
	OS/2 2.0: 12Mb
RAM on Workstation	640k (DOS), 6MB (OS/2)
Disk Space on Server	15Mb
UTILITIES PROVIDED	
Administration Utility	Yes
Interactive User Utility	Yes

Table 4.3

(continued)

UTILITIES PROVIDED	
Operating Systems/Environments Supported	DOS 3.1 or higher, OS/2 1.21 or higher
NATIVE LANGUAGES	
ANSI SQL	Level 2 with Integrity Enhancements
DB2 SQL Extensions	Yes
Other SQL	No
Non-SQL Language	No
MAXIMUMS	
Database Size	2G
Column Size	4,000 bytes, or 32,700 characters in a LONG VARCHAR
Row Size	4,005 bytes
# of Columns in Row	255 columns
# of Rows per Table	Limited by disk space
# of Rows per Database	Limited by disk space
# of Tables per Database	Limited by disk space
# of Views per Database	Limited by disk space
# of Tables per View	15

■ XDB-Server

XDB System's claim to fame has always been products and toolkits that let developers create, on a PC, DB2 applications that can easily be ported to the mainframe once they're completely designed and debugged. What many potential users may not know is that XDB also sells a PC-based database server that's 100 percent compatible with DB2; it can be used either to share data with DB2 databases or as a platform for downsizing them.

Significant Features

Ironically, XDB-Server Version 2.41 is more compatible with DB2 than IBM's Database Manager. This Class 2 RDBMS is 100 percent DB2 2.2 compatible in both SQL syntax and database structures. XDB-Server includes DB2's declarative referential integrity and domain integrity, and user-created rules can be added to the database to provide further data integrity. Version 3.0 for OS/2.0, due to be released in late 1992, will bring XDB-Server up to full compatibility with IBM's DB2 2.3 (the current release).

XDB-Server is available in DOS and OS/2 1.x versions; an NLM version is under development for release sometime in 1993. A stand-alone DOS SQL Engine is available for creating DB2 applications on a PC. The XDB-LINK package provides the capability of accessing DB2 databases from PC workstations running the SQL Engine or workstations using any of XDB's DB2 development tools.

XDB-Server supports a maximum of 256 total users per server. It also implements DB2's database location independence, which lets users transparently access multiple XDB-Servers at the same time. The server software's main screen includes a real-time monitor that lets the DBA examine the database's current workload so that it can be tuned as needed, as shown in Figure 4.3.

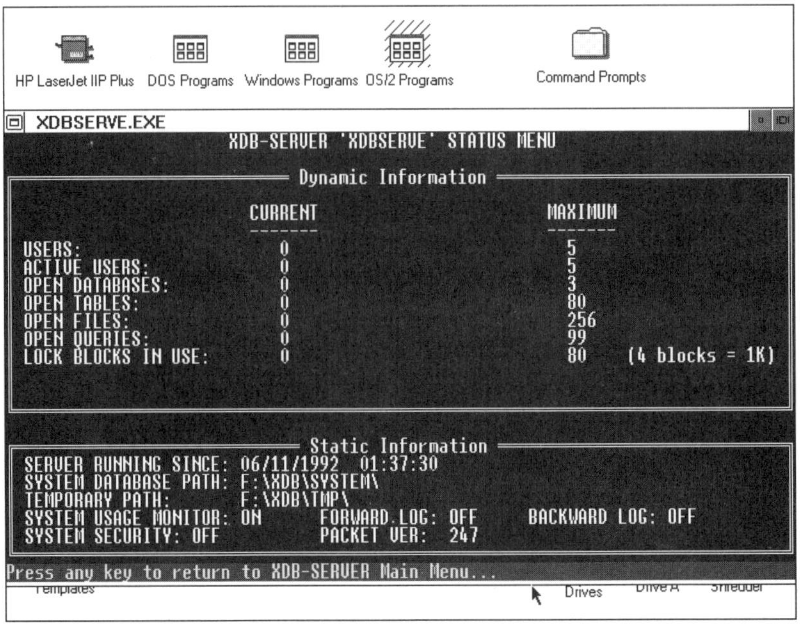

Figure 4.3

XDB-Server's real-time monitor screen lets the DBA keep an eye on the server's performance.

Hardware and Software Requirements

The DOS version of XDB-Server requires a 286 or better running DOS 3.1 or higher and at least 1.5Mb of RAM. The OS/2 version also needs at least a 286 with 4Mb of RAM; the NLM version will also require at least 4Mb of RAM on a 386 running NetWare 3.11. All versions take approximately 10Mb of disk space.

The OS/2 version uses either Named Pipes or NetBIOS as its network protocol, though XDB recommends using NetBIOS when accessing an OS/2 XDB-Server across a NetWare LAN. The other versions use NetBIOS as their communication protocol.

Native SQL Language

Almost everything I said previously about Database Manager's SQL applies to XDB-Server, the major difference being that XDB is 100 percent DB2 compatible. In addition, XDB offers the developer the option to switch the SQL syntax to SQL/DS or ANSI level 2 compatibility modes, letting her use the XDB tools to create applications for other back-ends.

Front-end Processors Provided

XDB-Server includes a character-based, full-screen interactive SQL query utility that can be used to create and access databases on the server. No other front-end processors are provided in the base package.

XDB does sell a number of other packages that can be used to create DB2 or XDB-Server applications. XDB-SQL Plus provides a report writer, menu generator, forms manager, and additional 4GL for creating XDB-Server applications. XDB-Workbench for DB2 lets developers create COBOL applications on a PC that access (or can be ported to) the mainframe. XDB-Tools is a prototyping toolkit that offers the same services as XDB-SQL Plus to DB2 programmers.

The XDB-C and XDB-Windows SDK give C programmers the ability to write DOS or Windows 3.x-based applications that can access the XDB-Server.

Advantages and Disadvantages

Like Database Manager, XDB-Server's greatest advantage is its 100 percent DB2 compatibility, which makes it an even better choice for IBM shops than IBM's own product, despite its extra cost. XDB-Server is ideal for use as a cost-efficient base for creating applications that access DB2 databases, and it can also be used as a downsizing platform. Unfortunately, it doesn't yet have the distributed processing capabilities present in IBM's products.

XDB-Server also suffers from a lack of third-party, front-end support; there are very few client applications outside of XDB's own. This can probably be attributed to XDB's emphasis on supporting DB2 applications development. In this light, XDB is a better choice for companies looking to integrate or downsize DB2 databases than for those seeking an overall Client/Server solution.

Table 4.4

XDB-Server Quick Summary

PRODUCT INFORMATION	
Name	XDB-Server 2.41
Vendor	XDB Systems, Inc.
Price	Unlimited users: $1,995 (DOS), $2,495 (OS/2)
OPERATING SYSTEMS	
On Database Server	DOS 3.1 or higher, OS/2 1.1 or higher
On LAN Server	Microsoft LAN Manager, Novell NetWare 3.11, IBM LAN Server, or any network that supports NetBIOS
On Workstations	DOS 3.1 or higher, OS/2 1.1 or higher
MINIMUM REQUIREMENTS	
RAM on Server	1.5Mb (DOS), 4Mb (OS/2)
RAM on Workstation	640k (DOS), 4Mb (OS/2)
Disk Space on Server	10Mb
UTILITIES PROVIDED	
Administration Utility	Yes
Interactive User Utility	Yes
Operating Systems/Environments Supported	DOS 3.1 or higher, OS/2 1.1 or higher
NATIVE LANGUAGES	
ANSI SQL	Level 2 with Integrity Enhancements

Table 4.4

(continued)

NATIVE LANGUAGES	
DB2 SQL Extensions	Yes
Other SQL	Yes
Non-SQL Language	No
MAXIMUMS	
Database Size	512Mb (DOS), 2G (OS/2)
Column Size	4,056 bytes
Row Size	32,767 bytes
# of Columns in Row	400 columns
# of Rows per Table	Limited by disk space
# of Rows per Database	Limited by disk space
# of Tables per Database	No limit
# of Views per Database	No limit
# of Tables per View	No limit, maximum 400 columns

■ INGRES for OS/2

Ingres has always been one of Oracle's biggest competitors in the VAX and UNIX RDBMS markets, and its QUEL language was one of the strongest competitors to SQL as the standard relational language during the early 1980s. Even though Dr. Codd (the developer of the Relational model) considers QUEL to be the better relational language to this day, for better or worse, SQL has become the industry standard. Ingres has since added SQL to its products, and the company now concentrates on creating both technically proficient database servers and advanced client application tools.

Significant Features

Ingres was the original developer of cost-based optimization in a RDBMS, a feature that has since become a standard throughout the industry. Their optimizer is still considered the industry's best, because it translates the SQL queries into a syntax-independent, set-based algebra that ensures the query will be performed as fast as possible, regardless of how it's constructed.

Ingres's Class 2 DBMS also supports the creation of user data-types, and it has the strongest domain integrity features of any RDBMS. It supports stored procedures, which Ingres calls "rules"; however, rules can only be called through embedded SQL commands, not interactively, as in SQL Server. INGRES also doesn't have support for triggers, so it's up to the application programmer to implement any type of RI.

INGRES is unique in that it supports four different types of data-storage methods. These are determined by the DBA when a table is created and can be changed at any time as the table grows or changes. Heap storage is designed for tables that will usually be accessed sequentially, and hashed storage is for fast random access with no keys or indices. ISAM storage is based on a key field in which the index is static, such as a table primarily used for data lookups, and BTree storage is designed for random access on indexed tables that are constantly being modified or updated.

INGRES for OS/2 has one serious limitation that the large system versions don't share: Users of the OS/2 version can't access non-OS/2 INGRES databases, even though they may exist on the same network. The OS/2 version is also limited to a maximum of 32 users. Many of the shortcomings in the 6.2 version will likely be corrected in INGRES 6.4, which is slated for release before the end of 1992.

Hardware and Software Requirements

INGRES for OS/2 requires OS/2 1.3 or higher, running on a 386 with at least 5Mb of RAM (though Ingres recommends 8Mb of RAM for proper performance). The database takes up only about 10Mb of disk space.

However, DOS clients are affected to a greater extent; the INGRES/ NET software that's needed for client communications requires not only at least a 286 system with 2Mb of RAM, but also takes up an incredible 6.3Mb of hard-disk space. At this time, the INGRES/NET drivers work only with NetBIOS or the IPX/SPX network protocols, and it comes at a price—the client-side communications software costs an additional $495 per user.

Native SQL Language

Ingres provides two versions of SQL; INGRES/SQL, which is ANSI level 1 compatible, and Open SQL, a subset that can be used with the INGRES/ Gateway product to query non-INGRES RDBMSs.

For backwards compatibility (and for those who still prefer it), Ingres continues to support QUEL across its entire line of products. Additional support is available for EQUEL, an enhanced version of QUEL that almost doubles the number of commands.

Front-end Processors Provided

INGRES comes with a rather limited OS/2 character-based, front-end administration tool that shows its VAX/VMS roots; the interface feels like it belongs on a dumb terminal, not on a PC. Doing even the simplest task, such as adding users to the database, requires a number of steps that don't seem to have any logical flow.

A command-line SQL query tool is also provided, to provide administrators and users with a simple way of executing SQL statements. It also shows its terminal-based roots by its command syntax, which is neither intuitive nor well documented. Ingres has a number of DOS and Windows 3.x based toolkits that are much easier to use than the provided utilities. However, they cost extra and are very resource intensive on the client side.

DOS versions of these utilities are included in the INGRES/Net client-side package. Custom access for creating client programs in C is provided by the INGRES/Embedded Language toolkit, which is also available separately.

Advantages and Disadvantages

As technically advanced as the INGRES system is, there's very little to recommend in the current PC-based version. The documentation is confusing and, in some cases, fails to include information needed to get the DBMS up and running. The OS/2 version lacks TCP/IP support, so it can't share data with other INGRES databases, and the IPX/SPX version of INGRES/Net still has a number of bugs that make it virtually impossible to use without a lot of help from Ingres' technical support department.

The current version is also still a 16-bit application, which arbitrarily limits the server to 32 users. A 32-bit OS/2 2.0 version, as well as a possible NLM version, are due for release with the next version of INGRES. Also, INGRES suffers from the same problem as XDB; a lack of support from third-party client applications. Ingres is trying to correct this by actively working with other front-end vendors to add INGRES DBMS support to their products.

Many of these problems are due to be corrected in Version 6.4. So until the new version is released, I'd recommend using one of the non-PC-based INGRES versions. The only use for the OS/2 version would be as a development platform for applications that will be used to access Ingres databases on a mini or mainframe.

Table 4.5

INGRES for OS/2 Quick
Summary

PRODUCT INFORMATION	
Name	INGRES for OS/2 6.2
Vendor	Ingres Corporation
Price	32 users: $1,995 plus $495 per client
OPERATING SYSTEMS	
On Database Server	OS/2 1.3 or higher
On LAN Server	Microsoft LAN Manager, Novell NetWare 3.11, IBM LAN Server, or any network that supports NetBIOS
On Workstations	DOS 3.1 or higher, Windows 3.x, or OS/2 1.3 or higher
MINIMUM REQUIREMENTS	
RAM on Server	5Mb
RAM on Workstation	2Mb (DOS), 4Mb (OS/2)
Disk Space on Server	10Mb
UTILITIES PROVIDED	
Administration Utility	Yes
Interactive User Utility	Yes
Operating Systems/Environments Supported	OS/2 1.3; DOS versions available as part of the client-side package
NATIVE LANGUAGES	
ANSI SQL	Level 1
DB2 SQL Extensions	Subset
Other SQL	Yes
Non-SQL Language	Yes, QUEL
MAXIMUMS	
Database Size	2G

Table 4.5

(continued)

MAXIMUMS	
Column Size	2,000 characters
Row Size	2,008 bytes
# of Columns in Row	127 columns
# of Rows per Table	8 billion
# of Rows per Database	8 billion
# of Tables per Database	Limited by disk space
# of Views per Database	Limited by disk space
# of Tables per View	No limit; views limited to 127 columns

NetWare SQL and Novell BTrieve

Novell is the leading vendor of LAN operating systems and has enhanced their line to include Client/Server products in an effort to become a one-stop vendor for all of their customer's network needs. Novell's BTrieve engine was actually one of the earliest implementations of a limited form of Client/Server database; it was first available in 1982, well before the term Client/Server was first used. It provided server-based data storage and indexing functions to any application that could use the BTrieve format.

As both SQL and C/S systems became prominent, Novell developed and released NetWare SQL, an SQL interface to the BTrieve database engine. Since then, the two products have become so intertwined that it now makes sense to discuss them together, even though third-party applications can still use the BTrieve engine without having to go through NetWare SQL.

Significant Features

The NetWare SQL/BTrieve combination is an interesting hybrid of Class 4 and Class 2 functions. In earlier versions, the BTrieve NLM provided data storage and indexing functions only, leaving it up to the client application (or NetWare SQL) to take care of the rest of the data integrity (DI) features. However, when NetWare SQL Version 3.0 was released in early 1992, a new version of BTrieve (6.0) was bundled with it, to handle many of the DI functions. Current versions of NetWare 3.11 still ship with BTrieve 5.15.

Previous versions of the NetWare SQL/BTrieve combination were criticized because they violated one of the primary DI rules, namely, they didn't prevent access to the data by any DBMS other than the one that created the database. Any application that used BTrieve files could access any file no matter who created it. BTrieve 6.0 tightens that up by moving the enforcement of data and referential integrity to the engine, where the rules are still active regardless of what application accesses the data. While this still isn't completely in line with the Relational model, it does provide more integrity than earlier versions.

NetWare SQL is one of only three C/S DBMSs to provide full declarative RI (Gupta and IBM are the other two) when used in combination with BTrieve 6.0.

Other RDBMS vendors criticize the NLMs because it is difficult to write them due to NetWare's nonpreemptive, unprotected architecture. Novell has an in-house program through which third-party vendors can have their NLMs certified as safe to run; however, no other DBMS has been fully certified to date. NetWare SQL doesn't have this problem for one very obvious reason—it comes from the same company that designed the NLM architecture in the first place. Because of this, the NetWare SQL/BTrieve combination is very tightly integrated with the network operating system itself, so as to take full advantage of NetWare's performance capabilities.

NetWare SQL supports stored SQL statements (similar to those implemented by Gupta and IBM) which are precompiled and stored with the database. Noninteractive client applications can then call the statements to be executed on the server. NetWare SQL also supports true scrollable cursors on the server, which Novell implements through a temporary response table (again, similar to how Gupta does it).

NetWare SQL supports on-line backups through an included backup utility that works with any storage device, including other hard disks and tape drives. A form of distributed processing is supported, in that NetWare/SQL can access BTrieve data residing on any server on the network.

Hardware and Software Requirements

NetWare SQL and BTrieve NLM require a 386 system running NetWare 3.11, at least 8Mb of RAM, and approximately 10Mb of disk space. Versions of NetWare SQL for more than 20 users include a run-time version of NetWare 3.11, eliminating the need for purchasing a separate copy of the NOS.

Client workstations communicate through the included NetWare SQL Requesters, which work with the IPX/SPX protocol only. In addition, Novell supplies a Data Access Language (DAL) NLM with the base package that lets Apple Macintosh systems access NetWare SQL/BTrieve data when used with NetWare for Macintosh.

Native SQL Language

NetWare SQL's language is based on DB2's syntax, which also makes it compatible with the ANSI level 2 with Integrity Enhancement standard. However, Novell chose to implement a syntax-based optimizer instead of the more advanced cost-based optimizer implemented by every other RDBMS except Oracle.

Front-end Processors Provided

NetWare SQL includes a number of utilities for administrating and maintaining databases. Foremost among these are Xtrieve PLUS, a character-mode, interactive data-query system that includes a report writer, and SQL Scope, a Windows 3.x-based interactive SQL utility.

The RIUTIL (Referential Integrity utility) program checks the consistency of database files by applying the RI rules to them when the BTrieve data is accessed from outside NetWare SQL; it then reports on any inconsistencies for further action by the DBA. There's also a utility to convert existing BTrieve data files to the format used by Version 6.0 and a monitoring program that provides real-time statistics on NetWare SQL and BTrieve performance.

A NetWare SQL Developer's Kit, available separately, lets programmers create client applications in C, Pascal, COBOL, and BASIC.

Advantages and Disadvantages

NetWare SQL's primary advantage is its ability to provide a SQL-based relational interface to BTrieve data, which should make it attractive to those who already have a large amount of data in BTrieve format. Unfortunately, it runs only on NetWare 3.11 and uses only the IPX/SPX protocol, which limits its market to those using Novell's networking products.

NetWare SQL's tight integration with NetWare also makes it both one of the fastest and most stable NLM-based database servers available. The fact that it's produced by Novell also ensures that future versions will be certified before they're ever released.

However, in addition to my previously stated concerns about basing mission-critical data on an NLM product, I'm not entirely convinced that the current NetWare SQL/BTrieve combination resolves all data integrity problems. The fact that any BTrieve-based application can access the data still introduces the potential for violating the database's integrity, even though much of the integrity processing has been moved to the BTrieve engine. For this reason, I'd recommend using NetWare SQL only if you already have a large investment in BTrieve files.

Table 4.6

NetWare SQL/BTrieve
NLM Quick Summary

PRODUCT INFORMATION	
Name	NetWare SQL 3.0 with BTrieve NLM 6.0
Vendor	Novell, Inc.
Price	5 users: $795
	10 users: $1,295
	20 users: $2,195
	50 users: $3,995
	100 users: $5,995
OPERATING SYSTEMS	
On Database Server	NetWare 3.11
On LAN Server	Novell NetWare 3.11
On Workstations	DOS 3.1 or higher, Windows 3.x, or OS/2 1.2 or higher
MINIMUM REQUIREMENTS	
RAM on Server	8Mb
RAM on Workstation	640k (DOS), 4Mb (OS/2)
Disk Space on Server	10Mb
UTILITIES PROVIDED	
Administration Utility	Yes
Interactive User Utility	Yes
Operating Systems/Environments Supported	DOS 3.1 or higher
NATIVE LANGUAGES	
ANSI SQL	Level 2 with Integrity Enhancement
DB2 SQL Extensions	Yes
Other SQL	No
Non-SQL Language	No

Table 4.6

(continued)

MAXIMUMS	
Database Size	4G
Column Size	32k for variable-length data
Row Size	4,090 bytes for nonvariable data
# of Columns in Row	Limited by disk space
# of Rows per Table	Limited by disk space
# of Rows per Database	Limited by disk space
# of Tables per Database	Limited by disk space
# of Views per Database	Limited by disk space
# of Tables per View	8

■ ORACLE Server 6.0

ORACLE is the last, though certainly not the least, of the major PC-based C/S databases discussed in this chapter. Oracle has the distinction of being the first company to create and sell a commercial RDBMS that used SQL, beating out even IBM by a few years. The early versions were developed on VAX/VMS systems, and VMS remains Oracle's primary platform; all new versions come out for VMS first.

Since the early 1980s, Oracle has committed itself to supporting a wide variety of platforms, and it was one of the first vendors to produce a DOS-based RDBMS. Oracle continues its string of firsts to this day, as it was the first vendor to release a full 32-bit OS/2 2.0 version of its DBMS. ORACLE's support for a variety of systems has made it the top-selling RDBMS in the world.

Significant Features

ORACLE's most powerful feature is its portability and scalability. Versions are available for virtually every major hardware and software platform in existence, including PCs, Macintoshes, mainframes, and most UNIX variants. Code written for one platform can easily be ported to another, due to Oracle's SQL precompiler. PC-based versions of ORACLE are available for both OS/2 2.0 and as a NetWare NLM.

ORACLE provides the strongest distributed processing support of any of the C/S databases available at this time. The key to this database distribution is Oracle's SQL*Net communication protocol, which is available for a number of connection protocols, including NetBIOS, IPX/SPX, Named Pipes, IBM's APPC and 3270, DECNet, and TCP/IP; there's even a version that supports asynchronous connections over a modem. Since multiple versions of SQL*Net can be run at the same time on an ORACLE server, it can handle links to remote databases without user intervention.

Oracle databases can be split among different disks or volumes, which limits them to a maximum size of 2G under OS/2 or 4G for the NLM version. However, one ORACLE server can connect to other ORACLE servers, which allows the DBA to create "virtual databases" many times larger than the size limitations imposed by a single server.

ORACLE Version 6.0 supports queries through database links only; data on the remote server can't be modified through the link. However, different versions of SQL*Net can be run on the client workstation simultaneously (subject to available memory), allowing the client to directly connect to different ORACLE databases at the same time. When done this way, each connection supports the full capabilities of the user's application, so the user can view and modify data on any of the connected databases.

Unfortunately, ORACLE 6.0 is over two years old and no longer leads the market in technical excellence. It lacks such commonly requested features as stored procedures, triggers, declarative referential integrity, and cost-based optimization. It's also a resource hog—every user accessing the server requires at least an additional 250k of RAM on the server, because each user connection starts a completely new server process. When the overhead of the NOS and the Oracle software itself is added in, a 16Mb server can effectively support only 16 to 20 users without slowing to a crawl. Because of this, the OS/2 version is limited to a maximum of 48 users, and the NLM version to a maximum of 96 users.

Version 7.0, which is under development at the time of this writing, will bring Oracle's software up-to-date with the latest advances in RDBMS and Client/Server technology. Oracle expects to release the VAX/VMS version in late 1992; the PC-based versions will come out sometime before the summer of 1993.

Hardware and Software Requirements

As mentioned previously, ORACLE demands a lot of memory resources from the server. The OS/2 2.0 version requires a minimum of 12Mb of RAM, although at least 32Mb is required to support the maximum number of users. The software itself takes up less than 10Mb of hard-disk space.

The NLM version requires a minimum of 16Mb of RAM; in this case, at least 64Mb is required to support the maximum number of 96 users without suffering severe performance degradation.

Oracle's SQL*Net communications drivers support every major network protocol, which allows ORACLE access to the widest available variety of client platforms. ORACLE is the only C/S database other than NetWare SQL to support access from Macintosh clients; when used with TCP/IP, even UNIX-based clients can access PC-based ORACLE servers. The SQL*Net drivers take up a moderate amount of RAM, so it's possible to run at least two different versions on the same DOS client. For example, a user can access a NLM database using SPX while simultaneously accessing an OS/2 version using Named Pipes.

Native SQL Language

Oracle's SQL is compatible with the ANSI level 2 standard. Though Version 6 includes some of the keywords specified by the Integrity Addendum, the DBMS doesn't enforce them—they're present only for DB2 syntax compatibility. The application programmer is still responsible for checking and enforcing relational and data integrity. The server-based integrity features will be a part of Version 7.0.

Oracle also provides its own extensions to SQL through its Procedural Language/SQL (PL/SQL). Developed as a response to Sybase's Transact-SQL, PL/SQL includes logic and branching commands, support for variables and arrays, and a variety of string and math functions that can be used with the base SQL statements to create complete applications without an external language.

Front-end Processors Provided

The only front-end provided with ORACLE is SQL*DBA, a character-mode, command-line interface that's used both to administrate and to query databases. In addition to executing directly entered SQL statements, SQL*DBA can execute a series of PL/SQL statements stored in a text file.

SQL*DBA has some built-in administration functions, including a real-time database monitor which lets the administrator examine current and historical database access, existing database locks, current user activity, and server performance statistics, as shown in Figure 4.4. SQL*DBA is available in DOS and OS/2 versions.

The base version of the server software comes with interface libraries for customizing applications in C using the Oracle Call Interface (OCI). In addition, a PL/SQL precompiler can convert the embedded SQL statements into C code, which can then be compiled with any C compiler into executable client applications. Libraries and precompilers are also available for COBOL, FORTRAN, Pascal, PL/I, and Ada.

Figure 4.4

Oracle's SQL*DBA command-line interface provides the DBA with a comprehensive system monitor.

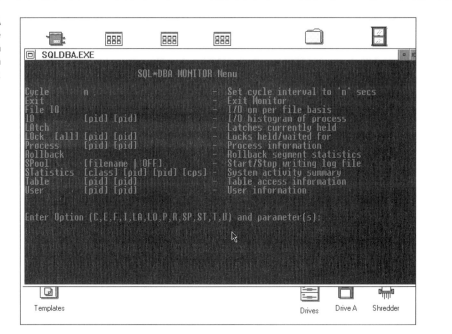

Oracle sells a complete application development kit called ORACLE Tools, which includes a menu generator, forms generator, report writer, and full-screen, interactive PL/SQL query utility.

Advantages and Disadvantages

Due to its widespread availability, ORACLE has the second-largest number of third-party, front-end support products. Only SQL Server has slightly more support.

ORACLE is the overall market leader for one simple reason—its scalability across a wide range of platforms. Corporations looking to create a complete Client/Server system including everything from PC LANs to mainframes can use ORACLE as the common RDBMS for all of their platforms, which reduces the need (and cost) of training programmers, developers, and support personnel in multiple database systems. In addition, ORACLE users can draw on a large pool of applications developers already familiar with the software when hiring new personnel.

Another advantage is ORACLE's support for almost all of the major procedural programming languages (only BASIC is missing). It's a relatively simple matter for an experienced programmer to learn PL/SQL and start creating ORACLE applications right away. ORACLE's support for Ada is unique among the PC-based C/S databases; Ada was designed by the U.S.

government as a replacement for COBOL, and at some point in the future, all new applications designed for the U.S. government will have to be developed in it. ORACLE is the top RDBMS used by the federal government.

ORACLE's drawbacks are its resource intensiveness and age, both of which will be corrected within the year upon the release of Version 7.0. It's also one of the more expensive of the C/S databases. However, if you have the computing and financial resources, you'll find ORACLE to be about the best platform for company-wide Client/Server databases available today. I recommend it without hesitation.

I can't finish this discussion without crediting the folks who wrote ORACLE's manuals. Not only do they cover every aspect of setting up, running, using, and programming for ORACLE, but they do it in a clear and concise manner. The manuals are so well written that they can serve as an introductory text to many of the concepts covered in this book, such as SQL, the Relational model, and the Client/Server database architecture. As I was reading them, I was tempted to include them in Appendix C as a reference for further reading—they're that good. Unfortunately, the only way to get the manuals is to buy the product.

Table 4.7

ORACLE 6.0 Quick Summary

PRODUCT INFORMATION	
Name	ORACLE Server 6.0
Vendor	Oracle Corporation
Price	8 users: $3,999 (OS/2 & NLM)
	16 users: $6,899 (OS/2 & NLM)
	32 users: $11,999 (OS/2 & NLM)
	48 users: $17,999 (OS/2 & NLM)
	64 users: $23,999 (NLM only)
	96 users: $35,999 (NLM only)
OPERATING SYSTEMS	
On Database Server	OS/2 2.0, NetWare 3.11
On LAN Server	Microsoft LAN Manager, Novell NetWare 3.11, IBM LAN Server, or any network supporting NetBIOS, Named Pipes, DECNet, or TCP/IP

Table 4.7

(continued)

OPERATING SYSTEMS	
On Workstations	DOS 3.1 or higher, OS/2 1.2 or higher
MINIMUM REQUIREMENTS	
RAM on Server	8Mb, plus 250k per user minimum
RAM on Workstation	640k (DOS), 4Mb (OS/2)
Disk Space on Server	10Mb
UTILITIES PROVIDED	
Administration Utility	Yes
Interactive User Utility	Yes
Operating Systems/Environments Supported	DOS 3.1 or higher, OS/2 1.2 or higher
NATIVE LANGUAGES	
ANSI SQL	Level 2
DB2 SQL Extensions	Yes
Other SQL	Yes
Non-SQL Language	No
MAXIMUMS	
Database Size	2G (OS/2), 4G (NLM)
Column Size	65,535 characters
Row Size	65,535 characters
# of Columns in Row	254 columns
# of Rows per Table	Limited by disk space
# of Rows per Database	Limited by disk space
# of Tables per Database	Limited by disk space
# of Views per Database	Limited by disk space
# of Tables per View	No limit, with 254 columns maximum per view

■ Class 3 C/S Databases for .DBF Files

Interest in expanding to the Client/Server architecture has extended into the dBASE-compatible world. There's a tremendous amount of PC-based data in the .DBF format, and companies whose primary databases reside in that format want to benefit from C/S computing without having to replace or reprogram all their existing applications. Three vendors have announced server databases that provide Class 3 C/S functions for .DBF files; two products are currently available (ExtendBase and XBase/Server), and the third (Quadbase) is due for release in late 1992. These database servers don't provide all of the benefits of the Client/Server architecture, and they also don't add much more than a limited amount of data integrity services to dBASE-compatible applications. However, they're perfectly acceptable for situations in which the power of a full C/S database is unnecessary. They're also good options for companies without the hardware or manpower resources to move existing databases and applications to a new platform.

ExtendBase for NetWare

ExtendBase for NetWare from Extended Systems was the first dBASE-compatible database server to reach the market. The $595 package runs as an NLM under NetWare 3.11, requiring a mere 200k of RAM on the server. ExtendBase uses dBASE-compatible programming commands to index, query, and report on .DBF files residing on the server.

Four different access interfaces are included in the package. ExtendBase USE emulates the dBASE dot prompt, allowing experienced dBASE users to access the data on the server by entering direct commands, as though the data resided in a local database. The ExtendBase Query Processor provides a menu-driven query interface for users unfamiliar with dBASE-compatible syntax. Extended Systems also provides a Lotus 1-2-3 DataLens interface module which lets 1-2-3 users query and extract data from the server to a local spreadsheet. (See Chapter 8 for more details on DataLens.)

ExtendBase's real power arises from its Clipper interface. (Clipper is a popular dBASE-compatible programming environment and code compiler.) The ExtendBase Clipper Interface adds a few simple commands to the Clipper language; the programmer just modifies the code where needed to access the remote data, and recompiles the program. Executable Clipper programs can then act as clients to the ExtendBase Server. Benchmark tests performed by *PC Magazine* and others have shown that moving .DBF files to an ExtendBase server generally reduces the time required to query or report on a database to a tenth of that required by dBASE or Clipper.

XBase/Server for DOS

Megabase systems has announced XBase/Server, a $99 dBASE-compatible database server that runs under DOS. XBase/Server, which requires a dedicated machine with at least 512k of RAM, will run on any network that supports DOS file- and record-locking protocols, such as Novell's NetWare, Microsoft's LAN Manager, and Artisoft's LANTastic.

Databases on the XBase/Server can be accessed from any PC application that uses the .DBF file format, including dBASE IV, FoxPro, Clipper, and R:Base 3.1. It adds a measure of data integrity through built-in security procedures, such as user IDs and an active database dictionary that implements some referential integrity features.

Because it's based on DOS, XBase/Server isn't designed for large databases or large numbers of users. Its low price and resource requirements make it ideal for small networks (generally under seven or eight users), which can benefit from the increased performance and security of a Client/Server system.

Quadbase-Server/NLM

The most interesting of these three products is the Quadbase-Server/NLM from Quadbase Systems. It bears a strong resemblance to the NetWare SQL-BTrieve combination in that it provides a SQL interface to .DBF files residing on a NetWare server. The databases can be accessed either from applications written in a dBASE-compatible language or through its own ANSI level 2-compatible SQL language.

Quadbase also provides more data integrity support than the other products in this class. It does so by running in "catalog mode," which prevents other dBASE-compatible programs from accessing the .DBF files while Quadbase is running. "Noncatalog mode" lets Quadbase share its database files with other applications and programs. It also provides multiuser concurrency control and true transaction processing through a transaction log. Quadbase-Server/NLM is due to be released in late 1992; the price has not been announced at the time of this writing.

- *Evaluating Client/Server Databases for UNIX Workstations and Minicomputers*

- *INGRES for UNIX and VAX/VMS*

- *ORACLE Server 6.0*

- *Sybase SQL Server for UNIX and VAX/VMS*

- *Gupta SQLBase for UNIX*

- *INFORMIX*

Client/Server Databases for UNIX Workstations and Minicomputers

ONE OF THE SURPRISING FINDINGS IN THE BRG STUDY I MENTIONED at the beginning of Chapter 4 was that minicomputers and "superservers" running UNIX had the smallest portion of the Client/Server market. Superservers, another name for RISC-based servers or high-end workstations, made up a mere 9 percent of the database server market. Minicomputers had 11 percent of the market, but that number is deceptive, as it represents *all* minicomputers, including those running proprietary operating systems. While the number of proprietary systems isn't specified, my guess is that they represent about half of all the minicomputers—which means that UNIX-based systems represent at most about 15 percent of the C/S database market.

Superservers and minicomputers, regardless of which operating system they run, fall into the middle of the computer spectrum in power and number of users. With PCs at the low end and mainframes at the high end, it's convenient to refer to the systems discussed here and in Chapter 6 as midrange computers.

With one exception, all of the RDBMSs considered in this chapter have PC-based versions, so many of the features, advantages, and disadvantages are the same. Rather than duplicate information already covered, I'll highlight the differences between the two versions and the advantages, if any, of using the UNIX version over the PC version.

■ Evaluating Client/Server Databases for UNIX Workstations and Minicomputers

If you're thinking of adding a UNIX DBMS to an existing PC-based LAN, you'll find yourself confronted with a bewildering array of hardware and software choices. In addition to choosing the DBMS that fits your needs, you'll have to find a compatible platform. Then you'll have to determine the size of the platform, which can range from a desktop RISC workstation to a minicomputer or superserver.

Or, if you already have UNIX systems, you may wish to extend their reach to the PCs in your organization. You'll find yourself faced with an entirely different set of considerations, not the least of which is which of several methods to use to enable the UNIX and PC networks to talk to each other.

Either way, you'll find that adapting a UNIX-based DBMS to a Client/Server system can be a much more complex undertaking than setting up the same DBMS on a PC platform. Paying careful attention to both the general and the product-specific information in this chapter can help you to successfully evaluate your options while avoiding some of the common pitfalls.

Advantages and Disadvantages

Why don't UNIX systems have a larger market share, especially when most of the PC-based RDBMS servers were ported down from databases that ran under UNIX? No conclusive study has been done to date; however, based on both my experiences in designing and setting up C/S systems, and on numerous conversations with others doing the same, I can make some educated guesses.

One major reason is UNIX's reputation as a hard-to-learn, hard-to-use "techie" operating system, particularly among those most familiar with PCs. This poor reputation is not altogether undeserved, though in recent years the rise of UNIX-based GUIs such as Motif and Open Look have given UNIX the same easy-to-use advantages that Windows and OS/2 have offered to PC users.

Another reason is cost, both in real dollars and in support resources. Prices for the entry-level (low-end) superservers and minicomputers generally start at around $20,000 to $25,000, and these systems are very limited in power and the number of users they support. High-end systems, which can support hundreds of users and/or multigigabyte databases, can run into the hundreds of thousands of dollars. As I mentioned in Chapter 2, the proprietary nature of these systems limits the market for third-party, add-on equipment, so options such as more RAM or disk space cost much more than the PC equivalents.

As for support, you'll find a smaller pool of UNIX-trained personnel to choose from, which means paying higher salaries for experienced personnel or spending more on training your existing technical staff.

UNIX software packages are also more expensive than their PC equivalents, due to both the smaller market (less demand) and the fact that the UNIX versions are multiuser. Another software problem is the lack of a standard version of UNIX; every hardware vendor has its own customized version, and slight incompatibilities between different versions force the RDBMS vendors to maintain numerous versions of their products. Software costs are a factor for database servers too, because most of the Client/Server RDBMS vendors charge considerably higher prices for their UNIX versions.

Many RISC workstation vendors are touting models priced in the range of high-end PCs as alternatives to PC-based systems. However, these RISC systems are really designed as single-user intelligent terminals on a network, rather than as database servers. They come with the bare minimum of RAM and hard-disk space needed to run UNIX. A standard RISC workstation would be acceptable as a client for a C/S database but not as a server. The high-end workstations that have the power to be database servers are more properly defined as RISC-based superservers.

The final reason for UNIX's smaller market share has to do with network protocols. The primary protocol for UNIX systems is TCP/IP and, until recently, the major PC LANs didn't support it as a native protocol. PCs on a network could use TCP/IP to communicate with UNIX systems, but only as intelligent terminals to the host system. In the early 1990s, Novell, Microsoft, and IBM began offering TCP/IP as a native protocol on their respective LANs, giving PC clients the ability to communicate with UNIX-based database servers. Soon the protocol problem will no longer be an issue.

However, some vendors' TCP/IP implementations take up a significant amount of RAM on PC/MS DOS systems, so it may not be feasible (or even possible) to run TCP/IP all the time. There are gateways available that translate the common PC LAN protocols to TCP/IP, which can be used as an alternative solution.

With all these drawbacks, why would anyone want to use a UNIX system as a database server? There are a number of reasons; most important, superservers and minicomputers are still much more powerful than PCs. This extra power translates into support for more users. Most PC-based C/S databases can realistically support no more than about 100 users per server, while a high-end UNIX system can support four to five times that number.

Speed is another reason. While the high-end PCs are closing the gap with RISC workstations, superservers and minicomputers are still much faster, which translates into faster response times for the same number of users. The higher speeds result from a number of factors, including the faster RISC chips or proprietary CPUs in the midrange systems. These systems can also use much more RAM than PCs—256Mb to 512Mb of RAM is not uncommon in the high-end minicomputers and superservers. This extra RAM provides the DBMS more room to work in memory, reducing the bottleneck of disk accesses for virtual memory paging or for querying commonly used data.

Another factor related to speed is the advanced forms of multiprocessing supported by most minicomputers and superservers. *Multiprocessing* means what the name implies—the system has more than one CPU, and the CPUs split different system tasks among themselves under the control of the operating system. There are two types of multiprocessing systems: asymmetrical and symmetrical. In an *asymmetrical multiprocessing* system, different CPUs handle different subsystems (that is, one CPU manages the central processing while another CPU runs the DBMS), and each CPU is dedicated to its own task. While asymmetrical multiprocessing systems are now available in all sizes of computers, symmetrical multiprocessing remains in the domain of midrange and mainframe systems.

In a *symmetrical multiprocessing* system, each CPU can handle any processing task independent of the other CPUs, as directed by the operating system. For example, a symmetrical DBMS system will route a user query to any available CPU, which is obviously much faster than if one CPU had to handle all the queries. Symmetrical multiprocessing systems have recently been outpaced by *parallel-processing systems* in which single computation requests are split among different CPUs for processing; the answer arises from the combination of results received from the different CPUs. Parallel-processing systems are in the domain of *supercomputers*, which are the fastest computers available. While they hold great promise for the future as platforms for advances in artificial intelligence, currently they have little impact on the C/S market.

UNIX is currently the only available operating system that fully supports symmetrical multiprocessing technology on a broad range of systems, offering advantages of power and speed for database servers. Just about all of the UNIX-based RDBMS vendors are committed to supporting multiprocessing in their software, so it appears that the midrange systems will retain their high-performance advantage in the foreseeable future. However, be aware that not all UNIX variants support multiprocessing. Applications have to include their own support for multiprocessing if the core operating system doesn't support it.

Another major advantage of midrange systems is their support for large amounts of disk space. Most PCs are currently limited to supporting less than 10G of disk space, and current PC-based C/S databases are limited by the operating systems to about 4G. Midrange systems usually start with 500Mb to 1G of disk space, and the higher-end systems easily support over 100G of hard-disk space. UNIX-based RDBMSs can take advantage of whatever disk space is available, so again, the midrange systems will have this advantage over PCs in the foreseeable future.

Security is also a factor in UNIX-based systems. When properly set up, a UNIX system can be as secure against unauthorized access as any proprietary minicomputer or mainframe operating system. The U.S. Federal Government is one of the largest UNIX users in the country. Under standards set by the Department of Defense, it has established a series of security ratings for use with classified data. The ratings are identified by a seven letter-number combination, with the C-1 rating being the lowest and A-1 the highest. A UNIX system or DBMS must go through a rigorous certification process before it can claim one of the security rankings. While most UNIX systems qualify for one of the rankings, no PC-based operating system does to date. Microsoft has announced plans to release a secure version of Windows/NT sometime in 1993 or 1994.

The government has also created a standard API for programming applications, called *POSIX*. The POSIX standard is intended to make it easier to move an application from one platform to another. In theory, the source code for an application written using the POSIX API can simply be recompiled for a different platform without major modifications. In actual practice, though, the POSIX standard is still evolving, and incompatibilities still occur between different implementations. Also, the POSIX API only addresses character-mode applications, so it has somewhat fallen behind the market's move to GUIs. At some future point, every application written for government use will have to follow POSIX; however, it won't have a major impact on the DBMS market, as most vendors handle porting their product to other platforms, which bypasses the need for POSIX compliance. The POSIX standard will have more of an effect on front-end application development.

Microsoft plans to include POSIX support in Windows/NT, and IBM has announced plans to release a POSIX version of OS/2 2.x sometime in 1993.

The concept of fault tolerance originated with the larger systems, and UNIX vendors were quick to add support for fault-tolerant features such as disk mirroring, disk duplexing, and on-line backups. Many vendors also provide support for CPU fault tolerance, whereby a failing processor is locked out of the data stream, and tasks destined for the failed CPU are automatically directed to a different still functioning CPU.

The final advantage of UNIX systems may, at first glance, not seem like an advantage at all—the fact that these systems are multiuser. While it may seem like heresy to say so in this book, not every database has to be a Client/Server database. There are many situations in which users only need access to the database and nothing more; a telephone order-taking department or warehouse inventory system comes to mind. The right solution for these circumstances, in many cases, is a multiuser system with dedicated terminals; a full Client/Server system would be overkill and may well introduce unnecessary complexities and expense.

The UNIX-based RDBMSs covered in this chapter give you the best of both worlds: They can be directly accessed through terminals by those who need database access only; and, at the same time, they can act as a database server to the folks in the administrative departments, who use their PCs to track and analyze the whole company's business.

Special Considerations

Running a Client/Server system on a UNIX-based system presents an almost completely different set of considerations than running one entirely on PCs. Again, the information in this section should be considered only a starting point for the questions you need to ask when designing your own system:

- **Hardware:** Do you have an existing midrange system that you want to turn into a database server? Doing so may cause more problems than it's worth, as discussed in a study of different Client/Server platforms in the premier issue of *PC Magazine*'s sister publication, *Corporate Computing* (July, 1992). Many older minicomputers can't match the power of current high-end PCs, and the cost of upgrading them is too high compared against the extra power gained in the upgrade. If your existing systems are more than five years old, you should consider replacing them completely or moving the database server to a different platform. However, the number of users you need to support may prevent a move to a smaller platform, so a newer version of the existing system is your only choice.

  If you're designing a completely new C/S system, getting the right hardware is less of a problem. Midrange system vendors and VARs usually have a lot of experience in configuring complete systems that include all the necessary parts, such as sufficient RAM, disk capacity, and backup systems. However, configuring C/S systems may also be very new to some vendors, and they might not have a lot of experience in the field yet. It would be a wise move to contact other customers and talk to them about their experiences with the vendor before making a final decision.

- **Compatibility with existing networks:** This is the most critical area and the one where the most mistakes are made. First, be sure that the hardware you're going to use supports the same network topology (for example, Ethernet or Token Ring) that you run your LANs on. While there are bridges that can connect different topologies together, using one may be an unnecessary complication. The process is much smoother when all the systems share the same topology.

  As mentioned previously, network protocol is a factor in setting up a C/S database on a midrange system. If your existing LANs can't support TCP/IP as a native protocol, you'll have to factor in the additional costs of either upgrading or replacing them. Upgrading may not be a big problem, but replacing them can carry many hidden costs, especially those involved in retraining both users and support staff on the new LAN software. If your LAN software does support a version of TCP/IP, make sure it's compatible with the TCP/IP used by the UNIX system. Every vendor implements TCP/IP in a slightly different way, and the differences can eventually cause problems that are hard to track down.

- **Support and training:** Most vendors of midrange systems have been around a long time and have extensive support operations that are well equipped to handle their customers' needs. Support plans usually include on-site vendor engineers who get the system up and running, and training classes for in-house staff to keep them running.

  However, such support doesn't come cheap, so make sure you find out all the different plans the vendor has available. Support plans are usually based on response time—a plan that provides four hour response time from support engineers can be considerably more costly to you than one that guarantees eight hour response time. Make sure you factor in how much downtime you can afford when you're comparing the prices of these different plans.

  As with PC-based systems, find out where the vendor's training classes are held, and include any transportation costs in your planning.

- **Performance monitoring:** This is much less a consideration with the midrange and large systems. These systems have been around for years (and even decades) in one form or another, and numerous third-party performance monitors exist to supplement those built into the operating systems.

- **Front-end software:** This is a much more critical factor in the midrange and large systems. Many PC-based front-ends work fine with the PC versions of the DBMSs, but won't work (or require special software to work) with the UNIX-based versions. Many front-ends require an additional gateway system to communicate with the non-PC versions, which adds extra hardware and software costs to the price of the system. Make sure you find out which front-ends are supported before making a final decision on the DBMS software.

Advice and Tips

Given the state of the Client/Server market, the best advice I can offer about UNIX-based systems is to ascertain whether you really need the features such a system provides. Various benchmark tests run by *PC Magazine, Corporate Computing,* and others have shown that PC-based systems are approaching, and in some cases surpassing, the performance of all but the higher-end superservers and minicomputers, at considerably less cost.

Midrange systems still offer the advantage of supporting a greater number of users per system, though this may be lessened as distributed database technology makes further advances. This is where scalability can play a significant role in your decision. Choose a DBMS that has a PC-based version, as it will make it easier to migrate to a distributed system in the future.

The other advantage to midrange systems is database size. While advances in hard-drive technology have made it possible for some high-end PCs to support up to about 20G of disk space (though the PC operating systems haven't yet caught up to this amount), it will be quite a few years before PCs can approach the 100+G disk space that high-end superservers and minicomputers support. If you expect to have such large databases, opt for a midrange system running UNIX.

I would also recommend a UNIX-based midrange system if you expect to have large amounts of highly confidential data in your databases or if you need to meet POSIX standards. Windows/NT won't be out until the early part of 1993, and it usually takes at least a year for an operating system to receive POSIX certification. It'll be at least 1994 before any PC-based systems are certified as matching the security and POSIX capabilities of a UNIX system.

Finally, don't forget that these midrange systems are multiuser and can be equally accessed by both dedicated terminals and PCs. The extra cost of a midrange system can sometimes be offset by the savings accrued in not having to give a PC to everyone who needs access to the database.

■ INGRES for UNIX and VAX/VMS

UNIX and VMS are the primary platforms for Ingres's RDBMS and distributed processing tools. The release of Version 6.4 in late 1992 promises to bring the OS/2 version up to the same capabilities as the midrange systems; however, it remains to be seen how well Ingres meets these promises. For now, UNIX or VMS remains the preferred platform. The features detailed in this section are those that the UNIX and VAX/VMS versions of INGRES has in addition to those found in the OS/2 version.

Significant Features

The midrange system versions of INGRES don't suffer from the 32-user limit of the OS/2 version. Depending on the hardware platform, INGRES for UNIX can support 300 or more users accessing the database from both client systems and dedicated terminals.

The real strength of the Class 2 UNIX/VMS versions of INGRES lies in their support for distributed processing, both with other midrange INGRES systems and with other VAX/VMS or mainframe-based databases. The INGRES/Star database-integration server distributes database queries to multiple INGRES databases, while appearing as a single database to the client system. INGRES/Star supports: a *distributed database dictionary*, which splits the dictionary across database servers; *distributed query optimization*, which optimizes the SQL statements and commands for the most cost-effective execution on databases split across different systems; and distributed transactions with *full two-phase commit*, which means a transaction isn't considered successful until all the individual modifications on the different databases are successfully completed.

INGRES/Star can also communicate with the INGRES/Gateway, which provides seamless access to DEC Rdb and RMS databases running on a VAX, Hewlett-Packard AllBase databases running on HP systems, and DB2 or IMS databases running on an IBM mainframe. INGRES/Star and INGRES/Gateway are available for VMS and various flavors of UNIX, including ULTRIX, SunOS, and AIX.

Hardware and Software Requirements

As with all UNIX and VMS systems, the amount of RAM and disk space needed by INGRES varies from platform to platform, so it's difficult to recommend minimum requirements. In addition to VAX/VMS, INGRES runs on over 30 versions of UNIX, including AT&T's System V, SunOS, IBM's AIX, DEC's ULTRIX, HP's HP-UX, and SCO UNIX. Ingres also offers versions specific to the European and Asian markets; those run on systems from Bull, Nixdorf, Siemens, and Olivetti, among others.

Communications Protocols

Communications between the clients and the server are provided by INGRES/Net running over TCP/IP for the UNIX versions, and DECNet or TCP/IP for the VMS version. For DOS-based clients, TCP/IP is the better choice unless you already have a DECNet-based LAN.

Native SQL Language

The UNIX/VMS versions of INGRES also support INGRES/SQL, Open SQL, and both QUEL and EQUEL.

Front-end Processors Provided

Ingres provides UNIX and VMS versions of the same front-end tools that come with the OS/2 version. In addition, any of the DOS-based front-ends can be used with the appropriate INGRES/NET drivers.

Version 6.4 will include the Interactive Performance Monitor (IPM), an additional administrative tool that allows the DBA to monitor the performance of any Ingres database server or INGRES/Star server on the network.

For an additional cost, developers can purchase UNIX versions of INGRES/Tools to create INGRES front-ends for RISC workstations. Also available is INGRES/Vision, an application generator that helps speed the process of developing both Client/Server and terminal applications on DOS and UNIX systems. INGRES/Windows4GL lets programmers create Windows 3.x front-ends for any Ingres back-end.

INGRES/Tools is regarded as one of the better application development tools in the industry, and many DBMS vendors have licensed versions that can be used for developing applications for their own products.

Advantages and Disadvantages

I've learned from some INGRES users that the company has a reputation for providing only fair support for their products. My own experiences with Ingres leads me to believe these reports are true. When researching prices for the quick summary chart, I had to speak to several Ingres representatives over a period of two weeks before getting the information. In the process, I did learn that Ingres plans to change their price structure to a per-user basis in late 1992. Keep this in mind when you're comparing INGRES to other platforms.

Ingres's strength lies in its midrange system versions, though they suffer from the same lack of third-party, front-end support that the OS/2 version suffers from. However, their distributed processing capabilities give the UNIX or VAX/VMS versions an edge over the OS/2 version for downsizing from mainframe systems. If you prefer to use INGRES as your DBMS, and particularly if you prefer QUEL to SQL, the UNIX version is your best bet.

Table 5.1

INGRES for UNIX and VAX/
VMS Quick Summary

PRODUCT INFORMATION	
Name	INGRES for UNIX or VAX/VMS 6.2
Vendor	Ingres Corporation
Price	Varies depending on platform; ranges from $1,000 for a single user to $400,000 for a top-end system with 300 users; additional users cost $1,000 each
OPERATING SYSTEMS	
On Database Server	30+ versions of UNIX, including AIX, SunOS, AT&T System IV, VAX/VMS
On LAN Server	Any network that supports TCP/IP or DECNet (may involve an additional cost of $100-$200 per workstation)
On Workstations	DOS 3.1 or higher, Windows 3.x, RISC-based UNIX
MINIMUM REQUIREMENTS	
RAM on Server	Varies by system
RAM on Workstation	2Mb (DOS), 4Mb (OS/2), 8Mb (UNIX)
Disk Space on Server	Varies by system
UTILITIES PROVIDED	
Administration Utility	Yes
Interactive User Utility	Yes
Operating Systems/Environments Supported	UNIX or VAX/VMS; DOS versions available as part of the client-side package

Table 5.1

(continued)

NATIVE LANGUAGES	
ANSI SQL	Level 1
DB/2 SQL Extensions	Subset
Other SQL	Yes
Non-SQL Language	QUEL
MAXIMUMS	
Database Size	Limited by platform's supported disk space
Column Size	2,000 characters
Row Size	2,008 bytes
# of Columns in Row	127 columns
# of Rows per Table	Limited by disk space
# of Rows per Database	Limited by disk space
# of Tables per Database	Limited by disk space
# of Views per Database	Limited by disk space
# of Tables per View	No limit; views limited to 127 columns

■ ORACLE Server 6.0

I can't say much more about the midrange system versions of ORACLE beyond what I already stated in Chapter 4. ORACLE is the dominant RDBMS in the UNIX and VMS markets, and the company has made sure that all versions share the same features.

Significant Features

ORACLE's scalability and portability features continue through the midrange systems. In addition to VAX/VMS (Oracle's primary platform), versions are available for over 30 versions of UNIX, including all the major variations such as SCO, AT&T System V, AIX, and SunOS. Oracle also offers a version that runs under Data General's proprietary AOS-VS minicomputer operating system. Any ORACLE version can be interconnected to any other version through SQL*Net, which makes Oracle the leader in the move to distributed databases. The long-awaited Version 7.0 will most likely serve to solidify Oracle's position as leader in the Client/Server and RDBMS markets.

Like Ingres, Oracle also has a number of products that let ORACLE users access data on non-Oracle databases. SQL*Connect to DB2 and SQL* Connect to SQL/DS link ORACLE databases to IBM's mainframe-based RDBMSs, and SQL*Connect to RMS links ORACLE to DEC's VAX/VMS-based RMS database.

As with any midrange system, the number of users per ORACLE database depends on the hardware and software platform.

Hardware and Software Requirements

Oracle's RDBMS runs on over 80 platforms, including DEC's VAX/VMS, IBM's mainframe VM and MVS, and all the major versions of UNIX, ranging from PCs to the high-end superservers. The resources required vary depending on hardware and software configurations; as with the PC-based versions, though, ORACLE has higher system resource requirements than the other RDBMSs in this chapter.

Communications Protocols

Oracle's SQL*Net provides Client/Server communications for all versions. UNIX and VAX/VMS versions of SQL*Net support TCP/IP, DECNet, APPC, and asynchronous (dial-in) connections. The Data General version of SQL*Net only supports TCP/IP. DOS, Windows, OS/2, and UNIX-based clients can use any of the supported protocols to communicate with any ORACLE database on the network.

SQL*Net 2.0 enhances ORACLE's distributed processing capabilities by implementing Oracle's Transparent Network Substrate (TNS), a common communications API that's protocol-independent. By using TNS-based versions of SQL*Net with Oracle's MultiProtocol Interchange, clients can access different ORACLE databases without regard to the underlying network protocol and without having to load multiple copies of SQL*Net.

Native SQL Language

Oracle's SQL and PL/SQL are compatible across the whole range of supported server systems. As long as the proper version of SQL*Net is used, any front-end that relies on Oracle's SQL or PL/SQL can talk to any ORACLE back-end.

Front-end Processors Provided

All versions of ORACLE include a version of SQLDBA appropriate to the particular operating system the server is running on. Any version of SQLDBA can talk to any ORACLE server using the proper version of SQL*Net. All of the programming tools and front-ends available for the PC-based versions of ORACLE support any of the back-end versions through SQL*Net. UNIX versions of the programming tools are also available.

Cross-platform compatibility is an important feature in Oracle's development tools, though it sometimes works better in theory than in practice. The source code precompilers make it fairly easy to move PL/SQL applications from one platform to another. However, many application programmers report finding incompatibilities between different platform versions of some of the other application development tools, such as SQL*Forms and SQL*Report-Writer. While none of the incompatibilities reported was major, they do require the developers to redesign or recreate portions of the application.

Advantages and Disadvantages

All of the midrange and mainframe system versions of ORACLE share the advantages of the PC-based versions: significant third-party front-end support, portable applications, and platform scalability. They also share the problems of high resource requirements and of being less than state-of-the-art, a condition that should change as multiplatform versions of ORACLE Version 7.0 are released in late 1992 and early 1993.

At this time, there are no ORACLE connections to DEC's Rdb or IBM's IMS, so INGRES wins out if you need to share data with these systems. Otherwise, ORACLE is the preferred platform for downsizing large-system databases to the midrange systems. It's also the best platform currently available for integrating databases across a wide variety of platforms.

Table 5.2

ORACLE 6.0 Quick Summary

PRODUCT INFORMATION	
Name	ORACLE Server 6.0
Vendor	Oracle Corporation
Price	Varies based on operating system and number of users; ranges from about $700 per user on a PC-based UNIX system to over $800 per user for the high-end systems

Table 5.2

(continued)

OPERATING SYSTEMS	
On Database Server	VAX/VMS, DG AOS-VS, IBM MVS and VM, 30+ versions of UNIX including AIX, SunOS, ULTRIX and AT&T System V
On LAN Server	Any network supporting APPC, DECNet, or TCP/IP (may involve an additional cost of $100-$200 per workstation)
On Workstations	DOS 3.1 or higher, OS/2 1.2 or higher, RISC-based UNIX, including the X-Windows and Motif GUI
MINIMUM REQUIREMENTS	
RAM on Server	Varies by system
RAM on Workstation	640k (DOS), 4Mb (OS/2), 8Mb (UNIX)
Disk Space on Server	Varies by system
UTILITIES PROVIDED	
Administration Utility	Yes
Interactive User Utility	Yes
Operating Systems/Environments Supported	DOS 3.1 or higher, OS/2 1.2 or higher, RISC-based UNIX
NATIVE LANGUAGES	
ANSI SQL	Yes
DB2 SQL Extensions	Yes
Other SQL	Yes
Non-SQL Language	No
MAXIMUMS	
Database Size	Limited by platform's supported disk space
Column Size	65,535 characters
Row Size	65,535 characters

Table 5.2

(continued)

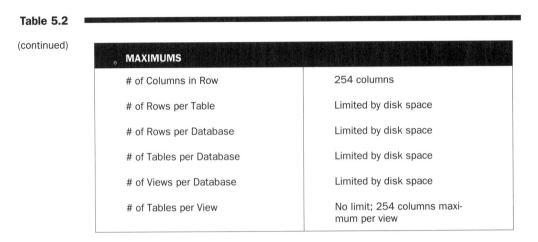

MAXIMUMS	
# of Columns in Row	254 columns
# of Rows per Table	Limited by disk space
# of Rows per Database	Limited by disk space
# of Tables per Database	Limited by disk space
# of Views per Database	Limited by disk space
# of Tables per View	No limit; 254 columns maximum per view

■ Sybase SQL Server for UNIX and VAX/VMS

Like ORACLE, Sybase SQL Server for UNIX and VAX/VMS shares the same features as the OS/2 and NLM versions covered in Chapter 4, so there's not much information to add here. SQL Server is Oracle's closest rival on midrange systems and is the technological leader on these systems (at least until ORACLE Version 7.0 is released).

Significant Features

SQL Server's most significant feature is the Virtual Server Architecture (VSA), Sybase's native support for symmetrical multiprocessing systems. First announced in 1990, VSA versions of SQL Server are available for various multiprocessing systems such as DEC VAXs, Sequent superservers, Sun 4/400 and 4/600MP SPARCServers, and AT&T StarServerE systems. Independent benchmark tests have shown SQL Server VSA to provide 30 to 50 percent performance increases over the regular UNIX or VMS versions, as well as the ability to support up to 1,000 simultaneous database users. Oracle has promised native symmetrical multiprocessing support for Version 7.0, but until it's released, SQL Server VSA is the only Client/Server DBMS on the market to take full advantage of these advanced systems, regardless of whether the operating system supports multiprocessing.

Sybase can also integrate data from other DBMSs with data on an SQL Server through their distributed processing Open Client/Open Server APIs. Open Client provides support for client access through different network protocols such as DECNet, TCP/IP, IPX/SPX, and Named Pipes. Open Server is the basis for a number of Sybase Open Gateways to non-Sybase RDBMSs, including Informix, Ingres, Oracle, DEC Rdb and RMS, and

IBM's DB2. The Open Gateways allow any Sybase client to access the other databases as if they were SQL Servers.

SQL Server shares ORACLE's portability and scalability, offering versions for VAX/VMS and most major UNIX versions, such AIX, AT&T System V, and the NeXT MACH operating system. Different versions can be linked together through a common protocol such as TCP/IP, and distributed processing is provided through both the Open Server facilities and SQL Server's support for Remote Stored Procedures (discussed in Chapter 4).

Hardware and Software Requirements

Sybase SQL Server runs on VAX/VMS systems and also supports over 30 major UNIX versions. It's unique in being the only RDBMS to have a version for the NeXT line of UNIX workstations. It's also the only one with full support for symmetrical multiprocessing systems such as the Sequent superservers. As always, the amount of RAM and disk space needed varies depending on the platform.

Communication Protocols

Sybase's Open Client API supports DECNet, TCP/IP, Named Pipes, IPX/SPX, and IBM's SNA. DOS and OS/2 clients can use DECNet or TCP/IP to communicate with SQL Servers on midrange systems.

Native SQL Language

All versions of SQL Server use TRANSACT-SQL as their native language, which includes support for stored procedures and triggers. Sybase has not yet adopted the support for scrollable cursors that was developed by Microsoft for their version of SQL Server. In addition, Sybase provides a number of UNIX-based application development tools that use APT-SQL, an enhanced 4GL version of SQL designed to speed application development.

Front-end Processors Provided

All versions of SQL server come with the character-mode ISQL utility. When used with the appropriate protocols, any front-end that supports the PC-based versions of SQL Server can be used to query and administrate midrange system versions.

The SQL Toolset uses both TRANSACT-SQL and APT-SQL, and includes: the APT Workbench, a *forms-based development environment* that lets the programmer create user query forms by painting them on the screen; Data Workbench, a *report writer* that programmers can use to create custom reports by again painting them on the screen; and APT-build, a *code generator* and applications prototyping utility. APT-build is particularly handy, as the code generator simplifies the application development process by letting the programmer describe the steps the application is to take through a series of menus and pick-lists; the generator then translates the actions into source code that can be modified or compiled as-is. The *applications prototyping utility* lets the developer test different actions and user screens prior to generating the code to make sure they work as expected.

Support is available for writing front-end programs on UNIX workstations in C, COBOL, and FORTRAN. Sybase also sells SQL Debug, a UNIX-based, interactive, source-level debugger for TRANSACT-SQL applications.

Advantages and Disadvantages

SQL Server on UNIX and VAX/VMS shares many of the same advantages as the PC-based versions, including the most third-party, front-end support of any of the Client/Server database systems. The one advantage unique to SQL Server is its support through VSA for true symmetrical multiprocessing, which can be a significant factor when you're looking for a high performance system that has to support up to 1000 users on a single server. However, many multiprocessing system vendors recommend ORACLE over SQL Server, because ORACLE works with the operating system's multiprocessing services, instead of providing its own multiprocessing support that bypasses the OS. The ORACLE method is generally better because it's always safer, for both the applications and the data, to work with the operating system instead of bypassing it. Bypassing the OS can lead to incompatibilities with the underlying hardware or to system crashes that occur when other applications don't know what the OS or DBMS is doing.

Sybase's Open Client and Open Server facilities also make it Oracle's strongest competitor in creating distributed processing databases. Sybase's gateway support for Informix, Ingres, and Oracle databases gives it a slight edge; however, if you want to integrate existing systems into a complete database network, either Sybase or Oracle can do the job. I have no reservations about recommending either of them.

Table 5.3

Sybase SQL Server for UNIX and VAX/VMS Quick Summary

PRODUCT INFORMATION	
Name	Sybase SQL Server 4.2
Vendor	Sybase, Inc.
Price	Varies based on operating system and number of users; ranges from about $600 per user on a PC-based UNIX system to a little over $300 per user for the high-end systems

Table 5.3

(continued)

OPERATING SYSTEMS	
On Database Server	VAX/VMS, most major versions of UNIX including AIX, AT&T System V, NeXT MACH, and Sequent Dynix
On LAN Server	Any network that supports DECNet or TCP/IP (may involve an additional cost of $100-$200 per workstation)
On Workstations	DOS 3.x or higher, OS/2 1.21 or higher, RISC-based UNIX, including the X-Windows, Motif, and Open Look GUIs
MINIMUM REQUIREMENTS	
RAM on Server	Varies by system
RAM on Workstation	512k (DOS), 6Mb (OS/2), 8Mb (UNIX)
Disk Space on Server	Varies by system
UTILITIES PROVIDED	
Administration Utility	Yes
Interactive User Utility	Yes
Operating Systems/Environments Supported	DOS 3.1 or higher, OS/2 1.21 or higher, RISC-based UNIX
NATIVE LANGUAGES	
ANSI SQL	Level 1
DB2 SQL Extensions	No
Other SQL Extensions	Yes
Non-SQL Language	No
MAXIMUMS	
Database Size	Limited by platform's supported disk space
Column Size	Normally 1,962 bytes; "image" and "text" data types store 2 billion bytes through pointers to external data
Row Size	1,962 bytes

Table 5.3

(continued)

MAXIMUMS	
Row Size	1,962 bytes
# of Columns in Row	255 columns
# of Rows per Table	Limited by disk space
# of Rows per Database	Limited by disk space
# of Tables per Database	2 billion
# of Views per Database	Unlimited
# of Tables per View	Unlimited tables, but only 250 columns per view

■ Gupta SQLBase for UNIX

SQLBase remains unique by being the only C/S database in this category to start as a PC-based RDBMS and move up to the UNIX platform. Although currently it only runs on the SunOS version of UNIX, Gupta has announced versions for the Univel UNIXWare and Solaris 2.0 UNIX variants, which will be released in early 1993.

Significant Features

SQLBase for UNIX's most significant feature is its price; at $9,995 for unlimited users, it's the cheapest of the database servers for UNIX. Except for the additional performance and database size provided by the Sun SPARCStation platform, SQLBase for UNIX is 100 percent identical to the PC-based versions. The UNIX version also supports the same gateways/routers as the PC-based versions, providing some distributed database capabilities.

Hardware and Software Requirements

SQLBase for UNIX requires a Sun SPARCStation or SPARCServer running SunOS 4.1.1 or newer, with at least 4Mb of RAM for the entry-level, five-user version. The software takes up approximately 10Mb of hard-disk space.

Communications Protocols

DOS and OS/2 workstations can communicate with a SQLBase for UNIX server via TCP/IP. The Gupta communications drivers have the same high-RAM requirement as the PC-based server drivers.

Native SQL Language

SQLBase for UNIX uses the same SQLTalk as the PC-based versions.

Front-end Processors Provided

Again, SQLBase for UNIX provides the same front-end utilities and capabilities as the PC-based versions. A UNIX version of SQLTalk/Character is also provided, and API libraries are available for creating UNIX front-ends in C or COBOL.

Advantages and Disadvantages

Gupta's SQLBase for UNIX's low price and front-end compatibility with the PC-based versions are its most notable advantages. The UNIX version is ideal for "upsizing" existing PC-based versions when greater performance or database size is needed.

The lack of versions for other midsize systems is a very significant disadvantage, so at this time I recommend SQLBase for UNIX only as an upgrade to existing PC-based servers which are reaching their performance limits. However, the release in early 1993 of the Solaris and UNIXWare versions may broaden SQLBase for UNIX's platform support and make it a competitor to other RDBMSs in this category.

Table 5.4

Gupta SQLBase for UNIX
Quick Summary

PRODUCT INFORMATION	
Name	SQLBase for UNIX
Vendor	Gupta Technologies, Inc.
Price	5 users: $995
	Unlimited:$9,995
OPERATING SYSTEMS	
On Database Server	SunOS 4.1.1 or higher
On LAN Server	Any LAN that supports TCP/IP (may involve an additional cost of $100-$200 per workstation)
On Workstations	DOS 3.1 or higher, Windows 3.x, SunOS 4.1.1 or higher

Table 5.4

(continued)

MINIMUM REQUIREMENTS	
RAM on Server	4Mb
RAM on Workstation	640k (DOS), 6Mb (OS/2), 4Mb (SunOS)
Disk Space on Server	10Mb
UTILITIES PROVIDED	
Administration Utility	Yes
Interactive User Utility	Yes
Operating Systems/Environments Supported	DOS 3.1 or higher, Windows 3.x, OS/2 1.0 or higher, SunOS 4.1.1 or higher
NATIVE LANGUAGES	
ANSI SQL	Level 2 with Integrity Enhancement
DB2 SQL Extensions	Yes
Other SQL	Yes
Non-SQL Language	No
MAXIMUMS	
Database Size	Limited by platform's supported disk space
Column Size	Limited by disk space (LONG VARCHAR data type)
Row Size	Limited by disk space
# of Columns in Row	250 columns
# of Rows per Table	Limited by disk space
# of Rows per Database	Limited by disk space
# of Tables per Database	Limited by disk space
# of Views per Database	Unlimited
# of Tables per View	Unlimited

■ INFORMIX

INFORMIX is the only UNIX-based RDBMS that doesn't have an OS/2 or NetWare NLM version. It has a DOS version, but it's primarily aimed at developers, and not for Client/Server users. Informix Software, Inc. was the first vendor to release a UNIX RDBMS, and in the mid-1980s, it added support for SQL. Although it has since been ported to other operating systems, UNIX remains INFORMIX's primary base.

Significant Features

Informix has two different Class 2 RDBMS which can serve as database servers: INFORMIX-SE and INFORMIX-OnLine. INFORMIX-SE is primarily a multiuser DBMS designed for small to midrange databases which can be used in a Client/Server system with the DOS-based INFORMIX-NET communications software. INFORMIX-OnLine has all the features of the SE version and provides greater performance and capabilities. Of the two, OnLine is the better version for Client/Server applications, so the remainder of this discussion will cover the more advanced version.

INFORMIX-OnLine Version 5.0 is designed for high-performance transaction processing systems, in which data integrity and high database availability are needed. One of the ways OnLine achieves its high performance is by circumventing the native UNIX file system and replacing it with its own disk-management routines that access the disk directly. This allows INFORMIX to replace the UNIX disk-caching routines with its own internal disk buffers, which are tuned for database performance.

OnLine also increases performance by providing limited support for parallel-processing on a symmetrical multiprocessing system. Parallel-processing is part of the data-sorting routines; different aspects of the sorting process are handled by different CPUs, and the results are combined before being written back to disk.

Database availability is provided through disk mirroring and on-line, real-time database backups to tape. Should the database system crash, INFORMIX-OnLine will automatically attempt to restore the database from the transaction logs when the system comes back up.

Data integrity is provided through a number of features, including stored procedures, business rules (similar to Sybase's triggers), and referential and entity integrity. INFORMIX's stored procedures are implemented in much the same way as Sybase's; the procedures are stored as part of the database and can be executed by any front-end application accessing the database. *Business rules* are user-defined, stored procedures limited to functioning at the column level, unlike Sybase's triggers, which can operate on a whole table or database. They can be used to specify such things as default column values or acceptable data values in a range.

While business rules can also be used to provide referential integrity, they're not necessary—INFORMIX provides full declarative RI that's compliant with the ANSI SQL Level 2 with Integrity Enhancements standard. Declarative RI is implemented as part of the table definition, along with options that determine how the RI is handled when a parent row is deleted (similar to Gupta's SQLBase implementation). In addition, INFORMIX provides *entity integrity*, in which the domain of a column is set when the column is defined. From that point on, the DBMS checks every INSERT or UPDATE action to ensure that the values being entered fall within the domain of the column.

INFORMIX-OnLine provides true support for *binary large objects* (BLOBs), which are text or graphics binary files up to 2G in size. Since BLOBs are implemented as pointers in the table columns to the external files, normal SQL commands can access the data. The BLOB data itself can be stored in a special disk area defined by the DBA. This provides additional performance, as the BLOBs are written directly to disk without having to go through INFORMIX's disk buffers. The INFORMIX-OnLine/Optical add-on lends OnLine the capability to store BLOBs on a write-once/read-many (WORM) optical drive. WORM drives, similar to CD-ROM drives, provide a large amount of storage space in a small package.

Client/Server capabilities and distributed databases are provided through INFORMIX-STAR, which provides full support for two-phase commits. INFORMIX-STAR lets the clients access, query, and modify multiple INFORMIX databases as if they were a single database.

Informix also sells INFORMIX-OnLine/Secure, a version designed primarily for government use. OnLine/Secure carries a Department of Defense B-1 security rating, which certifies it for use with top-secret data.

Hardware and Software Requirements

Version 5.0 of INFORMIX-OnLine is currently available for SPARC systems running SunOS, AT&T System V, and Hewlett-Packard's HP-UX. Version 4.1 is available for a number of other operating systems, including VAX/VMS and other UNIX versions, but it lacks many of the advanced features in the current version. A NetWare NLM version of INFORMIX-OnLine 4.1 has been announced and is due to be released in late 1992. Informix has also announced that most of the other platforms will eventually be updated to the 5.0 level.

Communications Protocols

INFORMIX-STAR uses TCP/IP to provide communications between
OnLine systems and client systems. DOS-based clients can use INFORMIX-
NET PC over TCP/IP to communicate with the INFORMIX-STAR system.

Native SQL Language

INFORMIX-SQL is compatible with the ANSI Level 2 with Integrity
Enhancements standard. INFORMIX uses a cost-based optimizer that can
return information to the application about how the SQL statement will be
optimized before actually executing it. This lets the DBA evaluate how the
command will affect system resources and postpone executing it if the performance of the system will suffer.

Front-ends Provided

INFORMIX-OnLine offers a number of UNIX-based administration utilities. DB-Monitor is a menu-driven utility that lets the DBA monitor the systems resource usage, start and stop on-line backups and restores, and adjust
system parameters.

Various command-line utilities provide the DBA with information about
disk fragmentation, and the abilities to both repair corrupted or damaged
index tables and view the contents of the transaction logs.

Libraries are available for creating front-end applications in C, COBOL,
and FORTRAN. Informix also has a number of application development
tools available, such as INFORMIX-4GL, a forms-based tool that uses an
enhanced 4GL version of SQL to create interactive applications, and ACE, a
report writer.

Advantages and Disadvantages

INFORMIX-OnLine suffers from the same disadvantage as INGRES—a
lack of support by third-party, front-end vendors. While this situation will
probably improve after the NetWare NLM version is released, potential
INFORMIX users are currently limited to custom-programmed client applications. Informix also has a reputation among users for providing poor support for its products.

Another disadvantage is that the technically advanced Version 5.0 currently runs on only three versions of UNIX. Again, this situation will likely
change over time; however, the lack of wide platform support limits
INFORMIX-OnLine's market appeal. Until more versions are available,
OnLine won't gain the support of third-party vendors that other C/S databases enjoy.

INFORMIX's greatest advantage is its OnLine/Secure version. OnLine/ Secure's high security rating makes it one of the few RDBMSs that can be used for top-secret government applications. This advantage is enhanced by the distributed processing capabilities provided by INFORMIX-STAR, which seamlessly ties multiple INFORMIX databases together.

Despite its advanced technology, I hesitate to recommend INFORMIX-OnLine for ordinary Client/Server use until Version 5.0 supports more platforms and third-party front-ends.

Table 5.5

INFORMIX-OnLine Version 5.0 Quick Summary

PRODUCT INFORMATION	
Name	INFORMIX-OnLine 5.0
Vendor	Informix Software, Inc.
Price	Varies based on operating system and number of users; ranges from $3,000 for a single-user version to $225,000 for an unlimited version on a high-end system
OPERATING SYSTEMS	
On Database Server	SunOS 4.1.1 or higher, AT&T System V, HP-UX
On LAN Server	Any LAN that supports TCP/IP (may involve an additional cost of $100-$200 per workstation)
On Workstations	DOS 3.1 or higher, RISC-based UNIX, including the Motif and DECWindows GUIs
MINIMUM REQUIREMENTS	
RAM on Server	8Mb
RAM on Workstation	640k (DOS), 8Mb (RISC-based UNIX)
Disk Space on Server	5Mb
UTILITIES PROVIDED	
Administration Utility	Yes
Interactive User Utility	No

Table 5.5

(continued)

UTILITIES PROVIDED	
Operating Systems/Environments Supported	SunOS 4.1.1 or higher, AT&T System V, HP-UX
NATIVE LANGUAGES	
ANSI SQL	Level 2 with Integrity Enhancements
DB2 SQL Extensions	No
Other SQL	No
Non-SQL Language	No
MAXIMUMS	
Database Size	Limited by platform's supported disk space
Column Size	32,767 bytes (2G in an external BLOB)
Row Size	32,767 bytes
# of Columns in Row	32,767 (241 BLOBs)
# of Rows per Table	4.278 billion
# of Rows per Database	Limited by disk space
# of Tables per Database	14.049 million
# of Views per Database	Unlimited
# of Tables per View	32,000 (The number of tables in use)

- *Evaluating Client/Server Databases for Proprietary Minicomputer Systems*

- *Rdb/VMS Version 4.0*

- *AllBase/SQL*

- *SQL/400 Version 2.1.1*

Client/Server Databases for Proprietary Minicomputer Systems

MANY PEOPLE IN THE COMPUTER INDUSTRY SAY THAT THE DAY OF the large computer systems (minicomputers and mainframes) has passed and that the future belongs to the PCs and RISC-based workstations and superservers. For the most part, I agree with this sentiment when it comes to Client/Server DBMSs; the previous two chapters have shown that the majority of the activity and advances in this arena are taking place on the smaller systems.

During the period from the early 1970s to the mid-1980s, minicomputer companies such as Hewlett-Packard, Digital Equipment Corporation (DEC), and Data General dominated what was then the low end of the computing market. These systems were proprietary, because they primarily ran the operating systems provided by the hardware vendor, and the vendor's operating system didn't run on anyone else's hardware. You could only access the computers through dedicated terminals. So, for example, if you wanted to run a VMS application, you had no choice but to purchase a VAX minicomputer and the VAX/VMS software from DEC.

The rise of microcomputers and UNIX-based RISC systems (usually referred to as "open systems") broke the stranglehold that the minicomputer vendors had on the low end of the market. The vendors scrambled to provide versions of UNIX for their hardware and to open up their systems to connections with PCs and workstations through LANs. Proprietary minicomputers were eventually squeezed into the narrow (and rapidly shrinking) portion of the computing spectrum between the superservers and the mainframes. In the late 1980s and early 1990s, the minicomputer vendors realized that their only hope of staying in the marketplace at all was to shift their focus from proprietary systems to open systems and reposition their minicomputers as superservers.

■ Evaluating Client/Server Databases for Proprietary Minicomputer Systems

Deciding whether to use a proprietary minicomputer as a database server boils down to one fundamental question: "Do I already have one of these systems running a database that LAN users need access to?" If the answer is no, there's really no need to look at these systems any further—you'll be better off investigating the systems covered in Chapters 4 and 5.

Advantages and Disadvantages

The proprietary minicomputers offer the same advantages as the UNIX-based superservers when it comes to the number of users supported and the potential database size. The larger minicomputers can support 500-plus users and databases well into the hundreds of gigabytes in size. However, the hardware required to do this is generally much more expensive than the same amount of computing power provided by the superservers (even those superservers sold by the same minicomputer vendor).

These minicomputers primarily support access through dedicated terminals, so you can mix dedicated and C/S database access on the same system. In this way, they share the mixed-use advantage of the larger UNIX systems discussed in Chapter 5.

Software license costs are also a factor. Not only are the proprietary operating systems more expensive, but they're usually licensed for a monthly fee instead of being purchased outright like the versions of UNIX operating systems are. This can add significantly to the cost of maintaining a proprietary minicomputer.

You should also consider the problem of support personnel. A programmer or system administrator familiar with one version of UNIX can usually adapt to another without too much additional training. Someone whose entire computer experience is with a proprietary operating system would probably have to be retrained on a different operating system, which increases the support costs. The pool of potential technical support employees is also predictably smaller; however, the decline in proprietary systems means fewer jobs available for those who haven't yet switched to a different system, so more experienced technicians and programmers may be available for hire.

The vendors of proprietary systems have also been somewhat slow in adapting their DBMSs to Client/Server capabilities. The independent DBMS vendors have beaten the minicomputer vendors to the market with versions of their own C/S DBMSs that run on the vendor's proprietary OS, or have produced gateway software that lets users of the third-party DBMS access data from the minicomputer's proprietary DBMS. For the most part, the proprietary systems fall into the Class 5 rating, supplemented by Class 3 capabilities provided by both the system vendor and third-party vendors.

In the long run, the major advances in Client/Server technology will primarily take place in the PC and UNIX systems and not with the proprietary systems. This should be particularly true for front-ends, as the third-party vendors expand their support of the more popular DBMSs.

The minicomputers have an advantage that they share with the high-end RISC and superserver systems: built-in CPU and disk fault tolerance. The systems, designed to stay up and running as long as possible, automatically correct or compensate for failures in most of the subsystems. PC and RISC system vendors are rapidly adding fault-tolerant features, though, so this advantage won't exist too much longer.

Here's the bottom line: You'll only benefit from these systems if you already have one that's loaded with critical data. You can then extend the system's reach to include Client/Server capabilities without having to transplant the data to a different DBMS.

Special Considerations

Once you've decided that you want to stay with an existing proprietary system rather than move your database processing to an open system, the main item to consider is network protocol. TCP/IP is the most common and is supported by the three systems discussed in this chapter, as well as by all the UNIX-based and PC systems. However, expect to pay a premium price for the hardware and software needed to add TCP/IP to an existing proprietary system. Also don't forget that the TCP/IP protocol stack usually takes up more RAM on the client systems than other protocols. A gateway can be used in most cases to translate between the LAN's native protocol and TCP/IP, though this adds a level of complexity to the system.

In general, networking between proprietary systems and PCs wasn't a priority for the system vendors until recently. The steadily growing market forced them to add network support; however, such support is usually grafted onto the minicomputer, instead of being designed as part of the system. This almost guarantees that problems will occur when you're setting up a Client/Server system between a minicomputer and PCs. Make sure your PCs can connect easily and efficiently with the DBMS you're thinking of using before committing time and resources to developing the C/S system.

Unless you already have the vendors SQL-based RDBMS software, make sure that your existing data can be imported into the DBMS's format without major modifications.

Finally, be prepared to develop your own front-end software; the majority of the front-ends available for these systems are provided by the minicomputer vendor. There are few direct (non-gateway) third-party front-ends available for two of the three DBMSs described in this chapter at the time of this writing.

While the minicomputer vendors usually have good technical staff ready to support customers, I have found that getting information about their products can be an exercise in frustration if you're not already a customer (which is reflected in the scarcity of information in some of the quick summary tables in this chapter). The problem seems to lie in the layers of bureaucracy that have built up over the years in the vendor's internal organizations. Local sales offices seem to be geared more toward buyers than shoppers, so in most cases they refer information inquiries to the national office. The national offices don't have one person responsible for simply providing information, and in every case they suggested contacting the local sales office. If you're already a customer, you shouldn't have too many difficulties obtaining information on DBMSs from local vendors. If you're not, be prepared to spend some time tracking down the information you need to make an intelligent comparison between these products and the third-party RDBMSs.

Advice and Tips

At the risk of sounding like a broken record, the best advice I can give is to avoid using a proprietary system for a Client/Server database if you can. The disadvantages of using one far outweigh the advantages. Unless you're already locked into one of the three systems discussed here (perhaps because of a non-DBMS application that only runs on the proprietary system), your best course of action would be to build your C/S system around one of the DBMSs in Chapter 4 or 5.

Alternatively, consider using one of the third-party RDBMSs that support the minicomputer's OS. As I mentioned in Chapter 5, Ingres, Oracle, and Sybase have VAX/VMS versions of their DBMSs which can be integrated into a distributed system with other platforms through TCP/IP or DECNet.

Ingres, Oracle, Sybase and Informix also have versions for Hewlett-Packard's HP-UX variant of UNIX—these are better alternatives to HP's own AllBase on HP-UX. The same is true for IBM AS/400 systems running IBM's AIX. However, if you're running HP's proprietary MPE/XL or IBM's OS/400 operating systems on their respective minicomputers, you're out of luck—your only choice is the respective vendor's SQL-based RDBMS.

■ Rdb/VMS Version 4.0

Digital Equipment Corporation (DEC) is the market leader in proprietary minicomputer systems, most of which run its VAX/VMS operating system. Both the Oracle and the Ingres RDBMSs were initially written for VMS, and it remains their primary home. In an effort to remain a player in the database market, DEC created the Relational Rdb/VMS in the mid-1980s.

Significant Features

DEC's strength has always been VAX/VMS, which was designed from the ground up as a multiuser, real-time access operating system. (When VMS was initially released, the dominant operating systems were designed for batch processing on mainframes.) VMS runs on any DEC system—from the roughly $5,000 MicroVAXs to the $10,000 DECStations to the $4,000,000-plus, mainframe-size VAX 9000 series. Because of this scalability, VMS has become a popular platform for a wide variety of multiuser applications, and DEC has become the largest minicomputer in the world. DEC was also an early pioneer in local area networks, using the ethernet topology and DEC-Net protocol to link any number of VAX systems together.

Rdb/VMS runs on any VMS system, and a run-time version is included with the operating system. This lets Rdb/VMS applications run on any VAX without your having to purchase the full product. The full Rdb system is necessary for developing applications and providing Client/Server access to the database.

Rdb/VMS uses a concept called *storage maps* to store its data, which lets the DBA allocate data space in a number of ways. Of particular interest is a storage method called horizontal partitioning. *Horizontal partitioning* lets the DBA create rules governing where Rdb stores particular types of data, providing a measure of automatic load balancing on the data disks and increasing data-retrieval throughput.

Also available is SERdb Version 4.1, an add-on to Rdb/VMS that provides U.S. Department of Defense security levels for federal government use. The enhanced security features are also useful for businesses dealing with highly confidential data, such as hospital patient records.

Another interesting module is Rdb/ELn, which provides real-time data capture capabilities for Rdb databases. Real-time data capture is useful, for example, in a laboratory to automatically gather test data from specialized testing machines or in a weather bureau to gather continuous radar updates.

Ironically, while UNIX was originally developed on early DEC minicomputers (the PDP series, predecessors to the VAX line), it never factored into DEC's marketing until recently. DEC does sell their own version of UNIX, called ULTRIX, but doesn't offer a version of Rdb for it. ULTRIX users can purchase a version of INGRES that DEC has customized called ULTRIX/SQL. DEC also sells ULTRIX/SQL Remote Access to Rdb/VMS, a module that lets ULTRIX/SQL users access Rdb databases, and a cross-compiler that lets programmers convert ULTRIX/SQL applications to Rdb/VMS applications.

DEC has also begun to move into the multimedia market with the SQL Multimedia for Rdb/VMS module, which lets client applications running on VMS, ULTRIX, PC/MS DOS, and Macintosh systems store and access large data objects, such as graphics and video, in an Rdb database. Informix is the only other RDBMS company providing similar capabilities at this time, though I expect it will become a feature in other DBMSs as multimedia applications become more common.

Hardware and Software Requirements

Rdb/VMS runs on any DEC computer that uses the VMS operating systems, including the DECStation workstations, MicroVAX superservers, and VAX minicomputers. The number of users supported depends on the capacity of the hardware platform.

A run-time version of Rdb is included with every VMS operating system package. The full Rdb/VMS system is available separately.

Communication Protocols

Rdb/VMS uses the DECNet protocol to communicate with other VAX systems running VMS or ULTRIX. The full Rdb package includes the VAX SQL/Services communication protocol, which provides network access to Rdb/VMS databases from applications running on DEC systems using VMS or ULTRIX. It also provides access from PC's running PC/MS DOS connected to the VAX over a DECNet LAN.

DEC provides their own gateway-like software, called SQL/Services, to assist third-party vendors in creating front-end applications for Rdb. One of the more notable products that uses SQL/Services is Novell's NetWare for VMS, a version of their popular LAN operating system that runs on VAXs. NetWare for VMS lets PC clients use the IPX/SPX protocol to access Rdb/VMS.

A few front-end vendors provide their own gateways to Rdb. Gateways are also available from other DBM vendors, such as Ingres, which use TCP/IP to communicate with Rdb. DEC supplies TCP/IP for the VMS systems as an additional cost module.

DEC is also the first third-party DBMS vendor to provide support for the Microsoft/Sybase Open Database Communications (ODBC) protocol. ODBC support can only help to make more third-party front-ends available for Rdb.

Native SQL Language

Rdb/VMS's current SQL implementation is compatible with the ANSI Level 2 with Integrity Enhancements standard. DEC also provides their own relational language, called RDML (Relational Database Management Language); however, it was never very popular, and DEC provides cross-compilers and program translators to help developers move RDML programs to SQL.

Rdb uses dynamic optimization to optimize SQL statements. *Dynamic optimization* is unique to Rdb (DEC has applied for patents on the process); it can dynamically switch between different search techniques based on the initial responses to a query. For example, Rdb starts a search by using the appropriate index for the table. If the number of rows that satisfy the query criteria exceeds a certain percentage of the total number of rows in the table, Rdb will switch to just scanning the whole table to complete the search. This method ultimately improves response time, since Rdb doesn't have to search in two separate places (the index and the actual table) for the data.

Front-end Processors Provided

The VAX SQL/Services included with Rdb/VMS provide an interactive character-mode administration utility for VMS, ULTRIX, and PC/MS DOS systems. Also included are a number of programming libraries for creating custom front-end applications on PC/MS DOS, Macintosh, and SUN systems.

DEC has licensed a number of the Ingres application development tools and adapted them for creating Rdb/VMS applications using the SQL/Services gateway. DEC also provides InstantSQL for Rdb/VMS, an ULTRIX-based development package that runs on the Motif GUI. The graphical interface allows users create applications that access Rdb without having to learn SQL.

Advantages and Disadvantages

The major advantage to Rdb/VMS is that DEC includes a run-time version with every copy of the VMS operating system. So anyone who has one or more VMS systems needs only one copy of the full version to create applications that can run on all their systems. The security enhancements and real-time data collection modules are also an advantage for those who need such capabilities.

Another advantage is the architecture of the VAX hardware systems. One of the primary features of the VAX/VMS systems is called *clustering*, in which multiple VAX computers can be linked together into one complex, and each computer has full access to all the disk drives and communications resources of the cluster. This offers users the ability to expand the processing power of the computer system without purchasing full VAX systems with their own disk drives and communications hardware. This option can amount to a significant cost savings. VMS automatically balances the workload between the different systems in the cluster to improve performance.

DEC provides fairly complete Client/Server capabilities for Rdb/VMS. There are a number of third-party front-ends available (though far fewer than for the DMBSs described in Chapter 4 and 5) that use either SQL/Services or their own proprietary gateways. Of particular interest is the number of Macintosh-based client applications available; there are at least twice as many for the Macintosh as there are for PCs. This is probably due to co-development agreements between Apple and DEC, which are designed to improve Macintoshs' access to VAX/VMS systems. A number of third-party gateways are also available, and DEC's ODBC support should help to increase the number of front-ends that can access Rdb/VMS directly.

However, unless you absolutely have to run Rdb/VMS (for example, if you already have a significant amount of data in a Rdb database), your best bet for integrating VMS systems into a company-wide Client/Server network is to use one of the third-party RDBMSs that have a VMS version. I recommend using ORACLE (which is the most popular VMS database), instead of Rdb, because it offers better built-in distributed processing capabilities, multiplatform support, and greater front-end support.

DEC is developing their own RISC CPU (currently called Alpha) and expects to release Alpha systems by mid-1993. They have announced plans to move their entire line of computers and operating systems to an Alpha-based architecture through the mid-90s. DEC has also announced plans to move Rdb to Alpha-based versions of VMS and UNIX and eventually to Microsoft's Windows/NT. Perhaps these efforts to make Rdb less proprietary will revitalize it and make it a more serious contender in the Client/Server market.

Table 6.1

Rdb/VMS Version 4.0
Quick Summary

PRODUCT INFORMATION	
Name	Rdb/VMS Version 4.0
Vendor	Digital Equipment Corporation (DEC)
Price	Ranges from $2,080 to $236,000 depending on underlying hardware platform
OPERATING SYSTEMS	
On Database Server	DEC VAX/VMS
On LAN Server	DEC PathWorks (DEC version of MS LAN Manager)
On Workstations	PC/MS DOS, ULTRIX, VMS
MINIMUM REQUIREMENTS	
RAM on Server	Varies depending on platform
RAM on Workstation	640k (DOS)
Disk Space on Server	Varies depending on platform
UTILITIES PROVIDED	
Administration Utility	Yes
Interactive User Utility	Yes
Operating Systems/Environments Supported	PC/MS DOS, ULTRIX, VMS
NATIVE LANGUAGES	
ANSI SQL	Level 2 with Integrity Enhancements
DB2 SQL Extensions	No
Other SQL	No
Non-SQL Language	RDML
MAXIMUMS	
Database Size	Varies depending on platform
Column Size	32,767 bytes; LIST datatype up to 2G

Table 6.1

(continued)

MAXIMUMS	
Row Size	65,291 bytes
# of Columns in Row	2,000
# of Rows per Table	Limited by disk space
# of Rows per Database	Limited by disk space
# of Tables per Database	4,096
# of Views per Database	4,096
# of Tables per View	4,096

■ AllBase/SQL

Hewlett-Packard (HP) was one of DEC's early competitors in the mini-computer market. They have the distinction of being the first vendor to release a minicomputer-based DBMS, called Image. Image was based on the Network Database model and ran on HP's 1000 and 3000 series computers.

HP moved their entire line to the RISC architecture in the late 1980s. They replaced the HP3000 operating system with their proprietary MPE/XL (which was backward-compatible with the earlier OS) and HP-UX—their own version of UNIX. At the same time, HP released AllBase, a RDBMS that runs under either operating system.

Significant Features

HP is unique in that it provides two different interfaces to AllBase/SQL. An Image interface presents the relational AllBase's data as though it were still based on the Network Database model; this gives it backward compatibility with Image applications. It also has an SQL interface for use in applications and Client/Server systems.

AllBase provides some distributed database processing by letting users of one AllBase database query data on remote AllBase databases as though they were part of the local database. HP still markets TurboIMAGE, the current version of their Network model DBMS, and also provides AllBase TurboCON-NECT, which lets AllBase users transparently access Image-based databases.

According to industry reports, the HP3000 and HP9000 RISC-based microcomputers provide an excellent price-to-performance ratio, and HP has started marketing them as alternatives to superservers for use as database servers. HP has aggressively pursued third-party vendors to provide Client/Server applications, front-ends, and development tools for AllBase. They've also encouraged other RDBMS vendors to port their products to HP-UX and to date, Oracle and Informix have answered the call. Ingres also provides a gateway to AllBase databases.

Hewlett-Packard's minicomputers are a hybrid of proprietary and open systems, as HP pushes both the proprietary MPE/XL operating system and the more open HP-UX UNIX variant. The only reason I've classified them as proprietary is that AllBase itself is limited to running on HP systems. Though they've not yet announced any plans to do so, HP's targeting of the Client/Server market suggests they may provide versions of AllBase for other UNIX systems.

Hardware and Software Requirements

AllBase runs on any HP3000 or HP9000 series minicomputer. Both the MPE/XL and HP-UX operating systems are supported. The number of users and the size of database supported depends on the underlying hardware platform.

Communications Protocols

HP supports TCP/IP for communications between clients and AllBase. User-transparent distributed database communications between different AllBase databases are provided by HP's own Network System (NS) protocol. Transparent communications lets users send a query to an AllBase server without considering where the data actually resides. The server passes the query on to the proper database and passes the response back to the user.

In 1991, HP introduced AllBase/SQL PC API, through which PC/MS-DOS applications communicate with AllBase databases over TCP/IP.

Native SQL Language

HPSQL is AllBase's native language, which is ANSI Level 2 compatible. Support is also available for accessing AllBase databases through the Image language, retaining the Network model interface and backward compatibility with Image applications.

Front-end Processors Provided

No real Client/Server front-end is provided; the administration utility that comes with AllBase runs on a directly connected terminal. However, HP has a number of development tools available, including AllBase/4GL (designed for creating on-line transaction processing applications) and AllBase/Query (a terminal-based query tool for creating ad-hoc queries and reports).

HP's aggressive marketing has also led to an increasing amount of third-party, front-end support, including such PC-based front-ends as Gupta's

SQL Windows and Powersoft's PowerBuilder (covered in Chapter 8). A UNIX-based version of INGRES/Tools is also available for creating AllBase client applications on RISC-based workstations.

Advantages and Disadvantages

AllBase is the rising star of the proprietary Client/Server RDBMSs, and Hewlett-Packard's continuing efforts to line up third-party support can only help to make it a challenger to the third-party UNIX-based C/S systems. Until DEC releases their Alpha-based systems, HP has no serious competition in the UNIX market for proprietary C/S database servers.

The downside is that AllBase is still a proprietary product, because you're limited to running it on HP computers. HP's continued encouragement for porting third-party RDBMSs to their HP3000 and HP9000 platforms makes me wonder if they're as serious about making AllBase a contender in the Client/Server market as their marketing approach makes them appear.

While AllBase is the second-best overall of the three databases in this chapter for Client/Server applications, I'd really like to see HP announce plans for supporting it on other platforms before giving it any kind of recommendation. Until then, you're better off using Oracle's or Informix's RDBMS on the HP platforms.

Table 6.2

AllBase/SQL Quick Summary

PRODUCT INFORMATION	
Name	AllBAse/SQL
Vendor	Hewlett-Packard Company
Price	Unlimited: Ranges from $10,000 to $48,000 depending on underlying hardware platform
OPERATING SYSTEMS	
On Database Server	MPE/XL, HP-UX
On LAN Server	Any LAN that supports TCP/IP
On Workstations	DOS, Windows, HP-UX

Table 6.2

(continued)

MINIMUM REQUIREMENTS	
RAM on Server	3Mb
RAM on Workstation	640k (DOS), 4Mb (HP-UX)
Disk Space on Server	10Mb
UTILITIES PROVIDED	
Administration Utility	Yes (terminal-based)
Interactive User Utility	No
Operating Systems/Environments Supported	HP-UX, MPE/XL
NATIVE LANGUAGES	
ANSI SQL	Level 2
DB2 SQL Extensions	No
Other SQL	No
Non-SQL Language	Image
MAXIMUMS	
Database Size	Varies depending on platform
Column Size	Not available
Row Size	Not available
# of Columns in Row	Not available
# of Rows per Table	Limited by disk space
# of Rows per database	Limited by disk space
# of Tables per Database	Not available
# of Views per Database	Not available
# of Tables per View	Not available

■ SQL/400 Version 2.1.1

Even though it's the largest computer company in the world, IBM hasn't had as great an impact (or market share) as DEC and HP when it comes to minicomputers. IBM's most successful minicomputers were the System/36 and System/38, released in the late 1970s. The System/3x computers were unique in that a DBMS was built into the operating system. Many of these systems were (and are) used in applications requiring dedicated database processing, for example, in warehouse inventory, and point-of-sale (POS), cash-register-type applications.

In 1990, IBM announced and released the first of the AS/400 line of mini-computers, which they've positioned as enhancements to and replacements for the System/3x line. The AS/400s are (for the most part) backward-compatible with System/3x applications and continue the System/3x tradition of having a DBMS as part of the operating system.

Significant Features

It's impossible to talk about the large IBM systems without briefly discussing IBM's System Application Architecture (SAA). During the mid-to-late 1980s, IBM found itself losing some of its large-system market share to DEC, primarily because IBM's systems lacked the ability to interconnect between the different-sized computers. DEC's VAX/VMS has built-in networking capabilities; these capabilities combined with VMS's ability to run on virtually every size of DEC's computers gave customers an easy way to link different department and corporate computers into a coherent company-wide system.

In an effort to counter DEC's networking advantage, IBM announced SAA in 1987. SAA isn't a particular application or operating system—it's a design specification for creating applications that can run on and access any of IBM's computers, no matter which platform was used to develop them. Along with SAA, IBM announced the SNA-based (System Network Architecture, the native networking protocol for IBM's mainframes) Application Program-to-Program Communications (APPC) protocol, which runs on any of their systems and allows applications running on one system to talk to those running on other systems. APPC is clearly designed as IBM's attempt to enter the Client/Server computing market.

SAA generated a lot of excitement when it was first announced, particularly among folks in MIS and IS departments whose entire computing power was tied up in IBM's mainframes. Their users were clamoring for a way to interconnect their desktop PCs with the company's central hosts, and SAA seemed to answer the MIS departments' prayers. However, it hasn't worked out quite so smoothly in practice, as IBM has been slow in implementing SAA across their entire range of systems.

So how does this relate to SQL/400? Well, one of the motivations for developing the AS/400 systems was to provide an SAA-compatible line of midrange computers to fill in the gap between OS/2 (the desktop portion of SAA) and IBM's DB2 (the only SAA mainframe DBMS to date). SQL/400 provides a nearly SAA-compatible SQL interface to the data on an AS/400, as well as some distributed processing and C/S capabilities.

The initial version of SQL/400 provided SAA-compatibility more in theory than in fact. Version 2.1.1, released in early 1992, significantly closes the gap by providing 98 percent compatibility with IBM's major SAA application, DB2. Unfortunately, the missing pieces make SQL/400 less capable as a Client/Server system than IBM's OS/2-based Database Manager (covered in Chapter 4). For example, one missing piece is the SQL command ALTER TABLE, which lets the database administrator change the structure of a table. Under SQL/400, the only way to change a table is to create a new one with the desired structure, copy the data from the old table to the new one, and delete the old table. This is not only time-consuming, it violates some of the database structure independence rules specified in the Relational model.

Otherwise, SQL/400 provides the same database structures as DB2 and the OS/2 Database Manager, so PC-based databases can be moved to the larger system as processing needs warrant. The additional power and disk-size capabilities of the AS/400 systems place them in between PCs and mainframes in user capabilities and maximum database size.

IBM also sells a version of their AIX UNIX variant that runs on the AS/400 systems. Ingres, Oracle, and Sybase all have AIX versions of their RDBMSs.

Hardware and Software Requirements

SQL/400 only runs with OS/400, the native operating system for the AS/400 line. The AS/400 systems range in size from the 9402 Model C04 that supports 12 users ($14,500) to the 9406 Model E90 that supports 240 users maximum ($900,000). OS/400 includes native DBMS capabilities; SQL/400 is an additional-cost module that provides an SQL interface to the underlying data.

Both AIX and OS/400 can run at the same time on the same AS/400, provided the system has enough RAM to support both operating systems. SQL/400 doesn't run on AIX, but the separately available AIX Viaduct for AS/400 module provides interprocess communications between AIX applications and SQL/400 databases.

Communication Protocols

SQL/400 communicates with other IBM systems through APPC. Unfortunately, APPC is memory intensive and takes up too much RAM on PC/MS DOS-based systems (over 300k) to be practical for DOS-based client systems.

TCP/IP is also available for the AS/400 systems and can be used by AIX and other TCP/IP workstations to communicate with SQL/400. IBM also sells the AIX AS/400 3270 Connection Program, which lets AS/400 systems running both AIX and OS/400 communicate with other SNA systems, such as an IBM mainframe or RS/6000 RISC workstation.

Native SQL Language

As I mentioned previously, SQL/400 is 98 percent compatible with IBM's DB2 SQL. This would make it mostly compatible with the ANSI Level 2 with Integrity Enhancement standard, as well as providing the DB2 SQL extensions. However, the missing 2 percent can cause complications when an application from another IBM SQL system is being moved to SQL/400.

The native language of OS/400 is the 3GL RPG/400, which was initially developed for the System/3x line. Support for COBOL is also available. The data on an AS/400 system can be accessed through applications outside of the SQL/400 interface, which implicitly violates the Relational model's data integrity principles. The system administrator can optionally prevent applications from reaching data without going through SQL/400, which partially resolves this problem.

Front-end Processors Provided

The AS/400 series is still primarily designed as a host system for dedicated terminals, so the only SQL/400 administration tools provided are terminal-based. Front-end, PC-based client support is available only through the Query Manager that comes with IBM's OS/2-based Database Manager.

Because of APPC's high RAM requirements, no PC/MS DOS-based front-ends are available at this time. While TCP/IP can be used by a DOS PC to communicate with an AS/400, there has been little demand for such products, so none exists.

Advantages and Disadvantages

At this time, an AS/400 system can serve as an upgrade to an existing System/ 3x minicomputer, which is the only real advantage to AS/400s. Upgrading to an AS/400 will provide additional processing capabilities and a limited form of Client/Server access to data formerly residing on the System/3x. The lack of 100 percent SAA and DB2 SQL compatibility prevents SQL/400 from neatly fitting into the midrange slot between the OS/2 Database Manager and DB2.

IBM also hasn't really clarified how the AS/400 systems fit into their product line, other than as replacements for existing System/3xs. IBM's line of RISC-based RS/6000 workstations and superservers provide as much (if not more) processing power than the AS/400s. The RS/6000s are generally less expensive and have the advantage of running AIX, so they're compatible with many third-party, UNIX-based RDBMSs. The only advantage that the AS/400s have over the RISC systems is that IBM has not yet announced how AIX will fit into SAA. SQL/400 maintains the advantage in providing some distributed database capabilities in a predominantly IBM environment.

Unless you're replacing a System/3x or need a midrange, terminal-based system that fits into an existing SAA environment, I'd recommend using one of the RS/6000 superservers with a third-party RDBMS over an AS/400 if you're looking for an IBM minicomputer.

Table 6.3

SQL/400 Version 2.1.1
Quick Summary

PRODUCT INFORMATION	
Name	SQL/400
Vendor	IBM, Inc.
Price	Unlimited: Ranges from $1,500 to $9,000 depending on underlying hardware platform
OPERATING SYSTEMS	
On Database Server	OS/400
On LAN Server	IBM LAN Server or any network that supports APPC; TCP/IP support optional
On Workstations	OS/2 1.3 Extended Edition; OS/2 2.0 with the Extended Services product
MINIMUM REQUIREMENTS	
RAM on Server	8Mb
RAM on Workstation	8Mb (OS/2)
Disk Space on Server	10Mb
UTILITIES PROVIDED	
Administration Utility	Yes (terminal-based)
Interactive User Utility	No
Operating Systems/Environments Supported	OS/2 1.3 EE; OS/2 2.0 with ES

Table 6.3

(continued)

NATIVE LANGUAGES	
ANSI SQL	Level 2 with Integrity Enhancements (98% compatible
DB2 SQL Extensions	Compatible
Other SQL	No
Non-SQL Language	RPG/400
MAXIMUMS	
Database Size	Varies depending on platform
Column Size	4,000 bytes, or 32,700 characters in a LONG VARCHAR
Row Size	4,005 bytes
# of Columns in Row	255 columns
# of Rows per Table	Limited by disk space
# of Rows per Database	Limited by disk space
# of Tables per Database	Limited by disk space
# of Views per Database	Limited by disk space
# of Tables per View	15

- *Evaluating Client/Server Databases for Mainframes*
- *SQL/DS*
- *ORACLE Mainframe Versions*

Client/Server Databases for Mainframes

I T MAY SEEM ODD, AT FIRST, TO CONSIDER MAINFRAMES AS A PLATFORM for Client/Server databases, since the main reason for moving to a C/S platform is to downsize corporate databases from large, expensive computers to smaller, less costly ones. However, the reality is that mainframes made up 23 percent of the Client/Server market in early 1992, as shown in the BRG study mentioned at the beginning of Chapter 4. The reason is simple: In many businesses, mainframes are the primary computer resource; it's easier to integrate them into a company-wide Client/Server system than to toss them out and start from scratch.

Another inescapable fact is that currently no other computers can handle the quantity of data and simultaneous users that a mainframe can. Mainframe architecture has evolved over the last 30 years to include support for multiple CPUs linked through high-speed data channels, attached to hundreds, if not thousands, of large capacity disk drives. Anyone who has ever been in a mainframe computer room containing rows upon rows of disk-drive cabinets can understand why they're commonly referred to as "disk farms."

For this reason, mainframes, expensive as they are to maintain, aren't going to disappear in the foreseeable future. However, their role in corporate computer operations is changing; increasingly, mainframes are viewed less as the primary computer resource and more as the central storage facility for data access through Client/Server or distributed database processing. Even IBM (the world's largest mainframe vendor) recognizes this and refers to their mainframes as the "data warehouses" of large corporations.

Although I primarily discuss IBM mainframes in this chapter, it's important to remember that companies such as Ahmdal, Hitachi, and others also make mainframes that run the same operating systems and software as IBM. However, since IBM has the largest share of the market and all mainframe software is written to the IBM standard, it's simpler to refer to mainframes as though they all came from IBM.

■ Evaluating Client/Server Databases for Mainframes

Evaluating a mainframe as a Client/Server platform is very different from evaluating the other platforms in this book. First, we have to work on the assumption that you already have a mainframe. With all the less expensive alternatives available, there's no reason to purchase a mainframe for the database server function alone—it just isn't cost-effective. With the advances being made in C/S databases available for the smaller platforms, it makes more sense to expand their capacity or add more database servers than to move all the data to a costly central platform.

Second, mainframe-based databases are, with one exception, designed primarily for access via dedicated terminals, with little built-in support for Client/Server communications. The primary way to access data on a mainframe from a PC or RISC client is through a gateway system. This system translates the communications across the different network protocols used by the client and the mainframe. Gateways also translate the client's SQL commands into a form of SQL which the mainframe databases understand, and translate the responses from the database into a form the clients can use.

The exception to this is ORACLE, which has versions for the two major mainframe operating systems, VM and MVS. ORACLE databases on the mainframe can share data with other ORACLE databases and can be accessed by clients, just like any other version of ORACLE, using the appropriate version of SQL*Net and network protocols.

Advantages and Disadvantages

The clear advantage of mainframe databases is the potential quantity of data and users supported. It's not unheard of for a mainframe database to hold terabytes (one trillion bytes) of data, which can be accessed by a thousand or more users at the same time. While advances in computing power and distributed databases may someday give the less expensive systems the same capabilities, the mainframes should continue to hold this advantage through most of the 1990s.

Of course, such power comes at a very high cost. It's not just the mainframe CPUs and disk drives that are expensive; there are numerous necessary add-ons, such as communications processors to connect to the dedicated terminals, banks of tape drives to back up all that data, and high-speed printers to produce reports from the data. There's also the cost of maintaining the special environment a mainframe requires: a raised floor in the "data center" for all the cabling and pipes to pass under; special air conditioning systems to keep the computer room at a constant temperature; water pipes for cooling the CPUs; and large generator-driven backup power supplies to prevent the computer from crashing when the main power goes out.

Then you must consider the personnel costs. Most MIS departments grew up around mainframes because of the number of different technical support staffs needed to keep the system running. There are systems programmers who tune the operating system and balance the load between different applications to obtain the best performance; systems analysts and application programmers who design, develop, and support the user applications; system operators who monitor the system and perform day-to-day maintenance tasks such as data backups; and network technicians who support and maintain the communications portion of the system.

There are also the complexities of sharing the data on a mainframe with client systems. Mainframe databases are just not geared toward C/S applications, so the previously mentioned gateways are usually needed to communicate between the client systems and the mainframe. IBM is making moves in the Client/Server direction with its two mainframe RDBMSs, but the problem is that the majority of mainframe databases are still running under the hierarchical IMS database (discussed in Chapter 1) or similar DBMSs and not under the relational DB2 or SQL/DS DBMSs. Special gateway systems are needed to translate the SQL commands into a form IMS can understand and respond to.

In addition to the need for gateways to handle the different communications standards or access non-SQL databases, there's the problem of character coding. Mainframes and other computer systems simply don't speak the same language when it comes to how standard characters are coded in binary form. *Character coding* is the way the letters, numbers, and symbols of the standard alphabet are assigned unique binary data values. By using a standard coding (usually referred to as a character set), every system that follows the standard agrees (for example) that a certain value represents a capital "A," while another value represents a lowercase "a." PC, UNIX, and VAX/VMS systems use a form of text coding called ASCII (American Standard Code for Information Interchange), while mainframes use EBCDIC (Extended Binary-Coded Decimal Interchange Code). Database gateways must translate the ASCII-coded SQL requests from the client systems into EBCDIC-coded SQL to pass requests to the mainframe, and then must reverse the process with the response. While this translation process sounds complex, it's actually based on common technology that has been available for years. So the process itself is fairly trivial to implement, and the net effect is a slight increase in processing overhead.

Mainframes do have an advantage when it comes to security. Decades of experience with mission-critical and/or confidential data translates into the highest security capabilities of any computer systems available. Mainframe hardware and software vendors provide a number of security packages that control access to the different applications and databases, and most of these packages meet the U.S. Department of Defense security standards. Mainframe support personnel also have the experience needed to maintain the security systems that are in place, and they are usually more aware of potential security problems than the majority of those who support the smaller systems—especially those who support PCs.

Finally, mainframes remain the most reliable computer systems currently available, primarily due to the large number of redundant components in the system. Mainframe designers have years of experience in determining which components are most likely to fail, and they have built in automatic systems that lock out a failed component and activate its backup. Many high-end minicomputers and superservers are closing the gap though, as their designers add the reliability features pioneered on the mainframes. I expect that most of these systems will match the mainframe's reliability within the next few years, reducing this advantage to a common feature.

Special Considerations

In various respects, mainframes and potential client systems don't speak the same language. Mainframes use the IBM System Network Architecture (SNA) protocol to communicate with dedicated terminals, with PCs acting as dedicated terminals through modems, or with terminal emulation boards. SNA isn't designed to accommodate the complex two-way communications necessary for true Client/Server applications.

One solution is the gateway systems mentioned earlier. A *gateway system* is generally a node on the LAN consisting of specialized software that talks to the mainframe through a terminal emulation board. The gateway is usually a dedicated system, due to the amount of processing needed to handle the translations between the different protocols and character codes. The clients either talk directly to the gateway or send the query to the local database server, which then passes it on to the gateway. Client communications use the normal LAN protocols, and the gateway translates the requests and sends them to the mainframe in the SNA protocol. A software application is usually running on the mainframe that's part of the gateway system; the software handles the interface between the data in the DBMS and the SQL commands passed along by the gateway. Needless to say, gateways are expensive and add a tremendous amount of complexity to the communications between the clients and the database.

Another alternative is to use a common network protocol, such as TCP/IP, to provide communications. While this may seem to be a better solution, it's not without its own complexities and costs. Adding TCP/IP to a mainframe involves using an expensive hardware/software combination. And some type of gateway application on the mainframe must still handle the application communications and character-set translations between the client and the database.

The real price for all this complexity is generally slower response time to database queries. Because of the number of layers a client request goes through to be processed, it takes longer to get a response from a mainframe database than to get the same response from a local database server.

I also encountered the same problems in acquiring information I mentioned in Chapter 6: Getting information from IBM about their two mainframe database products was almost impossible. Most of the information about DB2 and SQL/DS in this chapter was gathered from third-party sources—the "new," more open IBM may be in charge of the PC-based products, but the old IBM is still very much in control when it comes to large systems. Getting information from Oracle about their mainframe version provided a pleasant contrast to IBM's silence. Oracle's representatives were more than willing to provide any information I requested about their products; only IBM's OS/2 products division showed the same level of cooperation.

Advice and Tips

The whole point of moving to a Client/Server DBMS is to downsize from a large expensive system, so your first step should be to closely examine your current database processing system to see if it can be replaced by smaller, and possibly distributed, systems. It's entirely possible that you don't need to keep all the data in the mainframe active; you may be able to archive most of it on tapes and to restore it only for special processing runs such as quarterly or annual reports. It may also make sense to break up the data contained in one large database into smaller databases dedicated to a particular department or function. The data can then be combined through some type of distributed processing capabilities when needed for complex analysis or reports. However, be aware that breaking up a large database requires careful planning, including a complete rethinking of the database's structure. Such planning requires a great deal of expertise in database theory and design; in most cases, you'll be better off hiring a qualified consultant who has experience in downsizing large systems to help you in your efforts.

Distributed processing is really the preferred method of implementing a Client/Server system, whether you choose to archive or break up the data. If it's not possible to do either, the next step to consider is building a semi-distributed system. You can do this by maintaining parts of the database on superservers or high-power PC servers that the users actually access. At scheduled times during the day, the database servers can communicate with the mainframe and transfer any data modifications for integration into the central database. The mainframe can then pass back appropriate updates to the databases on the servers, so that users always work with the latest data.

Many companies with existing mainframes use a variation on this method. Instead of maintaining multiple copies of the database, the MIS department sets up a system that downloads the relevant portions of the data to a PC (usually in ASCII format). The user can then import the data into a PC-based application such as a spreadsheet or word processor, where he can further manipulate the data or create custom reports. This practice reduces the overhead of performing a number of queries on the mainframe itself. More importantly, it reduces the need to have expensive application programmers spend time and resources developing custom reports on the mainframe—reports that a user can easily create in a matter of minutes or hours with a familiar PC application.

The next alternative is to use a gateway system to allow direct client access to the mainframe databases. While this solution is complex and somewhat expensive, it may be the only choice if there's no logical way to break down the database or if confidentiality and security concerns require that all the data be maintained in a central place.

Finally, there's the same alternative that exists with the proprietary mini-computers—keep the mainframes, but switch to a DBMS more suited for Client/Server applications. Oracle sells a version of their RDBMS that runs on mainframes and can be connected to other ORACLE databases to share data and client access. IBM sells AIX (their version of UNIX) for their mainframes, and many of the UNIX-based DBMS vendors have versions that run under it.

The bottom line, though, is that the best way to approach using a mainframe for a database server is as a short-term solution. In the long run, it makes the most sense from both technological and cost perspectives to downsize your databases from the big systems in the "glass house" (slang for the computer center) to distributed servers running DBMSs that are designed for Client/Server computing.

DB2

Both the Relational model and SQL were developed at IBM, and IBM did most of the early research in implementing a Relational database with their System/R project in the mid-1970s. However, Oracle beat them to the market with a commercial RDBMS by almost two years. It wasn't until 1981 that IBM announced their first RDBMS (SQL/DS, covered later in this chapter). In 1983 IBM announced the first version of Database 2, more commonly known as DB2, and it has since become their flagship database product.

Significant Features

The current version of DB2 is Version 2, Release 3, which became available in 1991. All of IBM's current research and development advances in the Relational model and SQL are based on DB2, so it's the first to implement any new features that will eventually be added to IBM's other RDBMSs. Because of IBM's influence in the computer industry, DB2's SQL has become the de facto standard—the ANSI Level 2 SQL standard is predominantly based on the DB2 implementation of SQL, and many third-party database vendors make a point of supporting the extensions IBM has added to DB2's SQL since 1989.

DB2 was initially designed for multiuser access from dedicated terminals, and that remains its primary market. Until recently, the only way to access DB2 from a Client/Server system was through third-party gateways, which made it a Class 3 database.

In late 1991, IBM announced its "Information Warehouse" concept, a strategic plan for tying all its RDBMS products together with Client/Server capabilities. The basis of the Information Warehouse is the Distributed Relational Database Architecture (DRDA) specification, a portion of IBM's SAA network strategy (see the SQL/400 section in Chapter 6 for more details on

SAA). DRDA describes how RDBMSs on different platforms can communicate with each other in a Client/Server or peer-to-peer server capacity. These capabilities are implemented through a function IBM calls the Remote Unit of Work (RUOW), a fancy name for the simple process of creating a query on a client system and sending it to the database to be processed. With RUOW the client can either be a workstation or another RDBMS, blurring the line a bit in defining a client system under the C/S architecture. Confusing terminology aside, RUOW is IBM's first significant step toward implementing a distributed database system.

DB2 Version 2.3 was the first IBM database to implement DRDA. A significant number of third-party vendors have announced support for DRDA, and IBM is implementing RUOW capabilities in its other RDBMSs, so DB2 should continue its move toward being a true Class 2 C/S back-end over the next several years.

Location independence is another distributed database concept implemented by IBM in DB2 2.3. Simply described, *location independence* means that a user can query one or more tables in one or more DB2 databases at the same time, regardless of the data's location in the network. In standard SQL, a user can specify a particular table in a particular database by using both names in the query, separated by a period: *<database>.<table>*. Location independence extends this by adding a third name which specifies the database server plus the user's ID:

```
<server>.<authorizedID>.<database>.<table>
```

As you can see, specifying four names can become unwieldy, so DB2 includes support for aliases which let the DBA identify the *<database>.<table>* combination with a single name. This cuts the location identification down to a slightly more manageable construct:

```
<server>.<authID>.<table alias>
```

DB2 includes support for read-only databases, which prevents users from accidentally modifying the data. It also lets the DBA create and grant security permissions to groups of users (similar to Sybase), making it easier to administrate the database.

Hardware and Software Requirements

DB2 runs on the most recent versions of IBM's MVS mainframe operating system, MVS/XA and MVS/ESA. MVS runs on any of IBM's System/370–compatible mainframes, but it requires a lot of system resources to get decent performance. The majority of MVS systems are IBM's largest mainframes, the 3090 series or the high-end ES/9000 models.

DB2 itself also has a reputation as a resource hog, and the majority of users I've talked to say they wouldn't run it on anything but the most powerful of the 3090 or ES/9000 computers. However, the prices for just the mainframe range from about $3.5 million for a 3090 model 250J to over $22 million for an ES/9000 Model 900, so you can see why many businesses are seriously considering downsizing.

Communications Protocols

DRDA is a part of SAA, so all native communications are done through IBM's Advanced Peer-to-Peer Communications (APPC) protocol. APPC runs on any network protocol that supports it, though the dominant implementations are in IBM's LAN Server NOS and the SNA protocol used by the mainframes.

APPC requires a lot of RAM on the client, so it's not normally used on PC/MS DOS systems. DOS clients can access data in a DB2 database through a roundabout method, using NetBIOS to communicate with a Database Manager server on an OS/2 system. The Database Manager can then pass the SQL statements to DB2 using APPC, which effectively makes it a type of gateway system for DB2.

Gateways

Until more direct support exists for DRDA, the primary medium for client access to a DB2 database is a gateway. Many Client/Server DBMS vendors have their own gateways, such as Gupta's SQLHost/DB2, Oracle's SQL*Connect for DB2, and the INGRES/Gateway for DB2. These gateways run in conjunction with the vendor's respective database servers and translate the user's request for data from the SQL used by the third-party RDBMS to DB2's SQL before passing it on.

The best known third-party DB2 gateway is marketed by Micro Decisionware Inc. The gateway consists of two parts: the Database Gateway for DB2 that runs on a LAN-based OS/2 system, and the DB2-CICS Access Server that runs under MVS on the mainframe. This combination lets users of Microsoft's SQL Server query a DB2 database as if it were an SQL Server database. Database Gateway uses Microsoft's Open Database Connectivity (ODBC) API, so any front-end application that supports ODBC or SQL Server can use it to communicate with DB2. It supports data compression between the gateway and the host to cut down on transmission times, and it also lets the DBA transfer data from DB2 to an SQL Server in order to reduce mainframe network traffic and processing costs. The gateway automatically translates SQL Server remote stored procedures into DB2 RUOWs, and it provides SQL access to data stored in IBM's non-relational databases, such as IMS and VSAM.

Information Builders, Inc., the vendor of the non-relational FOCUS DBMS, has taken an interesting approach to providing client access to DB2. Their Enterprise Data Access/SQL (EDA/SQL) gateway is database-independent on both the client and server side, providing transparent access to over 50 different DBMSs. EDA/SQL provides this access through its own API, called API/SQL. Any client system that supports API/SQL can talk to any DBMS that EDA/SQL supports. The client-access portion of EDA/SQL runs on an OS/2 system and communicates with EDA software running on the DBMS host system. EDA/SQL is the first non-IBM product to fully support DRDA, and IBM is marketing it as one of its Information Warehouse products. EDA/SQL's database-independence may have an enormous impact on the Client/Server market over the coming years, as it gains support among front-end application vendors.

Using a gateway is an acceptable but expensive method of providing Client/Server access to DB2. For example, the Micro Decisionware Database Gateway for DB2 costs $3,495—which doesn't seem like much until you add the $24,000 to $70,000 for the DB2-CICS Access Server. A complete EDA/SQL setup can run as high as $115,000.

Native SQL Language

As I mentioned previously, DB2's SQL is the de facto standard by which all other SQL implementations are judged. The ANSI Level 2 with Integrity Enhancements standard is based in large part on DB2's SQL, and many third-party SQL databases are compatible with the DB2 SQL extensions. DB2's SQL query optimizer has a reputation for providing good performance, even though it's still syntax-based. DB2 also provides a number of other SQL performance enhancements to speed response time. However, these enhancements come at the price of requiring more system resources, particularly CPU processing power and additional memory.

Front-end Processors Provided

No front-end processors are provided. Instead, DB2 administration is handled through a dedicated terminal, which uses applications that run directly on the mainframe. IBM's OS/2 Extended Services Database Manager provides the only native client support for accessing and administering a DB2 database using RUOWS.

Advantages and Disadvantages

DB2's only advantage is that it runs on a mainframe—which gives it capabilities far beyond most other RDBMSs in terms of database size and the number of simultaneous users it supports. A few of the high-end superservers are beginning to approach mainframe capabilities at considerably less cost, but no system yet matches the computing power a mainframe provides.

But this power comes at enormous expense, in terms of hardware, software, environment, and personnel costs. While IBM is to be commended for finally "seeing the light" and making an effort to provide Client/Server access and distributed processing capabilities to their large-system DBMSs, the costs involved in maintaining a mainframe completely outweigh any capacity advantages. The C/S architecture was specifically designed for downsizing databases from the large systems while best utilizing the computing power of desktop PCs and RISC workstations.

DRDA may have a significant impact on the development of true distributed databases, primarily because of IBM's backing (I explore this further in Chapter 9). However, using DRDA or a third-party gateway to provide client access to DB2 is at best a short-term solution for most companies. Granted, there are databases that are, and will remain, so large that for the foreseeable future only a mainframe can provide the necessary processing power and disk capacity. Careful analysis of your current database processing needs is the only way to determine whether you absolutely need a mainframe. If not, your ultimate goal should be to move your databases to smaller Client/Server systems and pull the plug on the mainframe.

Table 7.1

DB2 Quick Summary

PRODUCT INFORMATION	
Name	Database 2 (DB2) Version 2, Release 3
Vendor	IBM
Price	Unlimited users: $113,400 to $244,850 initial cost, plus a $3,500 to $7,000 lease fee per month, depending on host system
OPERATING SYSTEMS	
On Database Server	MVS/XA, MVS/ESA
On LAN Server	Any network that supports APPC or an appropriate gateway
On Workstations	OS/2 1.31 or higher, with IBM's Database Manager; other operating systems through an appropriate gateway

Table 7.1

(continued)

MINIMUM REQUIREMENTS	
RAM on Server	Varies based on platform and number of users
RAM on Workstation	12Mb under OS/2
Disk Space on Server	Varies based on platform
UTILITIES PROVIDED	
Administration Utility	Terminal-based
Interactive User Utility	No; OS/2 Database Manager needed
Operating Systems/ Environments Supported	MVS; OS/2 1.21 or higher for Database Manager
NATIVE LANGUAGES	
ANSI SQL	Level 2 with Integrity Enhancements
DB2 SQL Extensions	Yes
Other SQL	No
Non-SQL Language	No
MAXIMUMS	
Database Size	Varies according to system capacities
Column Size	4,056 bytes; 2G in various LONG datatypes
Row Size	32,767 bytes
# of Columns in Row	750
# of Rows per Table	Limited by disk space
# of Rows per Database	Limited by disk space
# of Tables per Database	No limit
# of Views per Database	No limit
# of Tables per View	No limit, maximum 750 columns

■ SQL/DS

SQL/Data System (SQL/DS) is the direct descendent of IBM's System/R prototype RDBMS and was IBM's first commercial Relational database when it was released in 1983. It remained IBM's primary relational platform until the 1989 release of DB2 Version 2. Since then, SQL/DS has faded into the background, though many mainframe shops still prefer it to DB2.

Significant Features

There are actually two distinct versions of SQL/DS Version 3: SQL/DS 3.1 for DOS/VSE, and SQL/DS 3.3 for VM. DOS/VSE is an early mainframe operating system that still has widespread user support, despite IBM's best efforts to retire it. VM is IBM's preferred operating system for the smaller mainframes (the 438x series and the lower-end ES/9000 models), though there are some companies that prefer VM to MVS because VM offers better real-time transaction processing capabilities.

IBM has continued to enhance SQL/DS for VM to the point that it is, for all intents and purposes, a VM version of DB2. Released in March of 1992, Version 3.3 supports IBM's Distributed Relational Database Architecture (DRDA) and Remote Units of Work (RUOW), making it DB2's full partner in the Information Warehouse concept. It also provides 100 percent compatibility with DB2's SQL, so applications written for one can easily be moved to the other. However, it is still DB2's "little brother," so any advances IBM makes to RDBMS technology will show up first in DB2 and then be added to a later release of SQL/DS for VM.

SQL/DS for DOS/VSE still bears a strong resemblance to the System/R prototype, and IBM has implied that the VSE version will not become part of SAA nor will it support DRDA. Unless a significant number of users force IBM to bring SQL/DS for DOS/VSE into the SAA, I can safely say that it's a dead product as far as Client/Server database capabilities are concerned. SQL/DS for VM is the preferred platform for bringing the smaller mainframes into a C/S system.

Hardware and Software Requirements

IBM's VM operating system runs on any size System/370 mainframe, from the smallest 4381 and ES/9000 to the high-end 3090s and ES/9000s. However, its predominant market is the smaller systems ranging in price from about $400,000 to $4 million. Both VM and SQL/DS require fewer system resources than MVS and are more suited for smaller organizations with less than 500 users.

Communication Protocols

SQL/DS for VM uses the same protocols as DB2, so everything discussed in that section of this chapter applies here.

Gateways

Oracle is the only third-party RDBMS vendor to provide a gateway to SQL/DS. Their SQL*Connect to SQL/DS supports both current versions of SQL/DS, as well as older Version 2 databases, and it provides Client/Server capabilities from any front-end compatible with ORACLE Server.

Micro Decisionware's Database Gateway for SQL/DS is virtually identical to their DB2 gateway. However, currently it only supports the DOS/VSE version, through the SQL/DS-VSE Access Server. A SQL/DS-VM Access Server is planned, but no release date has been announced. Information Builder's EDA/SQL supports both versions of SQL/DS.

Native SQL Language

As I mentioned earlier, SQL/DS for VM is 100 percent compatible with DB2 SQL. It also maintains support for the native SQL found in SQL/DS for DOS/VSE to ease the transition between DOS/VSE and VM versions. The VSE version's SQL is compatible with the ANSI Level 1 standard.

Front-end Processors Provided

Again, everything described in the DB2 section on front-end processors applies to the VM version. The only user and administration tools provided for the DOS/VSE version are terminal-based.

Advantages and Disadvantages

SQL/DS for VM has only two advantages: It provides DB2 capabilities on a smaller system with fewer resources, and it's a part of IBM's DRDA. Unfortunately, SQL/DS's primary market is the smaller mainframes, which are rapidly being surpassed in power and capabilities by less expensive minicomputers and superservers. Since the DOS/VSE version is virtually a dead product, you should only use SQL/DS as a Client/Server database if you already have a significant amount of data in it. SQL/DS systems are prime candidates for downsizing to a less expensive platform.

Table 7.2

SQL/DS Quick Summary

PRODUCT INFORMATION	
Name	SQL/Data System (SQL/DS) Version 3, Release 1 and Release 3
Vendor	IBM
Price	Unlimited users: $17,470 to $230,850 initial cost, plus a $364 to $4,810 lease fee per month, depending on host system
OPERATING SYSTEMS	
On Database Server	DOS/VSE (Release 1), VM (Release 3)
On LAN Server	Any network that supports APPC (Release 3) or an appropriate gateway (Both)
On Workstations	OS/2 1.31 or higher, with IBM's Database Manager (Release 3); other operating systems through an appropriate gateway (Both)
MINIMUM REQUIREMENTS	
RAM on Server	Varies based on platform and number of users
RAM on Workstation	12Mb under OS/2 (Release 3)
Disk Space on Server	Varies based on platform
UTILITIES PROVIDED	
Administration Utility	Terminal-based
Interactive User Utility	No; OS/2 Database Manager needed (Release 3)
Operating Systems/Environments Supported	VM, DOS/VSE, OS/2 1.21 or higher for Database Manager (Release 3)
NATIVE LANGUAGES	
ANSI SQL	Level 2 with Integrity Enhancements (Release 3); Level 1 (Release 1)
DB2 SQL Extensions	Yes (Release 3)
Other SQL	Yes (Both)
Non-SQL Language	No

Table 7.2

(continued)

MAXIMUMS	
Database Size	Varies according to system capacities
Column Size	4,056 bytes; 2G in various LONG data-types (Release 3)
Row Size	32,767 bytes
# of Columns in Row	400 columns (Release 1); 750 columns (Release 3)
# of Rows per Table	Limited by disk space
# of Rows per Database	Limited by disk space
# of Tables per Database	No limit
# of Views per Database	No limit
# of Tables per View	No limit, maximum 400 columns (Release 1); 750 columns (Release 3)

■ ORACLE Mainframe Versions

You've probably noticed by now that Oracle is prominently mentioned in all four chapters of this book that cover Client/Server back-ends. The reason is simple: Oracle is dedicated to providing database solutions for every major computer platform available.

Significant Features

The only difference between ORACLE on a mainframe and ORACLE on other platforms is the operating systems they each support and the data capacities a mainframe provides. In every other respect, the ORACLE RDBMSs are the same.

The mainframe version of ORACLE runs under the MVS and VM operating systems. Like other versions, it uses SQL*Net to communicate with both clients and other ORACLE databases, providing both C/S and distributed database capabilities. Oracle's two mainframe gateways can run on the same system and provide ORACLE users with transparent access to SQL/DS and DB2 databases. Client systems simply send their SQL commands to the ORACLE database, and it passes the data requests through SQL*Connect for processing. Users can also communicate directly with the SQL*Connect gateways using ORACLE-compatible front-ends, bypassing the need for an ORACLE database on the mainframe.

By using various versions of the ORACLE RDBMS and one of the SQL*Connect gateways, an MIS department can create the most complete distributed database system available today. IBM's DRDA is only beginning to provide what Oracle has offered for two years or more. And ORACLE Version 7.0 will continue to enhance Oracle's lead in the Client/Server market by providing tighter links between different platforms, as well as their own support for DRDA.

Ironically, one of Oracle's greatest weaknesses is having so many different platforms to support. New versions are always released for the VAX/VMS platform first, and the expanding Client/Server market demands that Oracle will concentrate on porting Version 7 to PC-based and UNIX platforms next. It may be some time before Version 7.0 is ported to the mainframe operating systems; in the case of Version 6.0, the time lag between the initial VMS release and the release of the mainframe versions was more than a year.

For a more complete discussion of ORACLE's features and capabilities, see the ORACLE sections of Chapters 4 and 5.

Hardware and Software Required

Oracle's mainframe versions run on both VM and MVS, so they support the entire range of mainframe systems. A version for IBM's AIX is also available, though it's fairly unusual for an MIS shop to run UNIX on a mainframe. The mainframe versions share the same problem as the other versions: They tend to be resource hogs, and the system requirements are similar to those needed by DB2.

Communications Protocols

Every version of ORACLE uses SQL*Net to provide client access to the DBMS. The mainframe version of SQL*Net supports the APPC, TCP/IP, DECNet, SNA, and asynchronous network protocols, lending it the widest networking support of any RDBMS available. Other protocols are supported through links between different ORACLE databases; for example, a PC/MS DOS client can access ORACLE on a mainframe by using Named Pipes to talk to an OS/2 ORACLE database, which can then transfer the request to the mainframe over one of the other supported protocols.

Gateways

No gateways are needed for client access to an ORACLE database running on a mainframe, unless you need to interface between different network protocols. As noted previously, Oracle provides their own gateways to other databases, including DB2 and SQL/DS.

Native SQL Language

ORACLE's mainframe versions use the same SQL and PL/SQL as the other versions. Applications and front-ends written for one version can access any other ORACLE database through the proper SQL*Net drivers.

Front-end Processors Provided

The mainframe versions of ORACLE come with the version of SQL*DBA appropriate for the operating system. SQL*DBA is terminal-based on a mainframe, but any other platform's version can be used to query and administrate a mainframe-based ORACLE database through the proper SQL*Net drivers.

Advantages and Disadvantages

ORACLE is currently one of the best solutions for bringing a mainframe into a Client/Server system, due to its built-in distributed processing capabilities. Even with the advent of DRDA, it's still much easier to communicate with an ORACLE database than with IBM's RDBMSs, and the savings generated by the reduced complexity may be substantial. And Oracle doesn't charge an additional monthly license fee on top of the software costs, which saves even more money over the long run.

Using ORACLE on a mainframe will make it easier to move the data to a smaller platform when you decide to downsize your databases. Or, if you use Oracle's SQL*Connect gateway products, you don't even have to migrate data from your DB2 or SQL/DS databases to take advantage of ORACLE's communications capabilities. The gateways also ease the processes of downsizing a DB2 or SQL/DS database to an ORACLE database on a smaller platform.

Of course, the mainframe versions are expensive (as is everything else associated with a mainframe), but the software's cost may well be offset by the savings in personnel costs. If you absolutely have to have a database on a mainframe, ORACLE is your best choice. If you already have DB2 or SQL/DS databases, ORACLE provides Client/Server capabilities that surpass those currently available from DRDA or EDA/SQL. The combination of ORACLE and SQL*Connect is the best solution currently available for integrating your mainframe into a distributed database system. I fully expect Oracle to do everything they can to maintain their lead over other systems in the Client/Server and distributed database market.

Table 7.3

ORACLE Mainframe
Versions Quick Summary

PRODUCT INFORMATION	
Name	Oracle Server 6.0
Vendor	Oracle Corporation
Price	Varies based on operating system and hardware platform, ranging from $103,000 for a VM-based 4381 to $298,000 for a high-end 3090 or ES/9000 running MVS
OPERATING SYSTEMS	
On Database Server	MVS, VM, AIX
On LAN Server	Any network supporting APPC, DECNet, or TCP/IP
On Workstations	Any operating system supported by ORACLE front-ends
MINIMUM REQUIREMENTS	
RAM on Server	Varies depending on platform and operating system
RAM on Workstation	640k (DOS), 4Mb (OS/2); 8Mb (UNIX)
Disk Space on Server	Varies depending on platform and operating system
UTILITIES PROVIDED	
Administration Utility	Terminal-based
Interactive User Utility	Terminal-based
Operating Systems/Environments Supported	VM, MVS; any platform supported by ORACLE front-ends
NATIVE LANGUAGES	
ANSI SQL	Yes
DB2 SQL Extensions	Yes
Other SQL	Yes
Non-SQL Language	No

Table 7.3

(continued)

MAXIMUMS	
Database Size	Limited by platform's supported disk space
Column Size	65,535 characters
Row Size	65,535 characters
# of Columns in Row	254
# of Rows per Table	Limited by disk space
# of Rows per Database	Limited by disk space
# of Tables per Database	Limited by disk space
# of Views per Database	Limited by disk space
# of Tables per View	No limit, 254 columns maximum per view

- *How Front-ends Work*

- *Types of Front-ends*

- *Choosing the Right Front-end for Your Needs*

Front-end Processors for Client/ Server Databases

A CLIENT/SERVER DATABASE IS A WASTE OF HARDWARE AND SOFT-
ware if there's no way to access its data. The database vendors usually provide an interactive administration tool and user front-end,
but the real power in C/S systems arises from the variety of third-
party client applications and development software.

Front-end packages can be divided into four broad categories based on their primary function: add-ons to existing products, application development tools, query/reporting programs, and data integration and analysis tools. Add-ons are modules that enable existing PC applications such as dBASE or Lotus 1-2-3 to query the database server. Application development tools, used primarily by programmers, are designed to ease the process of creating custom front-end applications. Query/reporting tools make it easy for nonprogrammers to create queries for and reports from the data on the back-end. Finally, data integration and analysis tools are designed for managers and executives who need to examine data from a number of sources in order to make complex business decisions.

While front-end applications are available for just about every desktop platform currently sold, the vast majority support the Intel-based PCs and environments: DOS, Windows, and OS/2. This chapter concentrates primarily on those products, but the general principles of front-end operations apply to all platforms. Further, since many front-end vendors are porting their products to other platforms (a trend I fully expect to continue), this chapter will help you evaluate future products as they become available for other environments.

To describe every front-end application would take an entire book; a survey taken for *PC Magazine* in May of 1992 found over 400, and new products are being released all the time. This chapter describes a representative sampling of some of the more well-known products in each of the four categories. (Because of rapid market changes, the best sources for current information are magazines and trade publications such as *PC Magazine*, *PC Week*, and *Corporate Computing*. For example, you'll find the results of the *PC Magazine* survey in the September 29, 1992 issue.)

After describing the products, I'll provide some advice and tips on deciding which ones best meet your needs. The chapter closes with a table listing all the front-end applications covered here and the back-ends they support. Use this information to evaluate both the products listed here and others that you may come across. Also, please bear in mind that the presence or absence of a front-end application in this chapter implies neither an endorsement nor a silent critique; every client application has its strengths and weaknesses, and only you can decide which ones are right for you.

■ How Front-ends Work

Front-end applications can be either standard off-the-shelf software or custom programmed for a particular company or user. In either case, the client application looks and runs just like any other application the user has on his PC, Macintosh, or UNIX workstation. If the client software is designed properly, the only hint to the user that she's using a front-end to a remote database server occurs when she enters her security log-on ID and password.

The sequence of events that takes place when the user accesses the database server can be generalized into the six basic steps illustrated in Figure 8.1. For the sake of simplicity, the term "query" represents any action the user can take on the database, such as updating the data, inserting new data, deleting data, or requesting data from the database.

Figure 8.1

The general sequence of events that occurs when a user accesses a database server

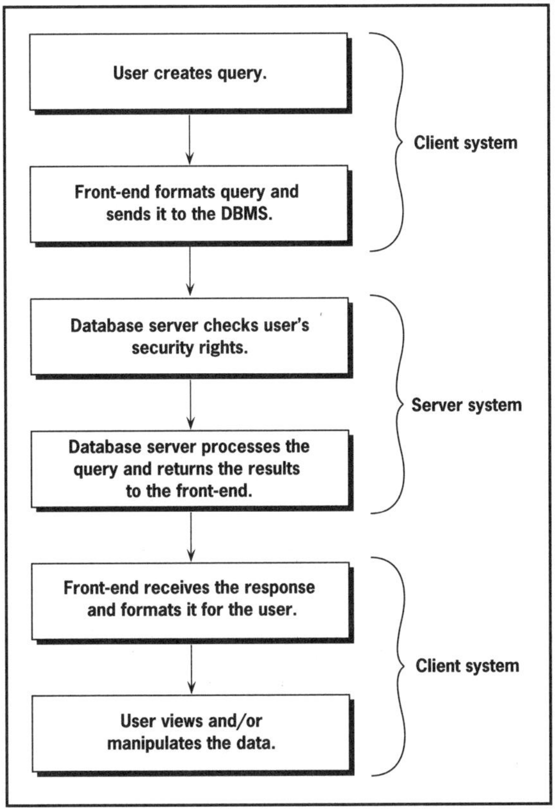

First, the user creates the query. It can either be created on-the-fly, frequently called an *ad hoc query*, or the user can run a preprogrammed or saved query that's part of the application. Next, the front-end application formats the query into the SQL used by the target back-end server and sends it out over the network to the server.

The server first verifies that the user has the proper security rights to the data being queried. If so, it then processes the query and sends the appropriate data back to the front-end. The client application receives the response data and formats it for presentation to the user. Finally, the user sees the response on the screen and can manipulate the data, or modify the query and start the process over again.

In the case of add-on front-ends, the process is usually more complicated at the user end. As Figure 8.2 shows, first the add-on module translates the query from the client's native language or menu format to SQL and then sends it on to the server. When the data is returned, the add-on processor translates the response data into the client's native file format. The user then views and manipulates the data as if it came from the front-end's own data files (which it now in fact does). All these translations add overhead to the process. This usually means that add-ons require more resources on the client system, particularly additional RAM and CPU power.

Figure 8.2

When the client software is an add-on to an existing application, the sequence of events in processing a query is slightly more complex.

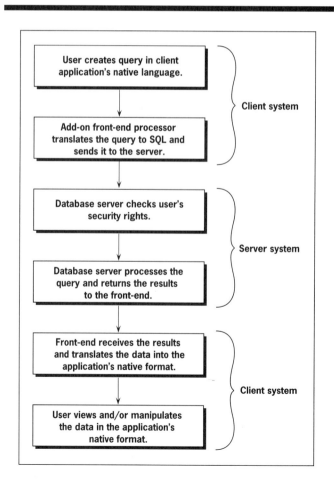

Many folks investigating Client/Server systems wonder why a particular front-end application can't access data on any vendor's database server. There are two reasons for this: the variations in SQL and communications protocols. As noted in Chapters 4 though 7, SQL isn't quite as standard as it should be; every DBMS vendor adds unique extensions or interpretations to SQL that make their version slightly incompatible with any other vendor's version. The developers of the front-end packages have to know every command used by a particular back-end in order to add support for that DBMS to their package.

In addition, every DBMS uses a different communications protocol between the client systems and the database server. It isn't sufficient for a client to speak the proper dialect of SQL; the front-end developers must also include the proper application programming interface (API) calls in their software to enable it to talk to the DBMS's communications driver.

Needless to say, front-end vendors are sometimes reluctant to invest the time and resources necessary to support every Client/Server DBMS available, so they support a few (or even just one) of the more popular back-ends. That's why it's relatively easy to find client applications that support the MS/Sybase SQL Server or ORACLE, while front-ends for DBMSs like INFORMIX-Online are somewhat rare.

Fortunately, this situation is rapidly changing. Client/Server database vendors recognize the advantages of working closely with the third-party front-end vendors and encouraging them to support the vendor's DBMS. I expect that by 1995 most of the front-ends that currently access only one or two back-ends will have expanded their support for other products on the market. The rise of database-independent APIs, such as the Microsoft/Sybase ODBC (mentioned in Chapter 4) and Information Builder's EDA/SQL or IBM's DRDA (discussed in Chapter 7), will also help front-end vendors broaden their support for different back-ends.

■ Types of Front-ends

As I previously mentioned, Client/Server front-end applications fall into four general categories: add-ons to existing products, application development products and toolkits, query/reporting programs, and data integration and analysis tools.

No hard and fast rules determine which category a product belongs in, and it's not uncommon for a front-end to have features that overlap different categories. For example, a good data analysis program can also have excellent reporting features, or an application that uses an add-on module to access a Client/Server DBMS can be the best query and reporting program for those familiar with its features.

In the next four sections I've categorized the front-end products according to their primary strength. Wherever possible I'll point out product features that properly belong to other categories.

Add-ons to Existing Products

It's only natural that the majority of add-ons exist for PC-based databases: After all, the majority of client systems are PCs, and just about every organization that has PCs also has PC databases. PC database vendors are eager to ensure that their products continue to be useful (and in demand) as more and more businesses move to the C/S architecture.

PC database add-ons also make it easier for those designing and developing Client/Server systems to integrate their existing databases into the new system. Front-end application development costs may be lower, because the users and programmers are already familiar with the existing database. With minimal training, they can usually adapt their existing skills to access the data from the server.

A PC database is also one of the more versatile front-end applications, primarily because it's a full DBMS in its own right. Most PC databases have a user-friendly interface, featuring menu-driven queries and complete reporting capabilities. PC databases also have fairly complex programming or script languages, which make it easy to create complete applications that can access and combine data from both native databases and database servers. The front-end features of a PC-based database could relegate it to any of the four categories.

On the other hand, a database add-on usually requires more system resources (particularly RAM) than a product designed as a front-end, due to the extra translation steps involved in converting queries and responses to the native format (see Figure 8.2 earlier). It's not uncommon for the database front-end to require 1Mb or more of extended or expanded RAM on the client system. The extra overhead also slows down the response time between the front-end and the database server.

However, when compared to the cost of developing an entirely new front-end application, the extra overhead of an add-on may be worth it. PC-based databases can serve as permanent solutions for creating client systems, if you realize problems may arise because these products are not primarily designed to be clients. The add-ons may not be tightly integrated into the product, which may require changes in how your applications function. PC databases may be more appropriate as a short-term solution while new front-ends are developed and the data is moved from the PC database to the database server.

Add-ons fall into three subcategories: external modules that are added to a product; modules that are included in the base version of the product; and modules that are released as part of a special version of the product.

dBASE Server Edition

The most eagerly awaited front-end add-on was one that gave dBASE developers and users access to a database server. Ashton-Tate was originally part of the group developing the PC version of SQL Server, but it dropped out before the product was released. In mid-1991, shortly before they were purchased by Borland, Ashton-Tate finally released the dBASE IV Server Edition 1.1. Borland has since released dBASE IV 1.5, but has not yet updated the Server Edition at the time of this writing.

The name Server Edition is somewhat misleading. It's actually a full dBASE package designed to provide access to data on the SQL Server from within dBASE; it doesn't offer any database server functions of its own. It requires at least 1Mb of extended memory to run, though the built-in DOS extender lowers its low RAM (below 640k) requirements to 60k.

First a dBASE command is issued against dBASE data and index files to store the appropriate information in the SQL catalogs. Then the built-in SQL commands can be used to access the data and files. However, once dBASE is in SQL mode (that is, once the familiar dBASE "dot" prompt changes to "SQL." in interactive mode), many dBASE commands and functions are disabled, and the behavior of others is changed. The general principle is that the SQL commands retrieve the data, and the dBASE commands process and format it for the screen or printing.

SQL programs and dBASE programs can be intermixed in the same application if they are chained to the different program modules. SQL programs can also use *dynamic SQL commands*—a subset of the dBASE SQL statements which are constructed and executed when the application is run. Standard dBASE commands are used to query the application's user for input; they then pass the input to SQL commands through variables. This lets the developer design ad hoc queries in the application. An additional parameter for the SQL SELECT command lets users save the results of a database server query in a local .DBF file, where the data can then be manipulated by the usual dBASE commands.

When SQL commands are issued against local .DBF files, the commands are internally translated to dBASE commands before being processed. However, when the SQL commands are issued against an SQL Server database, dBASE either passes them on directly or translates them to the appropriate TRANSACT-SQL commands. Because of this, transactions against a SQL Server database usually execute faster than they do against a local database containing the same data. The Server Edition also includes the SENDSQL command, which is used to send TRANSACT-SQL statements directly to the server for processing without syntax checking or translation by dBASE.

Borland also sells other specialized versions of dBASE that permit users to use familiar dBASE commands to access specific mainframe and minicomputer databases. For example, dBASE Direct for the 3270 accesses data in IBM main-frame databases such as IMS and DB2, and dBASE Direct for AS/400 provides similar access to IBM's minicomputer databases.

The dBASE IV Server Edition is a useful tool for dBASE programmers who wish to extend their applications to the Client/Server architecture. However, compared to other add-ons, its SQL implementation almost seems like a separate product and is not as tightly integrated into the system as it could be. It will be interesting to see if this changes when Borland releases the 1.5 version.

Programmers who want to use the dBASE language to access a database server, but prefer not to use dBASE itself, can use Computer Associates's Clipper. Clipper is a popular dBASE-compatible product that lets developers create and compile programs that use the standard dBASE file format. Clipper can also be used to create front-end applications for SQL Server, SQLBase, and NetWare SQL.

Paradox and Paradox SQL Link

Ironically, dBASE's closest competitor in the PC database market is Borland's Paradox. Paradox is well-known for its user-friendly Query-by-Example (QBE) interface and semirelational capabilities. In late 1990 Borland released Paradox Version 3.5 and Paradox SQL Link, which gave Paradox users the ability to access data from a database server. SQL Link currently supports IBM's Database Manager, SQL Server, NetWare SQL, and ORACLE, and support for other database servers is planned for a future release.

SQL Link requires Paradox 3.5 and a 80286 or better workstation with a minimum of 1Mb of RAM (1.5Mb for the ORACLE server). In order to access data from a SQL server, you must first run a utility provided with SQL Link that creates a replica table. *Replica tables* are used to translate the data between the server's format and Paradox's. Once the replica is created, Paradox translates requests for data from the server into a SQL statement and transmits it to the server. The response is sent back to Paradox and converted into a standard Paradox ANSWER table, using the replica table as a model. The ANSWER table can then be manipulated or saved locally, just like any other Paradox table.

SQL Link adds statements to the Paradox Application Language (PAL) that let the programmer access the database server through a custom application. SQL Link also allows programmers to send native SQL commands to the server from a PAL application; however, only one SQL command can be used at a time, and commands can't be nested. Paradox's real strength, though, is its QBE interface to SQL and SQL database servers, which makes it ideal for creating ad hoc queries.

DataEase SQL

DataEase is also known as an easy-to-use but powerful PC-based DBMS that uses query forms as its primary user interface. In 1990, DataEase International released DataEase SQL, a full version that currently provides access to ORACLE, SQL Server, Database Manager, and DB2 back-ends, as well as to native files and applications. DataEase SQL transparently integrates database server access into the forms-based DataEase environment. For example, when a user first creates a form, he specifies the source for data with which a form is associated; from that point on, the links to the data are made without user intervention.

The secret behind this is a DataEase facility called PRISM, the Processing Router for Integrated SQL Management. PRISM converts the DataEase functions and DataEase Query Language (DQL) statements into optimized SQL statements and transmits them to the database server. Application developers can also include native SQL statements in a DQL application.

Both DOS and OS/2 character-mode versions are available. DataEase SQL's forms-based environment makes it an able query and reporting tool. It can access multiple database sources from the same application, so it can also be used for data integration and analysis applications.

Superbase 4

Software Publishing Corporation's (SPC) Superbase 4 is a Windows 3.x database that makes designing databases, forms, and reports a mostly point-and-shoot affair. It provides full support for Dynamic Data Exchange (DDE) connections to other Windows applications. DDE is an interprocess communication protocol, supported by Windows and OS/2, that enables applications running on the same system to dynamically share data. The Superbase SQL Library is an optional module that links Superbase to XDB-DBMS, SQL-Base, ORACLE, and SQL Server.

In addition to accessing its own database files and data from a server, Superbase 4 can use dBASE III and dBASE IV data files for lookups and multifile reports on a read-only basis. It also supports its own type of BLOB data through an external-file field type, allowing the developer to link a particular record to an external text file, or more importantly, to an external graphics file. The graphic images are displayed on the screen along with the record they're attached to, which makes Superbase 4 ideal for such applications as personnel identification or parts inventories.

Its Database Management Language (DML) is a superset of structured BASIC and includes over 200 commands. Superbase 4 uses Windows to its best advantage; for example, the included Forms Designer module is a paint program that uses a toolkit bar, pop-up selections, and point-and-drag capabilities to create query forms. A form can access multiple data sources; the links, created between various files through pop-up selection lists, are graphically displayed for checking and reference. Reports can also be designed through the Forms Designer or programmed directly in DML. Like DataEase, Superbase 4's forms-based query and reporting features and its ability to link multiple data sources into a single query renders it equally at home in the other front-end categories.

Q&A

Symantec's Q&A is a flat-file database, or nonprogrammable database, that's primarily designed for managing simple tasks such as maintaining mailing lists or small databases. Like most nonprogrammable databases, its menu-driven primary interface allows users to easily create and manipulate databases. Unique among the nonprogrammable databases, its add-on module enables it to query and report on data from ORACLE and SQLBase servers. Symantec has promised support for other Client/Server databases in future releases. Figure 8.3 shows the streamlined menu interface that Q&A presents to the user. The Link-to-SQL module is available directly from Symantec; just send in a card that's included in the package.

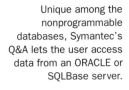

Figure 8.3

Unique among the nonprogrammable databases, Symantec's Q&A lets the user access data from an ORACLE or SQLBase server.

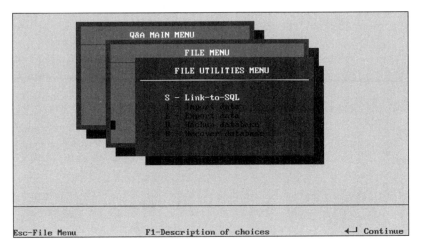

Q&A can also perform data lookups from external Q&A databases or directly from dBASE III and dBASE IV data files without having to import the data into the current database. Q&A has a complete built-in word processor that makes it easy to incorporate information from a database into letters and documents. It supports multiple printer fonts and has a built-in spell checker and thesaurus, all of which make it ideal for creating professional mail-merge letters.

Another of Q&A's unique features is its Intelligent Assistant, a natural language interface to the database that lets the user enter queries in plain English. With the Intelligent Assistant's Query Guide, users choose the data operators, the field names, and unique values for the fields from pop-up menus, greatly simplifying the process of creating an ad hoc query. Q&A is a great tool for users who have limited database needs, but who occasionally have to access a database server.

Advanced Revelation

A number of PC-based database packages are designed for application developers rather than end-users, and their vendors have jumped on the Client/Server bandwagon. Advanced Revelation is one example of a programmer-oriented database, and SQL is only one of the four programming languages it supports. Its primary language is R/BASIC, which has a wide range of functions for manipulating both the data and the Advanced Revelation environment. It also includes a variety of debugging routines and tools. Reports can either be designed directly through programming in R/LIST (the report writer language) or through the EasyWriter report generator, which creates R/LIST routines from your design. The Command Language (TCL), the master control language for all of Advanced Revelation, is a combination of a command line and job control language. TCL routines control the overall execution of applications by displaying windows and calling the appropriate R/LIST and R/BASIC modules.

Environmental Bonding refers to Advanced Revelation's ability to incorporate optional modules that let users access data files from other database systems (including database servers) in the external product's native format, using the standard Advanced Revelation languages and programming environment. Environmental Bonds for ASCII and dBASE III files are included in the product. Bonds for SQL Server, ORACLE, NetWare SQL, and DB2 are available from Revelation Technologies at an additional cost.

Clarion

Clarion is another PC-based database application development package that has a small but loyal following. Its add-on drivers allow application developers to access a wide variety of Client/Server DBMSs, including SQL Server, XDB-DBMS, INGRES, and ORACLE. Clarion has an IMAGE data type that's similar to Superbase 4's external file data type; it lets the programmer add graphics to the database.

PC/Focus and PM/Focus

Information Builders Incorporated (IBI) is best known as the vendor of Focus, a DBMS based on the Network Model that was designed for minicomputers and was ported down to PCs. Rather than creating their own Client/Server RDBMS, IBI is making its mark on the C/S market with EDA/SQL, the common SQL API discussed in Chapter 7. IBI is now positioning its PC/Focus (DOS) and PM/Focus (OS/2) databases as environments for creating front-end applications for the database back-ends supported by EDA/SQL. The two Focus versions can also access data on a SQL Server. PC/Focus and PM/Focus almost cross the line into being pure application development tools, but their continuing support for Focus databases keeps them in the add-on category for now.

Spreadsheet Add-ons

I can't close this section on add-on front-ends without mentioning the add-on modules that let spreadsheets query data from a Client/Server database. Spreadsheets are commonly used for analyzing, charting, and reporting on data, so they're a natural choice for users who are already familiar with the product and who need to analyze data that resides on a database server. The add-on modules translate the spreadsheet's requests into SQL and send them to the server. They then convert the server's responses into the spreadsheet's native format; the user can then manipulate the query's results just like any other spreadsheet.

Lotus Development Corporation has added this support to the DOS, OS/2, and Windows versions of 1-2-3 through its DataLens drivers. DataLens drivers for SQL Server, dBASE, and Paradox are included with 1-2-3 for Windows (see Figure 8.4) and are available for the other versions for an additional cost. Lotus has made it easy for other vendors to provide DataLens drivers for their own DBMSs, and Oracle Corporation sells a DataLens driver for their ORACLE DBMS.

Microsoft has also added support for querying SQL Server to Excel, their Windows-based spreadsheet. Excel accesses the server through a customized version of Pioneer Software's Q&E Database Editor (covered in the next section) which is included in the package. Additional back-end support is available by purchasing the full Q&E package.

Informix, more widely known as a DBMS vendor, has an interesting spreadsheet called Wingz. Wingz is unique in the spreadsheet market because versions are available for all the major GUI environments, including Windows 3.x, OS/2 2.0, Macintosh, the NeXT system's NeXTStep, and the UNIX-based Motif and Open Look. Informix provides back-end links through additional modules called DataLinks. Informix sells a DataLink for their own INFORMIX-Online DBMS and NetWare SQL. Fusion Systems Group is a third-party vendor that provides other DataLink modules which let Wingz access ORACLE and SQL Server databases.

Figure 8.4

Lotus includes DataLens drivers for dBASE, SQL Server, and Paradox with its 1-2-3 for Windows.

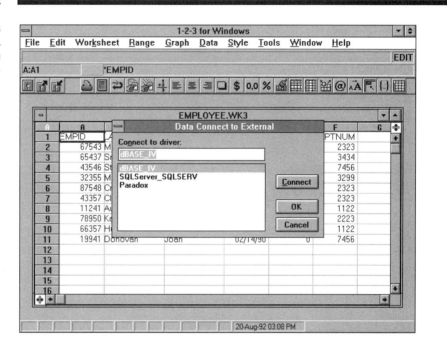

Application Development Products and Toolkits

Every Client/Server DBMS vendor has some type of programming toolkit available that can be used with a 3GL such as C or COBOL to create custom front-end applications. Many have also released their own application development products that make it easier to create custom query forms, reports, and user menus; Oracle's SQL*Forms and SQL*ReportWriter, and INGRES/Tools are prime examples. However, these toolkits are usually restricted to creating front-ends for the vendor's DBMS, or for other DBMSs whose vendors have licensed a version of the toolkit.

In the past few years, a number of third-party vendors have come out with application development packages that can be used to create front-ends for a variety of database servers. Some vendors have also released programming libraries that other vendors can use to let their own applications access data on a server. And programming language vendors have extended their languages' capabilities to include support for Client/Server databases.

Most third-party application development toolkits are based on Windows 3.x; its GUI eases the process of creating front-ends. Unfortunately, this can be a problem for many corporate front-end developers; since Windows users only represent about 10 percent of the PC market, many businesses have yet to upgrade to PCs that can run Windows, and many have decided not to use

Windows at all. Application developers for such companies will have to use the 3GL libraries and application toolkits provided by the DBMS vendors to create their own character mode front-ends.

Opinions are split among front-end developers on this issue. Some believe that the GUI tools make it easier to create front-ends and that this more than offsets the extra overhead a GUI requires. Others say that having to invest in hardware upgrades for a large number of client systems just so they can run a GUI-based front-end misses the point of Client/Server computing. I tend to agree with this second opinion; while GUIs have their place, potential front-end users shouldn't be forced to upgrade their systems solely to access a database server. Development toolkit vendors do their customers and potential customers a disservice by ignoring the large existing market for character-mode front-ends.

PowerBuilder

Powersoft Corporation's Windows-based PowerBuilder is a powerful object-oriented front-end developer's toolkit designed primarily for the corporate and MIS applications programmer. It supports SQL Server, SQLBase, ORACLE, XDB-DBMS, INGRES, AllBase, and DB2. The developer's package comes with support for one server, and additional interfaces are available at extra cost.

PowerBuilder has no native database manager and requires a connection to a database server to build and test applications. It takes full advantage of the Windows 3.x environment. All development is done through *painters*, the various PowerBuilder modules for creating the database, defining the menus and screen appearance, manipulating the data, and developing, debugging, and maintaining applications, as shown in Figure 8.5. While the modules' icons are displayed separately on the main menu, they're also tightly linked and can be executed from within each other as required. Underlying all the modules and tying the development environment together is PowerScript, PowerBuilder's C-like script language.

While prior knowledge of C or SQL isn't necessary to create applications in PowerBuilder, an understanding of how events and messages are passed in Windows applications will aid the development process. However, the manuals do discuss these concepts briefly and include many examples of the proper use of PowerScript statements and functions.

PowerBuilder makes excellent use of Windows graphics throughout the entire development process; for example, a key icon is attached to the appropriate columns to indicate which column the table is indexed on, and a view icon is connected to the tables that are part of a view. Bitmap graphic files (created externally or through the Picture Painter) can also be associated with a column in a database, regardless of the database server; the bitmap's file name is stored as the data in the column, and the bitmap is displayed by PowerBuilder when the row is retrieved.

Figure 8.5

PowerBuilder features a variety of application development tools called painters, in a tightly integrated programming environment.

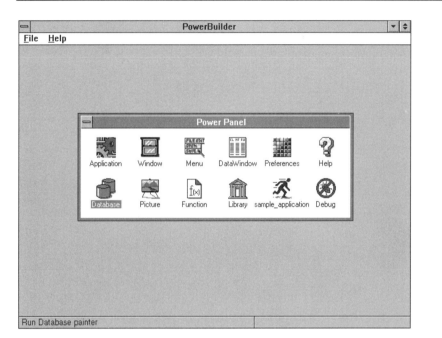

The database server can also be administered through PowerBuilder; the developer can enter SQL statements that are sent directly to the server to maintain users, groups, and security, and to execute stored procedures (if supported by the particular database server). PowerBuilder makes it easy to create common SQL statements through the SQL Painter which builds the statements through point-and-shoot pick lists.

The DataWindow Painter is the most powerful feature and the very heart of PowerBuilder. It's used in combination with SQL statements or PowerScript scripts to retrieve and manipulate one or more rows of data from the database server, providing a function similar to scrollable cursors. Data can be displayed in tabular rows or in a freeform window created by Window Painter. SQL statements can be custom-written or built through the SQL Painter, and the PowerScript Painter is used to create script files, drawing from over 70 built-in functions. User-defined functions are also supported and can be created through the Function Painter. Full DDE support is included, and external Windows or database server library functions can be called from within a script.

When development is completed, the developer uses the built-in compiler to compile the application into a run-time application file. When combined with the PowerBuilder run-time module (available at additional cost), the application can be used independently of the developer environment.

PowerBuilder includes two additional tools to make application development easier. The Library module is used to maintain application libraries, which can be browsed, separated, merged, or regenerated. They can also create a full report on a library's contents. The Debug module is a full debugger that supports single-step processing and breakpoints. It can be run on its own or from the various Painters during the development process.

SQLWindows

PowerBuilder's closest competitor is Gupta's SQLWindows, which can be used either as a user query tool or as an application development platform. Gupta includes a single-user version of their SQLBase DBMS in the package, which allows developers to create front-end applications without requiring a full Client/Server system. I've included it in this category because SQLWindows isn't limited to supporting SQLBase; developers can use it to create front ends for SQL Server, ORACLE, INGRES, Database Manager, NetWare SQL, AllBase, and SQL/400.

The SQLWindows programming environment is also object-oriented, but it isn't as tightly integrated as PowerBuilder's. As Figure 8.6 shows, SQLWindows uses a series of separate windows on the Windows desktop for designing and creating the application. SQLWindows lets you monitor the programming code it's creating in a separate window; it adds the appropriate SQLWindows Application Language (SAL) statements to the program each time the developer adds or modifies an object on the design screen. It has built-in debugging capabilities, and the developer can create a run-time application file that's used with the run-time module to execute the application outside of SQLWindows.

SQLWindows includes a couple of modules that let developers and users create front-end applications without writing code. Express Windows is used to create on-screen forms or table views of the database, and ReportWindows lets the developer create custom reports by painting the design on the screen. SQLWindows also provides DDE support so that data can be shared with other Windows applications.

SQLWindows and PowerBuilder both support a wide variety of backends, so deciding which one you should use depends on whether you prefer a tightly integrated development environment or a set of loosely coupled development modules. Both products also have a large following among front-end application developers, so it shouldn't be hard to find programmers familiar with either one. A large following also translates into easily accessible grass-roots support from user groups and on-line services.

Figure 8.6

Gupta's SQLWindows isn't as tightly integrated as PowerBuilder; however, one window (NEWAPP.APP) shows you the code being written as you add objects to the design screen.

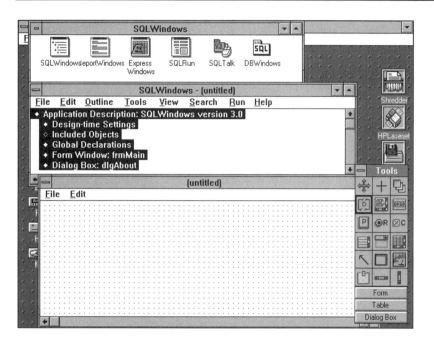

Q&E Database Editor and Library

Pioneer Software has approached the market for database server access modules from a slightly different angle. Pioneer's Q&E Database Editor for Windows or OS/2 is a query engine that can be used along with other applications to query and import data from a number of database servers, including SQL Server, NetWare SQL, INGRES, DB2, and Database Manager. The Q&E Database Library for Windows or OS/2 is a collection of function libraries that provide a standard API to be used with 3GLs to incorporate database server access into a programmer's application. Both products provide an easy method for other vendors to add front-end capabilities to their products. The Database Library supports the same back-ends as the Database Editor.

Q&E straddles the line between being a generic add-on and being an application development toolkit. However, the two packages are primarily aimed at providing software vendors and application developers with an easy way to access database servers, so I've included them in this category.

SequeLink

TechGnosis's SequeLink provides a development environment similar to IBI's EDA/SQL, in that it consists of a gateway and a host module that use a common API to provide access to a number of different DBMSs. However, it doesn't support as many back-ends as EDA/SQL; it is mostly known for providing Client/Server access to Rdb/VMS databases. SequeLink is a set of language libraries for Windows, Macintosh, OS/2, and UNIX systems that an application programmer can use to talk to the SequeLink Client/Server MiddleWare gateway. For whatever reason, SequeLink hasn't had as great an impact as EDA/SQL, even though it also provides a common interface for a variety of platforms. SequeLink could be quite useful for companies seeking to create front-end applications for a variety of client platforms.

Three GUI-based programming language environments also have Client/Server capabilities: Microsoft's Visual BASIC, Computer Associates's Realizer, and Borland's ObjectVision. Visual BASIC and Realizer are both Windows 3.x versions of the BASIC language that can be used to create custom front-end applications. Realizer uses its own drivers to access back-end databases; Visual BASIC uses the Q&E Database Library for the same purpose.

Borland's ObjectVision is an object-oriented application design and development platform, with versions for Windows and OS/2. ObjectVision can be used to create front-end applications that access database servers through Borland's SQL Link, which is very similar to the SQL Link for Paradox.

Query/Reporting Programs

Query and report writing programs are primarily end-user tools, designed to make it easy for the casual user and non-programmer to access data on a Client/Server database. Querying, which requests data and presents the response on the screen, and report writing, which sends the response to a printer, are actually two different functions, though just about every front-end program does both.

This type of front-end application usually doesn't have a built-in programming language, but may have a scripting or macro language that records the user's keystrokes so that common queries can be automated for later reuse. It may also save a query to a file so that it can be rerun when needed, or used in a report.

Query and reporting front-ends vary in their abilities to do one or the other. Some have excellent query interfaces with only minimal reporting capabilities, while others are more suited to report writing. As with any other application, which function you need more will determine which query/reporting program you should use.

Quest

Gupta checks into this category with Quest, a Windows-based query and reporting tool that uses dialog boxes to insulate the user from the underlying SQL requests. It also has a number of built-in functions to assist in analyzing the data. It can be used as a tool to pass query results to other Windows programs for further analysis.

Like SQLWindows, the single-user package comes with a stand-alone version of SQLBase, which lets the user create and use a local database or access an existing SQLBase server. Support for other back-ends such as ORACLE and SQL Server is supplied through the various routers and gateways that Gupta sells.

Quest's strength is its easy-to-use interface. A series of dialog boxes, pick lists, and drop-down menus leads the user through the process of choosing the database, tables, and columns to query. Through other dialog boxes, lists, and menus, users set the sort order and conditions for the query. Multitable joins are created through a dialog box that graphically links the columns of the tables to be joined. Quest's built-in intelligence automatically displays a link between columns in different tables that have the same name, and the user can either accept that link or create a new one.

Quest also provides a function editor, accessed by a dialog box, which offers a large number of math, string, date, and time functions. These functions can be used to create new columns in the result set for analyzing the data. Queries can be saved for reuse or reports once the user is satisfied they're working properly. Quest can also use DDE to pass the query results to another Windows program for further analysis or charting.

Reporting is another of Quest's strong features. It includes a full-screen report painter that presents dialog boxes for setting the report size and format. Reports are based on existing saved queries or local database files and can be previewed on the screen before printing.

Quest provides a number of formatting options, including adding graphic borders to fields, controlling blank lines, and printing different fields in different fonts. Bitmap (.BMP) graphics such as a letterhead can be added to a report for viewing or printing.

In addition to the numerous query functions, Quest has a set of aggregate and nonaggregate functions that can be used in a report. The report functions support data analysis of the components of the report using statistical functions such as minimums and maximums, sums, and data counts. They also provide numerous string functions for extracting portions of text fields or for converting fields between numeric and text formats. Quest's reporting functions also make it easy to create mailing labels or form letters that use the data in a database for the fill-in information.

Quest doesn't have a native programming or scripting language. It can be indirectly programmed through DDE links with Visual BASIC programs or through macro languages such as those in Microsoft's Excel or Word for Windows.

Quest's most serious limitation is that it doesn't directly support joins or views from multiple data sources, because it can only access one database at a time. The only way to create multidatabase joins is to query each database and save the results to a local database. Joins can then be made on the tables in the local database.

Quest is one of the better end-user tools available for creating queries and reports on Client/Server databases. It completely hides the SQL statements from the user, so it's ideal for nonprogrammers and casual users.

Personal Access

Spinnaker Software's Personal Access is a Windows-based application that extends the concept of hypermedia card stacks to user-oriented database access. Users can create cards that access data from a number of sources, including SQL Server, ORACLE, dBASE-type .DBF files, and Paradox data files.

Personal Access is actually an integrated front-end to Spinnaker's PLUS, a hypermedia applications development and management engine that also comes in a script-compatible Macintosh version. PLUS, an object-oriented system, lets users create stacks of cards that contain data objects such as text fields, data fields, graphics, and control buttons. However, the combination of Personal Access and PLUS is very resource-intensive, requiring at least a 80386 system with a minimum of 4Mb of RAM.

A PLUS stack, illustrated in Figure 8.7, consists of one or more cards that contain the actual data queries. Cards are created by placing various objects on either the foreground (present on only the visible card) or background (present on all cards in the same stack). A series of floating toolboxes make designing and placing objects easy. By itself, PLUS can only access data directly entered into the card stack.

Personal Access extends PLUS's cards utility by accessing external databases. Users can create queries through dialog boxes and pick lists, and a single card can contain queries from multiple databases. Up to 500 databases can be accessed through a single card to create complex lookups and interrelationships, which means Personal Access can perform data integration and analysis as well. The user isn't limited to working with only one type of back-end or database file at a time; if a common field exists, stacks can access data from different database formats at the same time.

Cards can be designed to show only one record at a time or to display multiple records in a table format. When a link exists between two or more databases, later cards in a stack can contain other fields that are linked to the fields on the first card, which gives the user the means to further examine the databases' contents. For example, the first card can contain a query of all the departments in a company; when a particular department is highlighted, the second card in the stack can contain the results of a query of all employees in that department.

Designing database card stacks is very easy using the point-and-shoot toolkits. Personal Access and PLUS also provide on-screen navigation menus that let the user move quickly around the stack. Floating toolboxes such as Quick Tools give the user easy access to the basic tools for creating and browsing through card stacks, adding fields to existing cards, or placing predefined action buttons on the card. All the toolkits can be toggled on and off, so they're not in the way when you're browsing data.

Figure 8.7

Personal Access and PLUS use hypermedia card stacks to provide access to a variety of data sources.

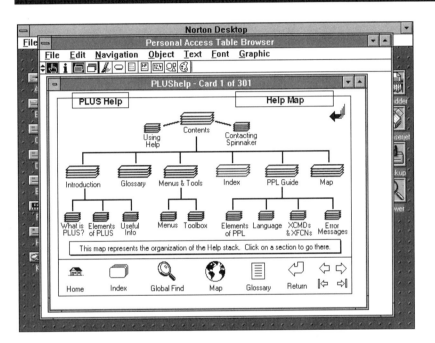

The PLUS Programming Language (PPL) is an event-driven scripting language that consists of over 200 command statements and functions that control Windows message handling, properties, navigation, visual and sound effects, menus, and other user-interaction tools. PPL scripts are automatically created when the cards are designed, and a built-in editor is included for more advanced customizing of precreated scripts or for custom programming of card stacks.

PPL also provides support for DDE with other Windows applications and can access external Dynamic Link Libraries (DLLs) for more complete control over the Windows environment. When used with PLUS, Personal Access adds additional PPL commands to the language to support external database access.

PPL scripts can be used with any version of PLUS, making it easy to create applications for both IBM and Macintosh systems that access the same database servers.

External utilities assist in database management and can be run directly from Windows or through Personal Access. The Table Maintenance utility lets the user create and change database files, and Joiner lets the user precreate links between different database tables for later use in PLUS card stacks. Index Finder manages dBASE-type indexes, creating the associations needed for accessing .DBF files through Personal Access.

The included PLUS Reports module is a full screen WYSIWYG report designer that lets the user create custom row-and-column or free-form reports, mail-merge letters, and forms from data contained in card stacks. Bit-map graphics from the clipboard can be included in reports, but only after they're copied to the clipboard from a card stack with a custom script. Reports can be printed or viewed in a window on the screen.

Also included in the package is PLUS View, which lets the user create dynamic row-and-column views of all the data contained in a particular stack. Views can be used as navigation tools or as a basis for quick summary reports of a stack.

Personal Access and PLUS are a powerful team for the easy creation of complex hypermedia card stacks for accessing existing databases. If you prefer a hypermedia interface or need to create database access applications that run on both the IBM and the Macintosh, the Personal Access/PLUS combination is a good choice.

Oracle Card

Oracle also provides Oracle Card, their own version of a hypermedia interface that uses the PLUS engine. Its scripting language, called Oracle Talk, is an enhancement of PPL which allows users and developers to issue PL/SQL and SQL commands from within a script. Oracle Card is similar to Personal Access, but is limited to accessing ORACLE databases. Many developers also feel that Oracle Card isn't as powerful as the Personal Access/PLUS combination and recommend using Personal Access instead of Card if you want to create hypermedia applications.

ClearAccess

ClearAccess Corporation offers a Windows-based query tool that's also designed to be a data link between a back-end and Microsoft Excel. Its ad hoc query capabilities are very easy to use, and queries can be stored for reuse through script recording. ClearAccess's greatest limitation is that it only supports ORACLE servers directly, and SQL Servers through Sybase's Open Client software.

From ClearAccess's main screen, users select icons to run a script, edit a script, connect to a database, query the database, and quit the program. Pull-down menus offer similar choices, as well as starting and stopping the script recorder, and creating a predefined JOIN of data from different tables.

The Query window is the heart of ClearAccess. Once a connection to a database is established, the Query window presents pick lists of all the accessible tables in the database. When a table is chosen, the columns in the table are displayed in a second pick list window. Queries are built by clicking on the columns and dragging them to a window on the right side of the query screen. The conditions and sorting options for the query are then chosen and entered, and the query is run. Users select other query options to format the results, create JOINs, and edit the various conditions before running the query. ClearAccess doesn't provide any statistical or mathematical functions beyond those provided by the supported back-ends.

The results can be returned either to the screen or to the Windows clipboard. Screen results are shown in a separate window that can be scrolled or enlarged; the results can also be saved to a file in ASCII, SYLK, or .WKS format for importing into other applications. Results from different databases can be joined by storing the different results sets in a local ClearBase database (ClearBase is ClearAccess's native database format) and creating a JOIN on the local tables. Or the results can be sent directly to the Windows Clipboard to be manually or automatically pasted into another Windows application.

The real power of ClearAccess arises from its scripting capabilities. The script language has over 50 commands, and scripts can be created by recording an ad hoc query or by direct editing in a text editor. Existing scripts, which can be edited through the built-in editor, are initiated from the RUN button on the main menu. For simple debugging, developers can pause scripts during execution or open a separate window to watch the actual dialog between the script and the database server. Using the script language, developers can prompt the user for values during script execution, allowing ad hoc queries to be created and run through the scripts.

The included ClearLinks module lets ClearAccess act as a direct automatic query link for Microsoft Excel and other Windows applications using DDE. Other Windows applications can be started and stopped by a ClearAccess script, which lets the developer completely automate the process of querying the database and moving the results directly to another application for reporting or analysis. Excel is supported directly through an included Excel Add-In document which lets Excel macro sheets directly access and run ClearAccess scripts to query databases and return the results to a spreadsheet. ClearAccess expects to add direct support for other Windows applications in the future.

ClearAccess is best used as a linking application; its strength lies in its ability to automate database access and automatically pass the results to other Windows applications for further reporting or analysis.

Data Integration and Analysis Tools

The last category of front-end applications covers data integration and analysis tools. Data integration and analysis are actually two parts of the same process—the user first queries data from different sources and then combines the data to analyze what it means.

The most common type of integration and analysis application is called an Executive Information System (EIS). EIS applications are designed to gather data from several different places in an organization and present the information to the organization's managers in a way that helps them make complex business decisions. For example, an EIS might combine data from the inventory, sales order, and personnel databases to help a manager create vacation schedules that have a minimum impact on filling orders.

Integration and analysis applications can also be used for statistical or scientific studies, for analyzing stock market trends, or whenever users need to combine and examine data from multiple sources. The proliferation of information in our modern businesses (and even our society) makes it very difficult to distinguish the important data from (for lack of a better term) "background noise," so in some respects, data integration and analysis is the most useful application a computer user can have.

LightShip

LightShip is a Windows-based data analysis package primarily designed for application developers who create EIS applications. The base package uses DDE as the source for its data, and the optional LightShip Lens module extends LightShip's capabilities to accessing data from other PC-based databases, such as dBASE, Excel, and Paradox, as well as SQL Server, ORACLE, and NetWare SQL. Although it allows the user to update the data in the source files, its primary function is to provide the user with different views of the data for analysis.

LightShip is object-oriented and uses a number of tools to create the different screen and data objects. The tools can either be accessed from the menu or from a floating icon tool bar. LightShip refers to data objects as documents and can place them anywhere on the screen. Each document can display data from only one source; the only way to combine and compare data from different sources is by creating an object for each source on the screen and manually comparing them.

Standard LightShip uses either directly entered data, a text file, or a Windows DDE link as the source for a document, which limits it somewhat as an analysis tool, particularly if you haven't moved your databases to Windows yet. The additional LightShip Lens module is essential for realizing LightShip's full power; once it's added to the system, it's automatically available and invoked as a data source when a new document object is created. Queries are easily created through a series of pop-up windows and pick lists that let the user or developer specify the data source, fields, and query conditions.

LightShip also has Hotspot objects, a facility that ties one or more actions to a particular object, or to an item in a document. When used in a document, a Hotspot lets the application developer create a pick list of items that the user can click on. The user can then view the document associated with that item in a separate object window on the screen.

One of LightShip's greatest strengths is its integration of screen displays and graphic image objects with data, as illustrated in Figure 8.8. .PCX, .BMP, and Clipboard images can be added to a screen for use as backgrounds to highlight different documents in different areas of the screen. A graphic object can also be used as a Hotspot indicator; clicking on the graphic brings up other screens that contain documents associated with the particular data being analyzed. LightShip also gives the developer complete control over the screen pallet for each object, which lets the developer highlight particular documents or portions of documents. This is particularly useful for creating data thresholds, where the color of an object can automatically change to reflect its value or status when it exceeds a programmer-defined limit.

Figure 8.8

LightShip uses Windows's graphics capabilities to the fullest and lets the developer mix both text and graphics on the same screen.

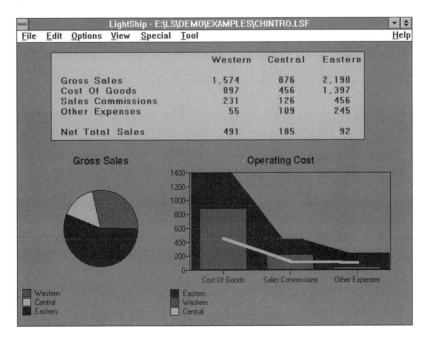

LightShip is primarily an application-building tool. While novice users can use it to query different data sources, building a complete analysis system isn't a simple process. LightShip is aimed at applications developers who want to create a simple-to-use EIS for their clients or upper management; it supports these capabilities by letting the developer create custom menus and screens with Hotspots that shield the user from the underlying program.

Developers use its debugging facilities to test-run the application and watch the values of defined variables and the actions being executed through a trace. Debug traces can be saved on disk or printed out to make it easier to correct problems or errors. The debug facility also gives the developer information on any image objects being used and on how they're used.

LightShip's most serious drawback is that it offers no easy way to create analysis links or show the relationship between different data documents. To analyze data, you must show different documents on the same screen and manually analyze what's being shown; data from different documents can't be joined into composite views or results.

LightShip's primary audience is developers of in-house EIS systems rather than end-users, and in that light it is a decent environment for creating data analysis applications. However, you must have the LightShip Lens module in order to access external data sources. Without it, LightShip is relatively useless.

Forest & Trees

Forest & Trees from Channel Computing, Inc. may be the easiest to use and the most powerful data analysis tool available in both DOS and Windows versions today. In the standard version, users can combine data from the most common PC file formats, including dBASE, Lotus 1-2-3, Excel, Q&A, R:Base, and Paradox. The Client/Server version adds the ability to integrate data from a number of back-ends, including SQL Server, ORACLE, SQL-Base, NetWare SQL, DB2 (through Micro Decisionware's Database Gateway), and Rdb/VMS. Its only limitation is that it's an analysis-only tool; it accesses the data sources in read-only mode.

As its name implies, Forest & Trees uses a tree metaphor. It collects data from various sources into data objects on the screen. Each object is a node in the tree diagram and can contain the results of a query on a particular data source, as shown in Figure 8.9. The objects can then be connected to other objects to create higher-level nodes based on formulas that analyze and combine the data from lower-level nodes. All the nodes ultimately connect to a top (root) level node which contains the complete analysis of the subnodes.

F&T doesn't have a programming or scripting language, so all data access and analysis is accomplished through objects, pick lists, and dialog boxes.

Figure 8.9

Forest & Trees lets the user view data from different sources and combine it for analysis.

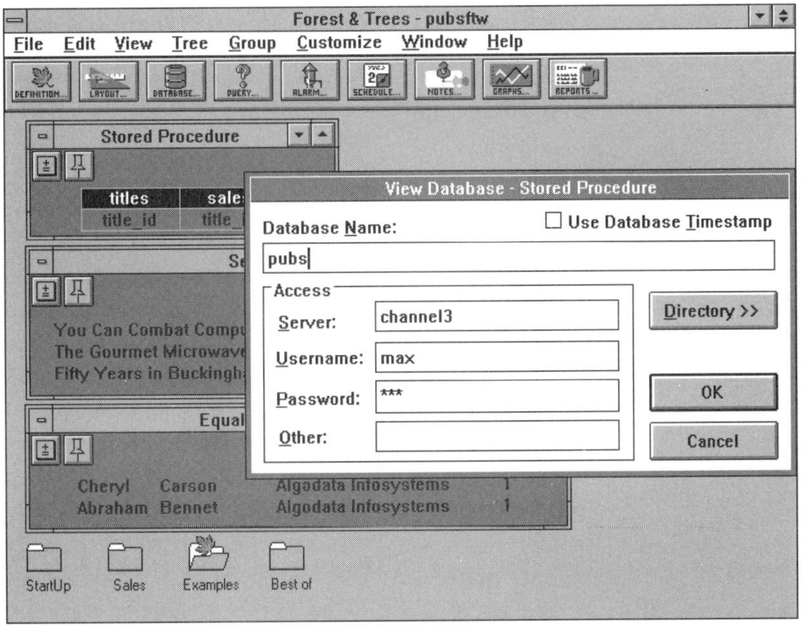

The easiest way to describe how F&T presents complex data for analysis is by example. Suppose a business owner wants to look at the cash flow of a business. The first step is to create objects that perform the queries and analyze the elements of cash flow, such as income received, outstanding invoices, inventory, taxes paid, expenses, cash-on-hand, and investments. Each particular node is created from a query on one data source for the item being examined. For example, the income data is from a set of Excel spreadsheets, while the inventory data is stored on a SQL Server database. Once the lower-level nodes are created, the user creates the second-level nodes that combine the results of the lower nodes into one node for income and one for expenses. Finally, a top node subtracts expenses from income to show the company's profits.

F&T presents all the nodes either as individual data objects or as a tree with connecting lines showing which nodes make up which portions. Navigating around the tree is easy—each node's display object has button icons that can be used to navigate up and down the tree to examine the data elements that compose the node. With other buttons, users create a graph or a report on the data the object represents; the user can even add pop-up notes to each node to clarify what the data means, to identify the assumptions behind the data query or calculation, or to alert managers to particular changes.

Forest & Trees is a powerful analysis tool because it provides real-time data results—which means users can examine the data as it changes. Application developers use F&T's scheduling tool to create a schedule for updating the data in an object. Automatic updating can occur daily, weekly, monthly, or yearly, or after a user-defined period of days, weeks, or months. If the application isn't running during a scheduled time, the updates are automatically performed the next time it's loaded.

F&T can also automatically save a history log of previous results from updates, so the user can view and analyze the changes in a particular data object over a period of time.

Along with scheduling, F&T users can set alarms for particular data conditions in each node. Alarms are indicated by color-coding the data displays in each object: Green means the data is OK, yellow means the data needs to be carefully monitored, and red means the data has triggered the alarm. Pop-up notes can be attached to the alarm to provide further information. Again using our example, you might set an alarm to indicate when expenses exceed 25 percent of total income, bringing the problem to the users' attention by turning the expense value red and displaying the alarm note.

Forest & Trees is simple enough for the novice to use, yet has enough built-in power and capabilities to create complex data analyses. Its data analysis capabilities are the best I've seen among all the front-end applications I researched for this book.

InfoAlliance

Software Publishing Corporation's (SPC) InfoAlliance is unique among the front-ends in this chapter, because it uses its own OS/2-based back-end server and data format, and supports user access to dBASE-type .DBF files, as well as Database Manager and SQL Server databases. SPC bills InfoAlliance as a "datasource integrator," because its primary function is to give users a way to integrate and examine or modify data from multiple sources in a single view or report.

The InfoAlliance system consists of three modules: the server, the front-end, and the SQL Connector. The NDSI server runs on any 80386-based OS/2 1.21 or higher workstation and supports access from workstations on Microsoft LAN Manager, IBM LAN Server, and Novell NetWare LANs. The NDSI server supplies security through user IDs and passwords, which are administered by the supplied OS/2 or Windows server administration program. Using the administration program, the database administrator can monitor activity on the server, such as determining the number of open files and identifying which files are being accessed by which users.

The second module is the user front-end—the heart of InfoAlliance. Both OS/2 and Windows versions are available. The front-end is primarily forms-oriented; users create and use data forms that can contain multiple fields from multiple databases. The forms are based on InfoAlliance views, which can link tables from any of the different data sources into one view (hence the term datasource integrator). Data reports and custom applications are also created and used through the front-end.

The third module is the Connector to SQL Server, which runs either with a stand-alone InfoAlliance Windows front-end, or as part of the NDSI server to give multiple users access to SQL Server data. The Connector handles all the translations to make SQL Server databases appear as InfoAlliance databases to the users; it can also copy the SQL Server data to any of the other supported data sources. With InfoAlliance's Connector, users can even create multitable views from tables residing on different SQL Servers, integrating the different tables into one form or report.

InfoAlliance uses the GUI capabilities of its host environment to the fullest, sparing users and developers from writing code. Bitmapped graphics and a number of built-in draw objects can be included in a form or report, and different sections and fields can be highlighted by different fonts and colors. Data may be viewed and manipulated through either a form or a table window; multiple data windows can be open at the same time, so data can be cut-and-pasted from one table to another for queries or updates.

Forms and reports are designed by first creating a data view through a combination of dialog boxes, menus, and pick lists. The data fields in the view can come from any of the supported data sources. The form or custom report is then designed using the fields in the view through a full-screen painter function. Quick reports can also be created from an existing form, and InfoAlliance includes a number of predefined standard mailing-label formats. There are no built-in charting functions, but InfoAlliance can export data in Harvard Graphics format for charting by that program.

InfoAlliance applications consist of a series of "actions," which are very easy to create. Applications are programmed through a series of menus, dialog boxes, and pick lists, so the developer never needs to write a line of code. Applications are stored in a proprietary format and can't be created or edited outside of InfoAlliance; however, the application file is compatible with both OS/2 and Windows versions and can also be compiled and used with a separate run-time module.

When it was first released in 1990, InfoAlliance was the only application that could combine data from a number of different sources into one view for analysis. Since then, many other products have matched and even surpassed its capabilities, so it's no longer unique. SPC also failed to gather much support for the NDSI server, and using a proprietary back-end in order to access other back-ends now seems to be unnecessarily redundant and complex. (Note: Shortly after this book went to press, SPC announced that they were discontinuing sales of InfoAlliance, and incorporating its analysis and reporting features into Superbase 4.)

■ Choosing the Right Front-end for Your Needs

As you can see, a wide variety of front-end applications are available, and more are appearing on the market all the time. The different front-ends also overlap in features and functions, so choosing the right one can be very time-consuming. In fact, it may turn out that there isn't just one that solves every problem you have, and you may have to use two or more front-ends depending on the needs of different users.

There are some broad principles you can use as a guide in evaluating front-ends. First, decide if you're going to use character-mode or GUI applications. If you want character-mode front-ends, you're essentially limited to using one of the PC database add-ons or writing your own custom applications in one of the 3GLs, because the majority of the other front-ends are based on Windows or OS/2.

If you want to program your own applications (or have the resources to do so), and you don't care if they're character- or GUI-based, you may want to use one of the database add-ons or application development tools. If you only want to create GUI front-ends, you should use one of the application development tools or one of the query/reporting tools which have a script language.

If your goal is to combine existing databases with a Client/Server system, you can use either the add-on front-ends or the data integration and analysis front-ends. If most of your data is already in a PC-based database, the add-on would be a better solution for most uses.

The query/reporting tools and integration and analysis tools should be used primarily for users who don't need to modify the data on the server. These tools are much better at retrieving the data than putting it in. You should use one of the add-on or application development front-ends for users that constantly modify the database.

Finally, you should definitely consider using at least one data integration and analysis application. They're the best way to combine and examine all the data in your organization, and they can help you discover relationships between the different parts of your business that you may never have thought existed.

Chart of Front-ends

Table 8.1 summarizes all the different front-ends covered in this chapter. It gives you a handy reference for which products fall into which category and the back-ends they support. Remember that the vendors are constantly adding new capabilities to their products, so you should use this chart as the starting point for your own investigations of the many front-ends available.

Table 8.1

Front-ends and the
Database Servers They
Support

	Supported Environments	SQL Server	ORACLE	SQLBase	INGRES
Add-ons					
Advanced Revelation	DOS, OS/2	x	x		
Clarion	DOS	x	x	x	x
Clipper	DOS	x		x	
DataEase SQL	DOS, OS/2	x	x		x
dBASE IV 1.1 Serv. Edition	DOS	x			
Excel	Windows	x			
Lotus 1-2-3	DOS, OS/2, Windows	x	x		
Paradox	DOS	x	x		
PC/Focus & PM/Focus	DOS, OS/2	x			
Q&A	DOS		x	x	
Superbase 4	Windows	x	x	x	
Wingz	Windows, OS/2, Macintosh, Motif, Open Look	x	x		
App. Development					
ObjectVision (w/SQL Link)	Windows, OS/2	x	x		
PowerBuilder	Windows	x	x	x	x
Q&E	Windows, OS/2	x	x	x	
Realizer	Windows			x	
SequeLink	DOS, OS/2, Macintosh, UNIX	x	x		x
SQLWindows	Windows	x	x	x	x
Visual BASIC	Windows	x			

	INFORMIX	Database Manager	XDB-DMBS	NetWare SQL	Rdb/VMS	AllBAse	SQL/400	SQL/DS	DB2	EDA/SQL
Add-ons										
Advanced Revelation				x					x	
Clarion		x	x	x						
Clipper				x						
DataEase SQL		x							x	
dBASE IV 1.1 Serv. Edition										
Excel										
Lotus 1-2-3										
Paradox		x		x						
PC/Focus & PM/Focus										x
Q&A										
Superbase 4				x						
Wingz	x			x						
App. Development										
ObjectVision (w/SQL Link)		x		x						
PowerBuilder			x			x		x	x	
Q&E		x	x	x						
Realizer				x						
SequeLink		x		x	x					
SQLWindows		x		x		x	x			
Visual BASIC				x						

Table 8.1

continued

	Supported Environments	SQL Server	ORACLE	SQLBase	INGRES
Query Reporting					
ClearAccess	Windows	x	x		
Oracle Card	Windows		x		
Personal Access	Windows	x	x		
Quest	Windows	x	x	x	x
Integration/Analysis					
Forest & Trees	DOS, Windows	x	x	x	
InfoAlliance	Windows, OS/2	x			
LightShip	Windows	x	x		

	INFORMIX	Database Manager	XDB-DMBS	NetWare SQL	Rdb/VMS	AllBASe	SQL/400	SQL/DS	DB2	EDA/SQL
Query Reporting										
ClearAccess										
Oracle Card								X	X	
Personal Access										
Quest	X	X					X			
Integration/Analysis										
Forest & Trees		X		X	X		X			
InfoAlliance		X								
LightShip				X					X	

- *Traditional Database Systems*
- *Client/Server Systems*
- *Object-oriented Systems*
- *Distributed Processing Systems*

CHAPTER

Future Trends in DBMS Technology

T HE FIRST PCS TO HIT THE MARKET IN THE LATE 1970S WERE
considered by most computer professionals as mere toys, useful
only to hobbyists. At the time, they were probably right—but IBM's
entry into the PC market in 1981 suddenly gave these toys respect-
ability. However, even IBM believed their early PCs were simply
super typewriters or intelligent terminals to the real computers
working in the data center. Few people involved in the computer
market in the early 1980s predicted the impact PCs would have on
the entire field.

Yet here we are, a bit more than a decade later, discussing how PCs and their bigger brothers (the RISC workstations and superservers) can be used to replace the mainframes and minicomputers that dominated the market just ten years ago. PCs and PC networks have come a long way since the days when they were primarily owned by hobbyists.

Ever-increasing abilities to handle larger databases with technically advanced DBMSs are the key behind the movement toward downsizing large systems to PC and RISC platforms. Traditional PC DBMSs have become more powerful and more capable of handling large databases for both the single user and small groups of users. The advent of Client/Server architecture has made it possible for PCs to both host and access databases that approach or match the data handling abilities and security features of the larger systems.

Object-oriented programming (OOP) has given programmers an entirely new approach to developing sophisticated user applications, both for character-mode systems and the increasingly popular GUIs. Many database theorists are looking for ways to adapt object-oriented principles to database design, which may well lead to a whole new model for database management.

Finally, the theories and practical experience behind Client/Server systems are being carried to their ultimate conclusion with distributed database processing. Distributed processing systems let users transparently access any data from any database on the network. They fulfill one of the primary goals of today's computer professionals—complete data independence, in which data can be accessed without regard to what system or DBMS it resides on.

This book has focused on the state of DBMS technology in general and Client/Server computing in particular during the early 1990s. Both fields are advancing at a rapid pace that shows no signs of slowing down. While I don't own a crystal ball and I can't claim to accurately predict the future, I can make some educated guesses about what advances the next several years will bring in the four major areas of DBMS technology: traditional database systems, Client/Server systems, object-oriented systems, and distributed processing systems. By combining the opinions expressed in this chapter with your own experience, you should be well on your way to judging what the trends are in the DBMS market and how they'll affect your present and future computer system plans.

■ Traditional Database Systems

Large system databases that are still primarily built on the Hierarchical or Network models should continue to gradually decline as more and more corporate users move to the Relational databases or replace the systems completely with Client/Server systems. However, a lot of corporate data still resides on mainframes and the larger minicomputers, and the short-term costs of migrating the data to other systems may convince many companies to move cautiously. I expect that the trend toward replacing older DBMSs with new ones based on the Relational model will continue as capabilities increase; IBM's push toward their Information Warehouse concept and DEC's inclusion of a run-time version of Rdb/VMS in every system should bolster the trend as well.

There's also the continuing problem of the size of existing databases; many are too large to be downsized yet. However, I firmly believe that a good portion of these databases may be so large simply because of the conservative attitude ("we've always done it that way") that is unfortunately still common in many MIS departments. You must carefully and completely analyze your company's data processing needs to determine if existing databases can be archived and/or proportioned out to smaller, less costly systems, or if they really do need to stay on the large systems for the time being.

Traditional databases will have a place on PCs throughout the 1990s, and the market will continue to develop in at least three different directions: nonprogrammable databases, dBASE-compatibles, and other PC DBMSs. On the bottom end, the nonprogrammable databases, such as Alpha Software Corporation's Alpha Four and Symantec's Q&A, will continue to enhance their user-friendly interfaces and data processing capabilities for those with simple database needs, such as maintaining mailing lists or small business inventories. The primary market for these packages will remain single-user systems and very small networks of 20 users or less.

I remember hearing someone jokingly describe the dBASE language as "COBOL for PCs." While this description may sound funny at first, it conveys a large element of truth. COBOL made large systems usable for day-to-day business data processing, and the dBASE language made data processing a reality on PCs. An enormous number of business applications are written in dBASE or dBASE-compatible code, and a whole cottage industry of database consultants do nothing but develop dBASE applications. Various surveys have shown that dBASE-compatible DBMSs and applications make up the lion's share of the PC database market. Efforts are underway to standardize all dBASE-compatible development platforms and languages into an "XBase" standard. (*XBase* is one of those unnecessary computer terms I absolutely despise and generally avoid using. It was a response to Ashton-Tate's attempts to prevent anyone else from using the word *dBASE* to describe its database language; however, if an XBase standard ever sees the light of day, we'll all have little choice but to refer to it to be understood.) Moves toward creating dBASE-compatible DBMSs for UNIX and VAX/VMS systems provide PC users with a growth path when the size of their databases surpasses what PCs can handle. A couple of vendors have also released products to extend Client/Server capabilities to the dBASE format; these were covered in the last section of Chapter 4.

Many dBASE-compatible vendors have attempted to keep up with the advances in DBMS technology—SQL in particular. Many products now understand and use SQL commands to access .DBF files. Adding SQL has usually meant merely grafting an SQL interpreter on top of the dBASE language; the extra overhead of translating the SQL into dBASE only slowed down the DBMS's response time. While these efforts were noble, by themselves they would only have postponed the eventual eclipse of dBASE technology by other DBMSs that more closely adhere to both the SQL standard and the data integrity features of the Relational model. However, several events that occurred in 1991 and early 1992 may serve to revive the dBASE market and keep it a serious contender throughout the decade.

The first of these events was the purchase of Ashton-Tate, the creator of dBASE, by Borland in 1991. Borland had already created a reputation for technically innovative PC products with its well-known 3GL compilers, and it had gained a significant share of the PC database market with Paradox, its mostly relational DBMS. Ashton-Tate was sliding into bankruptcy, in spite of (or perhaps because of) its merger with the Interbase Company, which was in the process of developing a Client/Server DBMS. Borland bought the ailing Ashton-Tate and proceeded to integrate the dBASE and Interbase development teams into its database systems division.

Some industry analysts speculate that the real reason Borland went after Ashton-Tate was to gain access to the Interbase technology, especially after Borland failed to make the Paradox database engine a standard platform for developing database applications. Whatever the real reason, the net effect is the same—dBASE is now owned and marketed by a company experienced in creating technically advanced database and language products. Future versions of dBASE will probably reflect that experience, and I wouldn't be surprised to see elements of both Paradox and Interbase incorporated in dBASE products. I also expect the Interbase server, now in development, to be well suited as a Client/Server back-end for dBASE applications.

Not to be outdone, in early 1992 Microsoft purchased Fox Software, makers of the popular FoxPro line of dBASE-compatible DBMSs. Previously, Microsoft had not released a DBMS, even though they dominated the PC operating systems market and held a significant share of the PC applications market. In fact, they've had a Windows-based DBMS in development for years; its current code name is Access, and it's scheduled for beta testing in late 1992 and for possible release in 1993. The purchase of FoxPro enhances that project by providing access to existing DBMS technology, particularly the Rushmore database indexing engine, developed by Fox, that has been benchmarked by *PC Magazine* as being more than twice as fast as dBASE.

I suspect the deal also provides Microsoft with a strategy for competing with their archrival Borland in the PC DBMS market in two ways should Access again be delayed. First, the Fox products establish Microsoft's presence in the database market. Second, Fox Software was working on their own Client/Server back-end database, though few details were available about whether it would be a relational, SQL-based DBMS or a C/S back-end for dBASE applications. If the rumors of a possible breakdown in Microsoft and Sybase's partnership in the development of SQL Server are true, Microsoft will have Fox's server technology to fall back on if forced to create their own back-end. At this point, it's too early to tell whether Microsoft will have a major influence on the dBASE-compatible market or if they'll just maintain a holding action with FoxPro by matching any new features and capabilities introduced by Borland in the original product.

The third event that may fuel a dBASE revival was Computer Associates's purchase of Nantucket, the vendors of the Clipper dBASE compiler. CA (as it's commonly called) is one of the largest vendors of mainframe software, after IBM, of course. Over the past several years, the company has attempted to make inroads into the PC market by buying PC-based software companies. CA hasn't quite shaken their mainframe roots, and the overall effect of their purchases has been a dcrease in their products' PC market share. Nantucket was the third-largest vendor of dBASE-compatible development systems, and I don't expect CA to have any more success with Clipper than it's had with its other products. The net result of this purchase will probably be to leave the future of the dBASE market in the hands of Borland and Microsoft—companies that understand the PC market very well and who have the means to keep some form of the dBASE language alive into the 21st century.

In the meantime, other PC DBMSs aren't standing still. Borland is continuing to enhance both the relational and development platform capabilities of Paradox; Version 4.0 is due out in late 1992 or early 1993, and early reports from beta testers say that it's significantly advanced in power and features over previous versions. Paradox has also been known for excellent LAN-based multiuser support (much better than dBASE's), and I expect that the new version will continue that support. Borland's LAN experience will most likely also improve network support for dBASE, which would resolve one of the most serious complaints dBASE users and programmers have had over the years.

Another company that may continue to have a major impact on the PC database market is Microrim, makers of R:Base. R:Base has always been known for being the most relational of the PC-based DBMSs, which is not surprising when you consider that Microrim was founded by some of the designers of the Relational Information Management (RIM) system developed by NASA in the late 1970s. It is also known for offering both excellent multiuser support and one of the best DBMS application generators available anywhere. R:Base was the first PC DBMS to support SQL as part of its native command language, and recent versions have been ANSI Level 2 compatible. Microrim was well on its way to entering the Client/Server market when it ran into financial difficulties in the early 1990s, and for a time it looked as if they would go out of business. Layoffs and cutbacks in mismanaged projects saved the company, and in June of 1992, Microrim released R:Base 4.0, a 32-bit PC/MS DOS and OS/2 2.0 version which has the distinction of being the first (and so far only) PC-based RDBMS to include built-in referential integrity rules. R:Base may well regain its former place as the DBMS of choice for those who want to use a highly relational or SQL-based database but don't yet need the features of a Client/Server system.

Traditional PC DBMSs will continue to dominate the market for single-user systems for obvious reasons. They will also remain the primary choice for small networks with 20 or fewer users, systems in which the power and complexities of a Client/Server or distributed database system is neither needed nor desired. I fully expect that the top PC-based DBMSs will continue to add relational features as PCs increase in power, lessening the impact of the additional overhead needed by the Relational model. I also expect that the DBMS vendors will continue to add features that make it easier for nonprogrammers to both develop and use database applications. The continually increasing acceptance of SQL as the standard DBMS language will also have an impact on PC-based databases; we'll see increasing support for SQL as either the primary or alternate language in PC databases in the future.

■ Client/Server Systems

In many ways Client/Server technology is still in its infancy. Client/Server RDBMS vendors are continuing to add new features and capabilities to their products, and other vendors are preparing their own entries into the field. The market for C/S systems is rapidly expanding as more businesses examine the technology as an upgrade path for database systems reaching their limits or as a cost-saving platform for downsizing existing large systems. The 1992 BRG study that I've frequently referenced throughout this book estimates that the Client/Server market is growing at the rate of 35 percent per year and will almost double by 1995.

A number of different trends will help fuel this growth. Chief among these is increasing front-end support for C/S databases and continuing enhancement of existing and new C/S DBMSs. PCs and RISC systems are also becoming more and more powerful, and the operating systems are finally catching up with the hardware systems they run on.

The trend toward adding Client/Server front-end capabilities to existing PC-based DBMSs and spreadsheets will continue over the next few years. As I mentioned in Chapter 8, most PC-based DBMSs and spreadsheets have support for at least one of the major back-end DBMSs. The next logical step for the vendors will be to expand their support for other back-end systems, which would give both their existing users and those developing C/S systems a wider choice in products on both ends of the cable. I also expect more vendors to include the Client/Server communication modules as part of their base product, instead of selling them as add-ons as most currently do.

Advancements in front-end technology over the next several years will continue to lie in products specifically designed to be front-ends, rather than in modules that enable existing applications to access a Client/Server database. Chief among these are the application development environments, the query/reporting programs, and the data analysis programs. Most of these dedicated front-end systems are designed for a GUI, which makes them much easier to use than character-based environments. Here too the vendors will continue to add support for different back-ends, as well as improving their products' abilities to combine data from different sources for queries and analysis.

The DBMS vendors won't be resting on their laurels, either. Oracle is poised to release a major enhancement of its RDBMS for all of ORACLE's supported platforms, which will only help solidify the company's position as the number one vendor in the total market and may well give it the opportunity to equal or surpass the Microsoft/Sybase team in the PC-based platform market. In late 1992, Ingres will release a new version of its DBMS that will represent a more significant and possibly more successful attempt at capturing a significant portion of the C/S market, particularly on PC platforms. And Informix should finally enter the PC market with its release of an NLM version in 1993.

Sybase is working hard on SQL Server 5.0 as well, which should be out in 1993. However, there's some confusion over which company (Microsoft or Sybase) will be releasing what operating system versions of the new release or if in fact the relationship between the two companies will continue at all. As it now stands, Microsoft will continue to support the OS/2 1.3 platform and to port SQL Server 4.2 and 5.0 over to Windows/NT. Sybase will release the UNIX and NLM versions, and it will port 5.0 over to OS/2 2.0. Sybase's DBMS technology and multiuser systems experience combined with Microsoft's PC and networking savvy creates a potent contender in the Client/Server market; it was Microsoft's marketing of SQL Server that brought the Client/Server architecture to the forefront of DBMS technology. It would be a shame (and rather silly) for them to go their separate ways over relatively inconsequential issues when they have the opportunity to either dominate or share dominance with Oracle of the entire Client/Server DBMS market for the rest of the decade.

The big unknowns are the two Client/Server DBMSs I mentioned in the previous section: the Interbase server from Borland and the former Foxbase server now owned by Microsoft. I fully expect Borland to forge ahead with work on Interbase by combining the development to date with the knowledge and experience it gained from both its own work on Paradox, and from the dBASE developers that have been absorbed into the company. When Interbase sees the light of day, it will be the second entry into the Client/Server market by a DBMS that started on PCs instead of on a large system; while much of the initial Interbase development was done under UNIX, I'd be surprised if Borland didn't release a PC-based version first.

The Foxbase server is more problematic, as Microsoft has not indicated whether they will continue to develop it and release it as a separate product, or will fold the work to date into their enhancements of SQL Server. A third possibility also exists: Microsoft and Sybase will go their separate ways, in which case the Foxbase server could become the foundation for an entirely new Client/Server DBMS. My guess is that the second scenario is the more likely of the three. Microsoft and Sybase share cross-development agreements in which advances to one side's products can be integrated into the other's; the two companies will patch up their differences and Microsoft will integrate the best aspects of the Foxbase server into SQL Server.

All the PC and UNIX DBMS vendors could stand to improve their technical support. Probably the most significant factor retarding the downsizing efforts of many MIS departments is the relatively poor support these vendors have for mission-critical systems. MIS folks are accustomed to receiving 24-hour-a-day, 7-days-a-week fast response support for their mainframes and large minicomputers. This level of support is vital to a customer whose database systems that just cannot go down for more than a few hours. Most PC and UNIX-based DBMS vendors don't provide this level of support yet, but it will become a critical factor in their success in the Client/Server market over the next few years. The vendors who match the support now available for mainframes will be the ones that will be around at the turn of the century; the ones that don't will become footnotes in C/S history.

Advances are also continuing in both the hardware and operating system software fronts. High-powered 32-bit PCs based on the Intel 80386 chip have been available since 1986, but it wasn't until April of 1992 that the first 32-bit PC operating system (OS/2 2.0) was released. While it's true that 32-bit versions of UNIX have been available for PCs for several years, UNIX has never had a big impact on the PC market; those who preferred UNIX purchased RISC workstations or minicomputers instead of PCs. However, newer versions of UNIX are adopting features such as multithreading that may give them another shot at the PC market.

The race to take advantage of the high-end PCs has started with IBM's OS/2 2.0 and will continue with the release of Microsoft's Windows/NT. Windows/NT may have a greater initial impact, because it's designed to run on both Intel-based and RISC-based systems, which will further blur the line between high-end PCs and UNIX workstations. IBM is continuing research on OS/2 3.0, which will also work on both PCs and RISC systems and should continue the competition between the two companies for dominance over the second generation of PC operating systems. Regardless of which company comes out on top, the real beneficiaries of the competition will be those looking to move to a high-powered, PC-based Client/Server platform.

The hardware continues to advance, gaining more power while costing less. Intel is currently developing the successor to the 80486, currently code-named the P5 chip, which will double or better the processing power of the current incredibly powerful CPU. Meanwhile, prices for PCs continue to drop, which makes them even more appealing as platforms for sophisticated multiuser and Client/Server databases.

RISC vendors continue to enhance the power of their chips as well, and significant advances are being made in the multiprocessor system field. DEC's Alpha chip may be the most significant advance in RISC systems when it's released in 1993. Alpha is a 64-bit CPU that will replace all the different CPUs in DEC's current systems, from desktop workstations to the top-of-the-line VAX mainframes. The Alpha CPU may have a tremendous impact on the Client/Server market, particularly because DEC and Microsoft are working on an Alpha version of Windows/NT. Alpha's scalability could make it the preferred platform for developing a C/S system with a built-in growth path.

High-end, multiprocessor-based UNIX systems are the most serious competition for mainframes when considering a platform for downsizing. While the Symmetry systems from Sequent are based on the Intel 80486 CPU, the top-end Symmetry 2000/700 and 2000/750 use up to 30 CPUs in a symmetrical multiprocessing architecture that can support up to 1000 users. They also support over 250G of disk space and come with Sequent's Dynix/pbx version of UNIX, which has built-in multiprocessing support. At a cost of around $800,000, the Symmetry 2000/700 has sufficient power to replace all but the most powerful mainframes. The bottom-end Symmetry systems cost about $35,000 for a 16-user, six-processor system with a 316Mb drive and are serious competitors for IBM's AS/400, and DEC's MicroVAX and MiniVAX systems for Client/Server database use.

Teradata is another well-known vendor of multiprocessor systems which provide mainframe power for minicomputer costs. ShareBase Corporation, a subsidiary of Teradata, manufactures computer systems specifically designed as database servers. The ShareBase SQL Server/8000 series is similar to the Symmetry computers; the Model 500 can also support up to 1000 users and more than 250G disk space for a cost of around $900,000.

What's even more impressive about these systems is that they provide all this computing power and require few of the environmental controls a mainframe must have. Prices will continue to drop as the cost of the CPUs decreases, a decline which will make the multiprocessor systems even more cost effective. They represent the future of high-end Client/Server database servers.

■ Object-oriented Systems

Every so often a concept is developed in the computer industry that gets elevated to the status of "buzzword," and suddenly, every vendor has to have a product that realizes the concept. Now, in the early 1990s, the hot concept is object-orientation (OO), both in programming languages and in databases.

Object-oriented programming (OOP) concepts have made significant inroads into the traditional 3GL market, encompassing such diverse development environments as the SmallTalk language, the C++ extensions to traditional C, and OO extensions to Borland's Turbo Pascal. OO principles are also appearing in the GUI interfaces, and in front-end development products (as mentioned in Chapter 8).

In its simplest form, the OO approach treats everything as an object that can be manipulated, or contained in other manipulatable objects. OOP has generated a whole new set of terms that define how objects are handled; unfortunately, different proponents of the OO approach agree neither on what the terms mean nor on an underlying theory of OO.

Nevertheless, both DBMS programmers and vendors are caught up in the OO hype, and they are attempting to apply OO principles to database management. At first glance, an OO database seems to be an ideal way to deal with a wide variety of data types—after all, a database record or field can be considered one type of object to be manipulated. In some ways, the OO approach solves some of the shortcomings of the Relational model, particularly when dealing with highly variable data types, such as large text fields. In many ways, the OO approach is ideal for such specialized databases as document management systems, which are designed specifically to manage all the text-based documents normally used by businesses.

When you dig deeper into what's being proposed as the foundation for OO databases, though, you find that the reality falls far short of the promise. And, in some ways, the OO approach represents a step back from the advances brought about by the Relational model.

DBMS theorists and vendors are primarily pursuing two different approaches to applying OO principles; one extends the Relational model by providing OO capabilities, and the other creates a whole new OO database model. Both approaches have their merits, but in my opinion the first will be more successful.

The Relational model has some weaknesses in handling large, variable data types and null values and is pretty much silent on the concept of user-defined data types. *Variable data types* are generally designed to accommodate data that doesn't fit into a rigid definition, in particular, large amounts of text and graphic images. RDBMS vendors have already begun to address this weakness with data types that fall under the generic heading of binary large objects, or BLOBs, which usually hold up to 2G of data. No RDBMS available today has a data type actually referred to as a BLOB; the vendors support BLOBs through such implementation-specific data types as LONG VARCHARS or IMAGE. Regardless of the actual name, the concept is the same.

The other problem with the Relational model lies with user-defined (sometimes referred to as abstract) data types. Current DBMSs define a set number of data types that can be used, such as TEXT, INTEGER, FLOAT, and CHAR. There are situations in which a user needs to store data that just doesn't fit into a rigid format—postal (zip) codes are a prime example. In the USA, all postal codes are composed entirely of numbers, or the more recent format of five numbers, a hyphen, and four numbers. However, in Canada and the U.K., the postal code is a combination of numbers and letters in two sets of three characters separated by a space. If a zip code field in a database has a numeric data type, it will reject Canadian postal codes. If it's defined as character or text, users may not get the results they expect from a sort based on the zip code field.

A user-defined data type would solve the problem. The database developer could create a new data type known as "zip," and define it as alphanumeric characters in the format of five numbers, or five numbers followed by a hyphen and four numbers, or three mixed characters followed by a space and three more mixed characters. If the user of the database expands operations to another country, the definition of the zip data type can also be expanded to accommodate the format of that country's postal code.

User-defined data types solve a very real business need but present enormous problems for RDBMS developers who must figure out a way to create an index on a user-defined data type. An index is necessary for performance, because the only purpose in having a user-defined data type is that the user needs to query the database based on that field. No currently available RDBMS addresses this problem, but the vendors and theorists are working hard on ways to adapt user-defined data types into the Relational model.

OO database proponents say that the solution is simple: Toss out the Relational model and design an entirely object-oriented database in which every data type is an abstract data type, whether it's built-in or user-defined. This approach sounds appealing, but there are two problems. First, there is, as yet, no theoretical foundation for an OO database. There's also little agreement on which OO concepts apply to database design or even on what the concepts are. Standard OO terms and concepts will evolve and come into use over time, so this problem will eventually be solved.

The lack of a theoretical foundation is a bigger problem. Every DBMS model has a clear theory behind it; for example, the Network model is based on set theory, and the Relational model is based on mathematical set logic. No such theory yet exists for OO databases. So far, some OO principles treat objects as sets, which is a step backward from the Relational model to the Network and Hierarchical models. OO languages are also more procedural than SQL, which is another step backward for the same reason.

A couple of DBMS vendors are marketing their products as object-oriented. However, if you look closely, you'll find that, like the words used by Humpty Dumpty in *Alice in Wonderland,* ("'When *I* use a word,' Humpty Dumpty said in a rather scornful tone, 'it means just what I choose it to mean—neither more nor less.'") what the vendors mean by OO is exactly what they say it means. They aren't, nor can they be, based on an OO standard or model, because one doesn't exist yet.

OO principles will affect the Client/Server DBMS market most significantly in developing and programming front-ends. The lack of an OO database model will prevent DBMS vendors from introducing a viable OO database for quite some time. Granted, the Relational model does have its faults and shortcomings, and it isn't the final solution for every data management need. However, it's still the most technically advanced and flexible database theory known today. A better DBMS theory may present itself in the next few years, but I don't believe object-orientation is it. For the time being, the better solution is being pursued by RDBMS supporters—extending the Relational model by integrating OO principles, primarily through BLOB and user-defined data types.

■ Distributed Processing Systems

The logical evolution of Client/Server systems is toward true distributed database processing. In a distributed processing system, the data can reside on any system, and the user can access the data she needs without regard to where it actually is stored. The user simply queries her local database server, and the server worries about where the data is located and how to get it.

The Client/Server architecture is a limited form of distributed processing, in which the front-end and the back-end share database processing duties. In order to avoid confusion, network and database professionals usually reserve the term *distributed processing* to define "back-end to back-end communications," and they refer to "user to back-end communications" as *Client/Server processing.*

Distributed processing systems are ideal for companies which already have a number of databases that they need to link together. They will also find a home in companies with offices scattered around the country or world that need to share common databases. They're also ideal for those who want to provide specific databases to different departments or activities of the organization, yet have the ability to link all the servers together for mass processing needs, such as quarterly or annual reports. Finally, distributed processing systems can provide greater performance (at significantly less cost) than a single mainframe or minicomputer by combining the processing power of a number of powerful PCs and RISC systems.

However, not every C/S system has to grow into a distributed system. There will still be many situations in which a single C/S database, perhaps running on a superserver, can fill an organization's entire data processing needs. Database administrators can allow database access for users who are outside the company's central location through remote dial-in links without the complexities of creating a distributed system.

The majority of Client/Server DBMS vendors are adding distributed database capabilities to their products. However, the bulk of these capabilities are offered with other versions of their own products; access to other DBMSs is provided by gateways. Linking even the same vendor's products together can be difficult, though, because of the different network protocols and operating systems involved.

Oracle is the farthest along of any of the C/S DBMS vendors in providing distributed database capabilities for their products, though they're currently at the read-only level for remote databases. Version 7.0 promises to bring full distributed processing to the ORACLE servers; we'll know for sure if they've succeeded in the next year or so.

The real success of distributed processing won't be realized if the DBMS vendors provide it only for their own products—they must also provide capabilities for passing queries on to other vendors' DBMSs for processing. While these capabilities currently exist through both vendor-provided and third-party gateways, the ideal solution is to roll the gateway's functions right into the DBMS itself. This would remove a level of complexity that only retards the move to Client/Server systems.

The key to this is through a database-independent API. Microsoft and Sybase are working in this direction with their Open Database Connectivity (ODBC) API. IBM is also attempting to create a distributed processing standard with their Distributed Relational Database Architecture (DRDA). And Information Builders is taking a unique approach with their EDA/SQL by providing a gateway API that currently supports over 50 DBMSs. EDA/SQL seems to be the best of the three; it isn't tied to any particular DBMS, so it's outside the reach of any one DBMS vendor's marketing efforts or control.

EDA/SQL also shouldn't be affected by the politics that usually accompanies the attempts of different vendors to work together on a common product. A number of third-party DBMS vendors have announced support for some or all of these APIs, and we should finally achieve true distributed database processing during the next three or four years.

The biggest remaining problem with distributed processing lies not in DBMS technology but in networking technology. Distributed processing works fine when all the database servers reside on a network that basically exists on one cable. The concept of "one cable" is more appearance than reality, as the network may actually consist of a number of different topologies and protocols. Network bridges, gateways, and routers link the different networks together, so that they appear to be one large network to users. Response time between the front-ends and the server is usually very good when all the linked networks exist in the same building.

However, the system starts to degrade when the network has to go outside of a single building, because of increasing limitations in data transfer speeds. If the systems being linked are close together (for example, two buildings on the same corporate campus), the problem can be solved by high-speed cabling between buildings. As the systems get farther apart, communication slows down to the point where the best a company can do on a cross-country link may be 14,400 bps (bits-per-second), the highest speed supported by current modems. While this may be fast enough for file transfers, it can have a significant impact on database performance, particularly when more than one database query or response is going over the link at the same time (which would not be uncommon). Database users will definitely complain about the slow response from remote databases, especially when compared to the speed of their local servers.

Networking companies are working on a number of different technologies and approaches for speeding up remote links, which are beyond the scope of this book (see Appendix C for recommended reading on this subject). However, the majority of these new technologies won't be in widespread use until at least the middle of this decade, so the speed problem will continue to hold back the implementation of distributed databases by companies with widely scattered offices for the next several years.

I hope you've enjoyed this tour through the current and future states of database and Client/Server technologies as much as I've enjoyed playing tour guide. The next step is up to you. Use the information in this book as the basis for your own explorations in how the Client/Server database architecture can best benefit your organization. I'm confident that the right system exists for your needs, and I wish you great success in finding and implementing it.

■ Appendix A

■ Quick Summary Charts

PRODUCT INFORMATION	PCs (Chapter 4)				
Name	SQL Server 4.2	SQL Server 4.2	SQLBase 5.0	OS/2 2.0 ES Database Manager	XDB-Server 2.41
Vendor	Microsoft Corporation	Sybase, Inc.	Gupta Technologies	IBM, Inc.	XDB Systems, Inc.
Price Range	$1,495–$7,995	$1,995–$29,995	$995–$4,995	$1,995	$1,995–$2,495
Operating Systems					
On Database Server	OS/2 1.21 or higher	NetWare 3.11	DOS 3.1 or higher, OS/2 1.0 or higher, NetWare 3.11	OS/2 1.31 or higher	DOS 3.1 or higher, OS/2 1.1 or higher
On LAN Server	MS LAN Manager, IBM LAN Server, Novell NetWare, or any other network that supports Named Pipes	NetWare 3.11	MS LAN Manager, IBM LAN Server, Net-Ware 2.11 or higher, Banyan VINES	MS LAN Manager, IBM LAN Server, NetWare 3.11, or any network that supports NetBIOS	MS LAN Manager, IBM LAN Server, Net-Ware 3.11, or any network that supports NetBIOS
On Workstations	DOS 3.x or higher, Windows 3.x, OS/2 1.21 or higher	DOS 3.x or higher, Windows 3.x, OS/2 1.21 or higher	DOS 3.1 or higher, Windows 3.x	DOS 3.1 or higher, Windows 3.x, OS/2 1.21 or higher	DOS 3.1 or higher, OS/2 1.1 or higher
Minimum Requirements					
RAM on Server	8Mb	12Mb	2Mb (DOS), 4Mb (OS/2), 8Mb (NLM)	8Mb (OS/2 1.3), 12Mb (OS/2 2.0)	1.5Mb (DOS), 4Mb (OS/2)
RAM on Workstation	512k (DOS), 6Mb (OS/2)	512k (DOS), 6MB (OS/2)	640k (DOS), 6Mb (OS/2)	640k (DOS), 6Mb (OS/2)	640k (DOS), 4Mb (OS/2)
Disk Space	20Mb	20Mb	10Mb	15Mb	10Mb
Utilities Provided					
Administration	Yes	Yes	Yes	Yes	Yes

PRODUCT INFORMATION	PCs (Chapter 4)				
Name	SQL Server 4.2	SQL Server 4.2	SQLBase 5.0	OS/2 2.0 ES Database Manager	XDB-Server 2.41
Interactive User	Yes	Yes	Yes	Yes	Yes
Operating Systems/ Environments Supported	DOS 3.1 or higher, OS/2 1.21 or higher, Windows 3.x	DOS 3.1 or higher, OS/2 1.21 or higher	DOS 3.1 or higher, Windows 3.x, OS/2 1.0 or higher	DOS 3.1 or higher, OS/2 1.21 or higher	DOS 3.1 or higher, OS/2 1.1 or higher
Native Languages					
ANSI SQL	Level 1	Level 1	Level 2 with Integrity Enhancement	Level 2 with Integrity Enhancement	Level 2
DB2 SQL Extensions	No	No	Yes	Yes	Yes
Other SQL	Yes	Yes	Yes	No	Yes
Non-SQL	No	No	No	No	No
Maximums					
Database Size	2G	32T	500G	2G	512Mb (DOS), 2G (OS/2)
Column Size	1,962 bytes; IMAGE & TEXT store 2G	1,962 bytes; IMAGE & TEXT store 2G	Limited by disk space. LONG VARCHAR stores 2G	4,000 bytes, or 32,700 char in LONG VARCHAR	4,056 bytes
Row Size	1,962 bytes	1,962 bytes	Limited by disk space	4,005 bytes	32,767 bytes
# of Columns in Row	255	255	250	255	400
# of Rows per Table	Limited by disk space	Limited by disk space	Limited by disk space	Limited by disk space	Limited by disk space
# of Rows per Database	Limited by disk space	Limited by disk space	Limited by disk space	Limited by disk space	Limited by disk space
# of Tables per Database	2 billion	2 billion	Limited by disk space	Limited by disk space	Unlimited
# of Views per Database	Unlimited	Unlimited	Unlimited	Limited by disk space	Unlimited

PRODUCT INFORMATION	PCs (Chapter 4)				
Name	**SQL Server 4.2**	**SQL Server 4.2**	**SQLBase 5.0**	**OS/2 2.0 ES Database Manager**	**XDB-Server 2.41**
# of Tables per View	Unlimited tables, but only 250 columns per view	Unlimited tables, but only 250 columns per view	Unlimited	15	Unlimited, maximum 400 columns

PRODUCT INFORMATION				RISC & UNIX (Chapter 5)	
Name	INGRES for OS/2 6.2	NetWare SQL 3.0 with BTrieve 6.0	ORACLE Server 6.0	INGRES for UNIX and VAX/VMS	ORACLE Server 6.0
Vendor	Ingres Corporation	Novell, Inc.	Oracle Corporation	Ingres Corporation	Oracle Corporation
Price Range	$1,995 plus $495 per user	$795-$5,995	$3,999–$35,999	$1,000 per user	$700–$800 per user
Operating Systems					
On Database Server	OS/2 1.3 or higher	NetWare 3.11	OS/2 2.0, Net-Ware 3.11	30+ versions of UNIX, including AIX, SunOS, AT&T System IV, VAX/VMS	VAX/VMS, DG AOS-VS, IBM MVS and VM, 30+ ver-sions of UNIX, including AIX, SunOS, ULTRIX, and AT&T SV
On LAN Server	MS LAN Man-ager, IBM LAN Server, Net-Ware 3.11, or any network that supports NetBIOS	NetWare 3.11	MS LAN Manager, IBM LAN Server, NetWare 3.11, or any network sup-porting NetBIOS, Named Pipes, DECNet or TCP/IP	Any network that sup-ports TCP/IP or DECNet	Any network that supports APPC, DECNet, or TCP/IP
On Workstations	DOS 3.1 or higher, OS/2 1.3 or higher	DOS 3.1 or higher, Windows 3.x, OS/2 1.2 or higher	DOS 3.1 or higher, OS/2 1.2 or higher	DOS 3.1 or higher, Win-dows 3.x, RISC-based UNIX	DOS 3.1 or higher, OS/2 1.2 or higher, RISC-base UNIX, includ-ing the Motif GUI
Minimum Requirements					
RAM on Server	5Mb	8Mb	8Mb, plus 250k per user	Varies by platform	Varies by platform
RAM on Workstation	2Mb (DOS), 4Mb (OS/2)	640k (DOS), 4Mb (OS/2)	640k (DOS), 4Mb (OS/2)	2Mb (DOS), 4Mb (OS/2), 8Mb (UNIX)	2Mb (DOS), 4Mb (OS/2), 8Mb (UNIX)
Disk Space	10Mb	10Mb	10Mb	Varies by platform	Varies by platform
Utilities Provided					
Administration	Yes	Yes	Yes	Yes	Yes
Interactive User	Yes	Yes	Yes	Yes	Yes

PRODUCT INFORMATION				RISC & UNIX (Chapter 5)	
Name	**INGRES for OS/2 6.2**	**NetWare SQL 3.0 with BTrieve 6.0**	**ORACLE Server 6.0**	**INGRES for UNIX and VAX/VMS**	**ORACLE Server 6.0**
Operating Systems/ Environments Supported	OS/2 1.3 or higher; DOS versions part of client-side package	DOS 3.1 or higher	DOS 3.1 or higher, OS/2 1.2 or higher	UNIX or VAX/VMS; DOS versions part of client-side package	DOS 3.1 or higher, OS/2 1.2 or higher, RISC-base UNIX
Native Languages					
ANSI SQL	Level 1	Level 2 with Integrity Enhancement	Level 2	Level 1	Level 2
DB2 SQL Extensions	Subset	Yes	Yes	Subset	Yes
Other SQL	Yes	No	Yes	Yes	Yes
Non-SQL	Yes, QUEL	No	No	Yes, QUEL	No
Maximums					
Database Size	2G	4G	2G (OS/2), 4G (NLM)	Limited by platform's disk space	Limited by platform's disk space
Column Size	2,000 characters	4,090 bytes; 32k for variable length data	65,535 characters	2,000 characters	65,535 characters
Row Size	2,008 bytes	4,090 bytes	65,535 characters	2,008 bytes	65,535 characters
# of Columns in Row	127	Limited by disk space	254	127	254
# of Rows per Table	8 billion	Limited by disk space	Limited by disk space	Limited by disk space	Limited by disk space
# of Rows per Database	8 billion	Limited by disk space	Limited by disk space	Limited by disk space	Limited by disk space
# of Tables per Database	Unlimited	Limited by disk space	Limited by disk space	Unlimited	Limited by disk space
# of Views per Database	Unlimited	Limited by disk space	Limited by disk space	Unlimited	Limited by disk space
# of Tables per View	Unlimited, maximum 127 columns	8	Unlimited, maximum 254 columns	Unlimited, maximum 127 columns	Unlimited, maximum 254 columns

PRODUCT INFORMATION				Proprietary Mini-computers (Chapter 6)	
Name	**SQL Server 4.2**	**SQLBase 5.0**	**INFORMIX-Online 5.0**	**Rdb/VMS**	**AllBase/SQL**
Vendor	Sybase, Inc.	Gupta Technologies	Informix Software, Inc.	Digital Equipment Corporation (DEC)	Hewlett-Packard Company
Price Range	$300–$600 per user	$995–$9,995	$3,000–$225,000	$2,080–$236,600	$10,000–$48,000
Operating Systems					
On Database Server	VAX/VMS, most major versions of UNIX including AIX, AT&T SV, NeXT MACH, and Sequent Dynix	SunOS 4.1.1 or higher	SunOS 4.1.1 or higher, AT&T System V, HP-UX	DEC VAX/VMS	MPE/XL, HP-UX
On LAN Server	Any network that supports DECNet or TCP/IP	Any network that supports TCP/IP	Any network that supports TCP/IP	DEC PathWorks, or any network that supports DECNet or TCP/IP	Any network that supports TCP/IP
On Workstations	DOS 3.1 or higher, OS/2 1.21 or higher, RISC-base UNIX, including the Open Look and Motif GUIs	DOS 3.1 or higher, Windows 3.x, SunOS 4.1.1 or higher	DOS 3.1 or higher, RISC-based UNIX	PC/MS-DOS, ULTRIX, VMS, Macintosh	DOS 3.1 or higher, Windows 3.x, HP-UX
Minimum Requirements					
RAM on Server	Varies by platform	4Mb	8Mb	Varies by platform	3Mb
RAM on Workstation	512k (DOS), 6Mb (OS/2), 8Mb (UNIX)	640k (DOS), 6Mb (OS/2), 4Mb (SunOS)	640k (DOS), 8Mb (UNIX)	640k (DOS)	640k (DOS), 4Mb (HP-UX)
Disk Space	Varies by platform	10Mb	5Mb	Varies by platform	10Mb
Utilities Provided					
Administration	Yes	Yes	Yes	Yes	Yes (terminal-based)
Interactive User	Yes	Yes	No	Yes	No

PRODUCT INFORMATION				Proprietary Mini-computers (Chapter 6)	
Name	**SQL Server 4.2**	**SQLBase 5.0**	**INFORMIX-Online 5.0**	**Rdb/VMS**	**AllBase/SQL**
Operating Systems/ Environments Supported	DOS 3.1 or higher, OS/2 1.21 or higher, RISC-base UNIX	DOS 3.1 or higher, Windows 3.x, OS/2 1.0 or higher, SunOS 4.1.1 or higher	SunOS 4.1.1 or higher, AT&T System V, HP-UX	PC/MS-DOS, ULTRIX, VMS	HP-UX, MPE/XL
Native Languages					
ANSI SQL	Level 1	Level 2 with Integrity Enhancement	Level 2 with Integrity Enhancement	Level 2 with Integrity Enhancement	Level 2
DB2 SQL Extensions	No	Yes	No	No	No
Other SQL	Yes	Yes	No	No	No
Non-SQL	No	No	No	Yes, RDML	Yes, Image
Maximums					
Database Size	Limited by platform's disk space	Limited by platform's disk space	Limited by platform's disk space	Limited by platform's disk space	Limited by platform's disk space
Column Size	1,962 bytes; IMAGE & TEXT store 2G	Limited by disk space. LONG VARCHAR stores 2G	32,767 bytes; BLOB stores 2G	32,767 bytes; LIST stores 2G	Not available
Row Size	1,962 bytes	Limited by disk space	32,767 bytes	65,271 bytes	Not available
# of Columns in Row	255	250	32,767 (241 BLOBs)	2,000	Not available
# of Rows per Table	Limited by disk space	Limited by disk space	4.278 billion	Limited by disk space	Limited by disk space
# of Rows per Database	Limited by disk space	Limited by disk space	Limited by disk space	Limited by disk space	Limited by disk space
# of Tables per Database	2 billion	Limited by disk space	14.049 million	4,096	Not available
# of Views per Database	Unlimited	Unlimited	Unlimited	4,096	Not available

PRODUCT INFORMATION				Proprietary Mini-computers (Chapter 6)	
Name	**SQL Server 4.2**	**SQLBase 5.0**	**INFORMIX-Online 5.0**	**Rdb/VMS**	**AllBase/SQL**
# of Tables per View	Unlimited, maximum 250 columns	Unlimited	32,000 (# of tables In use)	4,096	Not available

PRODUCT INFORMATION		Mainframes (Chapter 7)		
Name	**SQL/400**	**Database 2 (DB2)**	**SQL/Data Systems (SQL/DS)**	**ORACLE Server 6.0**
Vendor	IBM, Inc.	IBM, Inc.	IBM, Inc.	Oracle Corporation
Price Range	$1,500–$9,000	$113,400–$244,850, plus $3,500–$7,000 monthly fee	$17,470–$230,850, plus $364–$4,810 monthly fee	$103,000–$298,000
Operating Systems				
On Database Server	OS/400	MVS/XA, MVS/ESA	DOS/VSE, VM	MVS, VM, AIX
On LAN Server	IBM LAN Server, or any network that supports APPC, TCP/IP support optional	Any network that supports APPC or an appropriate gateway	Any network that supports APPC or an appropriate gateway	Any network that supports APPC, DECNet, or TCP/IP
On Workstations	OS/2 1.3 EE, OS/2 2.0 ES	OS/2 1.31 or higher with Database Manager, others through a gateway	OS/2 1.31 or higher with Database Manager, others through a gateway	Any operating system supported by ORACLE front-ends
Minimum Requirements				
RAM on Server	8Mb	Varies by platform and number of users	Varies by platform and number of users	Varies by platform and operating system
RAM on Workstation	8Mb (OS/2)	12Mb (OS/2)	12Mb (OS/2)	2Mb (DOS), 4Mb (OS/2), 8Mb (UNIX)
Disk Space	10Mb	Varies by platform	Varies by platform	Varies by platform and operating system
Utilities Provided				
Administration	Yes (terminal-based)	Yes (terminal-based)	Yes (terminal-based)	Yes (terminal-based)
Interactive User	No	No	No	Yes (terminal-based)
Operating Systems/ Environments Supported	OS/2 1.3 EE, OS/2 2.0 ES	MVS, OS/2 1.21 or higher for Database Manager	VM, DOS/VSE; OS/2 1.21 or higher for Database Manager	DOS 3.1 or higher, OS/2 1.2 VM, MVS, any platforms supported by ORACLE front-ends

PRODUCT INFORMATION		Mainframes (Chapter 7)		
Name	**SQL/400**	**Database 2 (DB2)**	**SQL/Data Systems (SQL/DS)**	**ORACLE Server 6.0**
Native Languages				
ANSI SQL	Level 2 with Integrity Enhancement (98% compatible)	Level 2 with Integrity Enhancement	Level 2 with Integrity Enhancement	Level 2
DB2 SQL Extensions	Yes (98% compatible)	Yes	Yes	Yes
Other SQL	No	No	Yes	Yes
Non-SQL	Yes, RPG/400	No	No	No
Maximums				
Database Size	Limited by platform's disk space	Varies by system capacities	Varies by system capacities	Limited by platform's disk space
Column Size	4,000 bytes, or 32,700 characters in LONG VARCHAR	4,056 bytes; 2G in various LONG data types	4,056 bytes; 2G in various LONG data types	65,535 characters
Row Size	4,005 bytes	32,767 bytes	32,767 bytes	65,535 characters
# of Columns in Row	255	750	750	254
# of Rows per Table	Limited by disk space	Limited by disk space	Limited by disk space	Limited by disk space
# of Rows per Database	Limited by disk space	Limited by disk space	Limited by disk space	Limited by disk space
# of Tables per Database	Limited by disk space	Unlimited	Unlimited	Limited by disk space
# of Views per Database	Limited by disk space	Unlimited	Unlimited	Limited by disk space
# of Tables per View	15	Unlimited, maximum 750 columns	Unlimited, maximum 750 columns	Unlimited, maximum 254 columns

■ Appendix B

■ Listing of Vendor Information

The following is an alphabetical list of all the Client/Server vendors mentioned in this book. Each listing includes a representative sampling of the vendor's products. This list is for information purposes only, and the presence or absence of a product or company in no way implies a recommendation or endorsement.

Borland International, Inc.
P.O. Box 660001
1800 Green Hills Road
Scotts Valley, CA 95066-0001
(408) 438-8400
Products: ObjectVision, ObjectVision SQL Connection, Paradox, Paradox SQL Link, dBASE IV Server Edition, dBASE Direct

Channel Computing, Inc.
53 Main Street
Newmarket, NH 03857
(603) 659-2832
Products: Forest & Trees, Forest & Trees for Windows

Clarion Software, Inc.
150 E. Sample Road
Pompano Beach, FL 33064
(305) 785-4555
Products: Professional Clarion

Computer Associates International, Inc.
One Computer Associates Plaza
Islandia, NY 11788-7000
(516) 342-5224
Products: Clipper, Realizer

DataEase International, Inc.
7 Cambridge Drive
Trumbull, CT 06611
(203) 374-8000
Products: DataEase, DataEase SQL Connect

Digital Equipment Corporation (DEC)
146 Main Street
Maynard, MA 01754-2571
(508) 493-5111
Products: VAX/VMS, Rdb/VMS, ULTRIX, DECNet; DECStations, MicroVAX, MiniVAX, and VAX computer systems

Extended Systems
6123 North Meeker Avenue
Boise, ID 83704
(208) 322-7575
Products: ExtendBase

Fusion Systems Group, Ltd.
225 Broadway
24th Floor
New York, NY 10007
(212) 285-8001
Products: Wingz DataLink for Oracle, Wingz DataLink for Sybase

Gupta Technologies, Inc.
1060 Marsh Road
Menlo Park, CA 94025
(415) 321-9500
Products: SQLBase, SQL Windows, Quest

Hewlett-Packard Company
3000 Hanover Street
Palo Alto, CA 94304
(415) 857-1501
Products: AllBase/SQL, AllBase/4GL, AllBase/Query, MPE/XL, HP-UX; Apollo workstations, HP3000 and HP9000 series

IBM Corporation
Old Orchard Road
Armonk, NY 10504
(914) 765-1900
Products: OS/2 2.0, OS/2 2.0 ES Database Manager, DB2, SQL/DS, SQL/400, AIX, MVS/XA, DOS/VSE, PC-DOS; PCs, minicomputers, and mainframes

Information Builders, Inc.
1250 Broadway
New York, NY 10001
(212) 736-4433
Products: EDA/SQL, Focus, PC/Focus

Informix Software, Inc.
4100 Bohannon Drive
Menlo Park, CA 94025
(415) 926-6300
Products: INFORMIX-SE, INFORMIX-OnLine, INFORMIX-OnLine/Secure,
INFORMIX-STAR, INFORMIX-Net, Wingz, Wingz DataLinks

Ingres Corporation
1080 Marina Village Parkway
Alameda, CA 94501-1041
(510) 769-1400
Products: INGRES Server, INGRES/Star, INGRES/Gateway, INGRES/Tools,
INGRES/Net

Lotus Development Corporation
55 Cambridge Parkway
Cambridge, MA 02142
(617) 577-8500
Products: 1-2-3, DataLens Driver for SQL Server

Megabase Systems, Inc.
415 Clyde Avenue
Suite 106
Mountain View, CA 94041
(415) 960-3575
Products: XBase/Server

Micro Decisionware, Inc.
2995 Wilderness Place
Boulder, CO 80301
(303) 443-2706
Products: Database Gateway for DB2, Database Gateway for SQL/DS, Database
Gateway for DBC/1012, PC/SQL-Link

Microsoft Corporation
One Microsoft Way
Redmond, WA 98052-6339
(206) 882-8080
Products: Windows 3.1, MS-DOS 5.0, LAN Manager, MS SQL Server, FoxPro,
Excel, Visual BASIC, MS C 7.0

Novell, Inc.
122 East 1700 South
Provo, UT 84606-6914
(801) 429-7000
Products: NetWare 3.11, NetWare SQL, NetWare BTrieve

Oracle Corporation
500 Oracle Parkway
Redwood Shores, CA 94065
(415) 506-7000
Products: ORACLE Server Version 6.0, ORACLE Card, ORACLE for 1-2-3
DataLens, SQL*Forms, SQL*ReportWriter, SQL*Plus

Pilot Executive Software
40 Broad Street
Boston, MA 02109
(617) 350-7035
Products: LightShip, LightShip Lens

Pioneer Software, Inc.
5540 Centerview Drive
Suite 324
Raleigh, NC 27606
(919) 859-2220
Products: Q+E Database Editor, Q+E Database Library, Q+E Database Library
for Windows, Q+E Database/VB for Windows

PowerSoft Corporation
70 Blanchard Road
Burlington, MA 01803
(617) 229-2200
Products: PowerBuilder for Windows, PowerBuilder DB2 Interface, Powerbuilder
XDB Interface

Quadbase Systems, Inc.
790 Lucerne Drive
Suite 51
Sunnyvale, CA 94086
(408) 738-6989
Products: QuadBase-SQL, QuadBase-Server/NLM

Revelation Technologies, Inc.
181 Harbor Drive
Stamford, CT 06902
(203) 973-1000
Products: Advanced Revelation, DB2 Bond, ORACLE Server Bond, SQL
Server Bond

Sequent Computer Systems, Inc.
15450 S.W. Koll Parkway
Beaverton, OR 97006-6063
(503) 626-5700
Products: Symmetry series multiprocessor superservers

ShareBase Corporation (Subsidiary of Teradata Corp.)
2055A Logic Drive
San Jose, CA 95124
(408) 369-5500
Products: SQL Server/8000 series multiprocessor superservers

Software Publishing Corporation (SPC)
3165 Kifer Road
P.O. Box 54983
Santa Clara, CA 95056-0983
(408) 986-8000
Products: InfoAlliance, Superbase 4, Superbase SQL Library

Sybase, Inc.
6475 Christie Avenue
Emeryville, CA 94608
(800) 879-2273
Products: Sybase SQL Server

Symantec Corporation
10201 Torre Avenue
Cupertino, CA 95014-2132
(408) 253-9600
Products: Q&A

TechGnosis, Inc.
301 Yamato Road
Suite 2200
Boca Raton, FL 33431
(407) 997-6687
Products: SequeLink, SequeLink Engine

XDB Systems, Inc.
14700 Sweitzer Lane
Laurel, MD 20707
(301) 317-6800
Products: XDB-Server, XDB-LINK for DB2, XDB-Workbench for DB2

■ Appendix C

■ Suggestions for Further Reading

The fields of database and network technology are enormously complex and cover a broad range of theories and real-world experience. Though I've tried to present as complete an overview as possible, no one book can cover it all. Here are some suggestions for further reading in the areas of databases, SQL, and local area networks, with a brief description of what's covered in each book or article.

Database Theory

Codd, E.F., "A Relational Model of Data for Large Shared Data Banks," *Communications of the ACM*, Volume 13, No. 6, June 1970. This is Codd's first paper, which laid the groundwork for the Relational model.

Codd, E.F., "Is Your DBMS Really Relational?," *Computerworld*, October 14, 1985; "Does Your DBMS Run by the Rules?," *Computerworld*, October 21, 1985. This two-part article first laid out the now-famous "12 Rules" for determining how closely a DBMS fits the Relational model.

Codd, E.F., "The Relational Model for Database Management, Version 2," Addison-Wesley Publishing Company, July 1990. This book details Codd's latest revision of the Relational model, based on further study and real-world experiences.

Date, C.J., "An Introduction to Database Systems, Volume I, Fifth Edition," Addison-Wesley Publishing Company, February 1991. This book thoroughly covers the entire range of database models and theory. It also contains some interesting discussions on Date's disagreements with Codd over the practicalities of the Relational model. Date is the cofounder of Codd and Date International.

Flores, Ivan, "Data Base Architecture," Van Nostrand Reinhold Company, Inc., 1981. Though somewhat dated and mainframe-oriented, this book has very clear and detailed explanations of the theory behind data management, as well as of the Relational, Hierarchical and Network models.

Pascal, Fabian, "SQL and Relational Basics," M&T Books, 1990. Aimed primarily at PC users, this book provides a detailed explanation of the Relational model through the "12 Rules" plus the basics of SQL. Of particular interest are the chapters that evaluate how well PC-based databases follow the Relational model.

SQL

ANSI, "American National Standard for Information Systems—Database Language—SQL with Integrity Enhancement," Publication ANSI X3.135-1989, American National Standards Institute, October 1989. This ANSI booklet details the latest version of the SQL standard, otherwise known as the ANSI Level 2 with Integrity Enhancement, or ANSI-89, standard. Though it's somewhat dry reading, anyone evaluating a SQL-based RDBMS should have a copy.

Date, C.J., "A Guide to the SQL Standard, Second Edition," Addison-Wesley Publishing Company, 1989. This book translates the ANSI Standards document into a more readable form and provides practical examples.

Hursch, Dr. Carolyn and Dr. Jack, "SQL—Structured Query Language, Second Edition," Windcrest Books, 1991. This book is an advanced and theoretical discussion of SQL. It includes details on some commercial implementations, and what's required to conform them to the standard.

Networks

Derfler, Jr., Frank J., "PC Magazine Guide to Connectivity, Second Edition," Ziff-Davis Press, 1992. Derfler is the senior networking editor for *PC Magazine*. His book is the best available introduction to the subject of PC-based networks.

Derfler, Jr., Frank J., "PC Magazine Guide to Linking LANs," Ziff-Davis Press, 1992. Another excellent book by Derfler that covers the different aspects of using bridges, gateways, and routers to link networks.

■ Glossary

ANSI Level 2 Integrity addendum   The portion of the ANSI Level 2 SQL standard document that describes how referential integrity should be implemented.

ANSI Level 2 with Integrity Enhancement   The current American National Standards Institute (ANSI) standard for the SQL language, issued in 1989. Sometimes referred to as the ANSI-SQL/89 standard; replaced the previous Level 1 version, the ANSI-SQL/86 standard.

application prototyping utility   A type of code generator that assists programmers in designing and testing the screens, reports, etc. for an application before they write the program code. The utility may also contain a code generator, or it may just outline the final application (called a *skeleton code*).

asymmetrical multiprocessing   A multiprocessing system in which each CPU is responsible for a different task. For example, one CPU handles the operating system while another runs the DBMS.

back-end   Common term for the database server or application in a Client/Server system.

bridge   A hardware/software combination connecting two LANs using the same or different topologies and the same network protocol. A bridge simply combines two or more smaller LANs into one large LAN and passes all network traffic through to both parts. Some modern bridges also have the ability to filter network traffic or route different protocols between the individual LANs. Bridges that also have these routing features are usually referred to as bridge/routers or brouters.

bus   The part or subsystem of a computer that connects peripherals to the main CPU. Also known as the data bus.

business rules   SQL statements and commands that enforce a user's rules specifying the values for one or more columns in a database. A business rule's values are usually more restrictive than is the domain of the column. For example, the domain of a salary column may be "$0 to $99,000," but the business rule may restrict the maximum value according to the employee job classification.

character coding   A standard method of translating characters such as alphabetical letters, numbers, and symbols into a binary code for storage and manipulation on a computer. The two current standards are ASCII and EBCDIC.

Client/Server database   A database system in which the database engine and database applications reside on separate intelligent computers that communicate with each other through a network. In this system, the processing power is split between the two CPUs. The user's workstation is the client, and the DBMS runs on the server.

clustered index   A method of indexing a database, in which the data in a table is physically arranged on the disk to closely match the index order. Reduces delay in accessing data from large tables.

clustering   The linking of two or more DEC VAX/VMS systems to automatically share CPUs and resources and to create a larger computer complex. The linked computers appear as one system to users.

coaxial cable   An electrical networking cable that has an insulated center core surrounded by an exterior braid and additional layers of insulation. Cable TV systems' cabling is a familiar example.

code generator   An application development tool (usually menu-driven) that helps users create DBMS applications without writing programming code. Users lay out the steps they want an application to take, and the code generator writes the code that carries out those steps.

cost-based optimization   An advanced method of optimizing SQL statements before execution. In a cost-based system, the DBMS analyzes the amount of CPU time and resources needed to fulfill a particular SQL statement using various methods. The DBMS then determines the "least costly" method and executes the statement accordingly.

daisy chain   A network topology, usually thin Ethernet, in which the cable runs from node to node of the network in a chain-like configuration.

data compression   Reduces the size of data packets for storage or transmission, using one of a number of methods. A compression algorithm shrinks the data to the smallest size possible without losing or damaging it.

data integrity (DI)   The overall guiding principle behind the Relational model and the specific sections of the model that define how the database protects the data it contains, and how it prevents inadvertent or unexpected modifications or damage to that data.

data integrity rules   The SQL statements or commands in a particular RDBMS that provide DI services.

data redundancy   The duplication of data in a database or application. Undesirable within a single database because data redundancy decreases available disk storage space and usually slows down data access. Desirable when duplicating an entire database on a different device in order to provide backup and database integrity services. This type of data redundancy is also known as fault tolerance.

database   A set of information, defined by the user's criteria, that is electronically organized, stored, accessed, and updated.

database administrator (DBA)   The technical support person who typically assigns user IDs and data access permissions, creates new databases, removes databases no longer in use, and monitors the database's disk storage usage and performance.

database application   A computer program designed to provide user access to the data in a DBMS, through data entry forms, query forms, and reports.

database dictionary   A specific type of system table that stores information about the structure of a particular database. Primarily used in relational DBMSs to store the names and data types of the tables and columns in a database.

database engine   The portion of a DBMS that stores and manipulates the data according to commands issued from a database application.

database integrity (DI)   The general theory of protecting and preserving data in a database that is realized in particular hardware and/or software methods. Database integrity may be implemented by the DBMS itself, or through administrator intervention, such as tape backups.

database management system (DBMS)   A computer application designed for the specific purpose of collecting and storing data. It always includes a database engine and may include an application programming language or interface for users to create applications.

database server   A computer in a Client/Server system that primarily runs the DBMS and processes user queries.

declarative referential integrity   The most advanced type of referential integrity (RI), which requires that rules for handling deletions be declared in the table definition, instead of being implemented through stored or precompiled SQL procedures by the application programmer.

disk duplexing   A method of providing database integrity whereby the application or platform automatically writes the data to two different disks on the same controller at the same time. If the primary disk fails, the system automatically switches to the duplexed disk and continues operating. Duplexing provides no protection against failure of the controller card.

disk mirroring   A method of providing database integrity whereby the application or platform automatically writes the data to two different disks on two different controller cards at the same time. If one disk or card fails, the system automatically switches to the mirror disk and continues operating.

distributed database   A database that resides on two or more servers, yet appears to users as a single large database.

distributed database communications   The means by which two or more databases pass queries or data between themselves.

distributed database dictionary   A database dictionary that is stored on two or more database servers and is automatically updated when any changes are made to any of the databases associated with it.

distributed processing   A method of sharing application processing between two or more computer systems. Client/Server databases are a basic form of distributed processing.

distributed query optimization   A method of SQL command optimization designed to speed queries on distributed databases.

distributed transactions   Database transactions that are split between two or more databases in a distributed system. All portions of the transaction must be successfully completed before the whole transaction can be considered successful.

domain (data domain)   The permitted range or set of values of a particular data item in a particular field or column. For example, the domain of a column of last names could be, "Words containing the characters A to Z in upper- and lowercase."

domain integrity   A principle of the Relational model that governs how the DBMS ensures that each value in a column fits in the domain of the column.

downsizing   A computer industry buzzword that describes the process of moving applications from large systems (usually mainframes) to smaller, less expensive systems (usually PCs or superservers).

dynamic optimization   A type of SQL statement optimization developed by DEC for their Rdb/VMS DBMS. It dynamically changes the type of search it performs on a table based on information or statistics gathered while performing the query.

encrypted file storage   A method of coding a file to prevent access by those who don't have the proper password or decoding "key."

Enhanced Industry Standard Architecture (EISA)   A 32-bit data bus developed as an enhancement to the ISA bus and an alternative to the MCA bus. The EISA bus is backward-compatible with ISA cards.

entity integrity   A term used by some DBMS vendors to refer to domain integrity.

fiber-optic cable   Networking cable that consists of one or more clear fiber threads inside a protective insulator. Fiber-optic cables use intense light or lasers instead of electrical currents to transmit the signal. Fiber-optics suffer less from signal strength loss than do electrical cables and are generally immune to outside interference.

field   One specific piece of information or item of a database, such as a manufacturer's part number or an employee's Social Security Number; referred to as a column in the Relational model.

file server   A computer (usually a PC) that provides the primary shared resources on a LAN that can be used by all the workstations or nodes on the LAN. Shared resources usually include hard-disk space and printers.

forms-based development tool   An application development tool that lets the programmer develop user interface screens by painting a data entry form on the screen.

fourth generation language (4GL)   An advanced computer programming language designed for creating a particular type of application, such as a database application. Examples of 4GLs include SQL and the dBASE-compatible programming languages.

front-end application   An application that runs on a client system and is designed primarily to serve as an interface between a database user and the database itself.

front-end processor (FEP)   A hardware system that handles communications with non-standard devices, usually for a mainframe. The FEP is primarily used for dial-in access through modems and LAN attachments.

gateway systems   A hardware and software system used to link two or more networks that use different protocols. Gateways are usually used to link PC-based LANs to a mainframe.

Graphical User Interface (GUI)   A general term used to define a class of operating systems or operating environments that base their user interface on graphics instead of text. Examples include Windows 3.1, OS/2 2.0's Workplace Shell, and the interface on the Apple Macintosh.

hard-disk subsystem The combination of one or more hard disks and the controller card that connects them to the rest of the computer.

hashed clustered index Hashing is a method of creating a smaller index by substituting binary values for common elements in the index. A hashed clustered index combines a hashed index with clustered data.

host Another term for a central computer system, such as a minicomputer or mainframe, that runs all the user and database applications. Users generally communicate with the host through terminals.

index A method used to speed up access to individual data items by creating a separate construct that only contains information on one or more fields in the database, sorted in a user-defined order. The index is searched, and a pointer leads the DBMS or application to the particular record the index refers to.

index file Some DBMSs store the index as a separate file on the disk, instead of storing it as part of the file that holds the database's records.

index pointer A programming construct that's included in the index. It's used by the DBMS to find the particular data record on the disk that the indexed item refers to.

Industry Standard Architecture (ISA) A term used to describe the data bus pioneered by IBM in the PC-AT systems, that has since become the standard 16-bit bus in the industry.

Information Warehouse IBM's marketing term for their concept of a distributed processing system in which data can be stored on and accessed from any computer on a network.

interface card A hardware card that plugs into a PC's bus and connects the CPU to peripheral devices. Examples include the disk interface card (commonly called the disk controller) for connecting the CPU to the hard disks, and a parallel interface card for connecting the PC to a printer.

interprocess communications Data communications among different processes running on the same computer system. A process can be a user application, a system function, or even different functions within the same application.

leaf In the Hierarchical model, a leaf is the very last data node on the lowest level of a database tree.

library   A collection of programming routines that can be included in custom-written applications to provide specific functions, or to speed the process of application development.

local area network (LAN)   A combination of hardware (such as interface cards and cabling) and software that lets two or more computers (usually PCs) communicate with each other to share resources.

Location Independence   An IBM term distinguishing the ability of DB2 users to access data residing in any accessible database that can participate in the Information Warehouse concept, regardless of the database system's location on the network.

Management Information Systems (MIS)   The usual name of the corporate department in charge of supporting computer resources. Sometimes shortened to Information Systems (IS).

MicroChannel Architecture (MCA)   A 32-bit data bus invented by IBM for their third-generation microcomputers (the PS/2 series). MCA was developed to enhance and replace the ISA bus and is not backward-compatible with ISA cards.

motherboard   A generic term that describes the primary circuit board in a computer. The motherboard usually contains the support circuitry for the CPU, external ports, and data bus.

multiprocessing system   A computer system with two or more CPUs that share processing duties.

multitasking operating system   An operating system designed to perform one or more computer tasks, such as running different applications, at the same time. OS/2, Windows/NT, and UNIX are examples.

multithreaded operating systems   A type of multitasking operating system that supports threads of execution which let applications multitask within themselves. OS/2 and Windows/NT are examples.

multiuser operating system   An operating system designed for running applications that are accessed by multiple users simultaneously through terminals and that are usually run on minicomputers and mainframes. UNIX, VAX/VMS, and IBM's MVS are examples.

NetWare Loadable Module (NLM)   A program or application that executes on a file server running under the Novell NetWare 3.11 and higher LAN operating system.

network administrator   The technical support person responsible for maintaining the network. Usual administration tasks include assigning network user IDs, monitoring disk space and network traffic, and ensuring network backups are performed properly.

Network Interface Card (NIC)   An interface card designed to attach a PC to a LAN through the PC's bus. Software drivers that tell the PC how to "talk" to the card and the network are usually provided with the card or with the network software.

network topology   The cabling scheme used for a computer network, consisting of the type of cables and the way the cables are interconnected. Ethernet and Token Ring are two types of network topologies.

network traffic   The amount of data that passes through a network during an arbitrary period of time. The traffic indicates the network's workload versus its capacity.

node   In the Hierarchical and Network models, another term for a particular data item or field. Node is also used in networking to describe a single computer on the network.

normalization   Used in the Relational model to describe the process of designing a database's structure to reduce the amount of duplicated data.

off-the-shelf software   A generic term used to describe any commercial software package that can be purchased in a software store or by mail order; distinct from those applications that are custom-written for a single company or industry.

one-to-many relationship   A term from database theory that identifies the structure of the relationship between one data item and multiple different data items. For example, a department supervisor has a one-to-many relationship with the employees in the department.

one-to-one relationship   A term from database theory that identifies the structure of the relationship between a data item that only relates to one other data item. For example, there's a one-to-one relationship between an employee's name and Social Security Number.

open systems   Refers to operating systems that will run on any of a class of computer hardware, regardless of vendor. PC/MS-DOS, OS/2, and UNIX are examples of open systems.

parallel-processing system   An advanced form of multiprocessing in which a task is divided among different CPUs for processing. Each CPU handles a portion of the computations, and the final result is derived by combining all the separate calculations.

parent-child relationship   A database term that defines how two pieces of data relate to or depend on each other in a particular database. A child record contains data that's also contained in the parent record.

platform   A general term that refers to the hardware/software combination that a particular application runs on. Specifically, the platform consists of the computer hardware and operating system.

plug compatible   A term used to describe third-party hardware systems that are compatible with IBM mainframes. Called *plug compatible* because they use the same input/output plugs as IBM hardware.

population   A term that describes the specific group of information contained in the database. For example, the population of an employee database is "All the people who work for the company."

POSIX   A U.S. Federal Government standard for computer operating systems sharing the same Application Programming Interface (API). The goal of POSIX is to allow programmers to write one application that can then be compiled and run on any POSIX-compliant system.

precompiled procedure   An SQL procedure that's compiled and stored on the same computer system as the DBMS and that can be used by any application accessing the database. Unlike a stored procedure, it's not part of a particular database. Precompiled procedures are executed on the client system instead of the server.

preoptimized procedure   A precompiled or stored procedure that's optimized prior to use. Preoptimization saves CPU time and increases DBMS performance by eliminating the need to optimize a statement each time it's executed by a client application.

program analyst   A senior applications programmer who determines the end-user's application needs and designs the program to fill those needs. The analyst then gives the design to the application programmers for development.

proprietary operating systems   Computer operating systems designed to run only on a specific vendor's hardware. Digital Equipment Corporation's VAX/VMS is an example of a proprietary operating system.

record   A record is comprised of all the fields that contain information about a particular individual item in a database; also referred to as a row in the Relational model.

Reduced Instruction Set Computer (RISC)   A type of CPU designed to perform high-speed processing by reducing the number of internal instructions the CPU must process to carry out a computation task. RISC CPUs are usually found in UNIX-based workstations and superservers.

referential integrity (RI)   A principle of the Relational model. Referential integrity is the part of data integrity that specifies how the DBMS should respond to a user's attempt to delete a parent row (record) in one table that has dependent (child) rows in another table. A proper implementation of RI ensures that child rows are never orphaned.

referential integrity rules   The SQL statements or commands in a particular RDBMS that provide RI services.

report writer   An application or application development tool primarily designed to assist the user or programmer in creating reports from a database. Report writers usually let the user or programmer create the report layout by painting it on the screen.

router   A hardware/software combination that joins two or more LANs. A router can link LANs using different topologies and protocols. Routers also reduce network traffic by only passing the data destined for the interconnected LAN(s), while filtering out data that should remain on the source LAN.

scalability   The characteristic of applications or databases that run on multiple platforms of varying sizes; for example, an ORACLE database can run on a PC or a VAX.

scrollable cursor   A SQL construct that allows the user to browse forward and backward through all the data returned in response to a query, instead of receiving and viewing the query results one row at a time.

sibling relationship   The characteristic of two or more pieces of information that are related to one another and are equal in importance. It's another way of describing the fields in a record; for example, the name, address, and phone number of an employee are each in sibling relationships with one another and with any data describing that employee.

Small Computer Standard Interface (SCSI)   A standard method for connecting data peripherals to a microcomputer, usually used for storage devices such as disks, tape drives, and CD-ROMs.

star configuration   A type of network topology in which the cables that connect the nodes to the network emanate from a central hub, with one cable per node. Sometimes referred to as a "hub-and-star" configuration.

stored procedures   SQL procedures that are stored as part of the database and executed entirely on the back-end system. Using stored procedures allows more of the database processing to be moved from the client to the server.

supercomputers   High-speed, high-powered computers predominantly used for intense scientific calculations, such as weather predictions and engineering design.

symmetrical multiprocessing (SMP)   A multiprocessing system in which processing tasks are divided between various CPUs. Each new task is routed to the CPU with the lowest workload at the time of processing.

syntax-based optimization   The original method of optimizing SQL statements whereby the DBMS analyzes the commands for the most logical order of executing them, without regard to the CPU time and resources needed. Syntax-based optimizers are generally slower and more resource-intensive than cost-based optimizers.

system tables   A special database used by some DBMSs to store information about the whole database system; for example, it identifies which individual databases are contained in the system and records user security access information. Primarily used in DBMSs that follow the Relational model.

terminal controllers   A hardware subsystem that handles the communications between terminals and the central host. Usually used with minicomputers and mainframes, a terminal controller can connect up to 64 terminals to the host through a single host connection.

terminal, dumb   A dedicated system connected to a central host that typically consists of only a display screen and keyboard. It sends keystrokes to the host and displays the screen information sent back from the host.

terminal, intelligent   A type of terminal connected to a central computer host that has its own CPU for handling some of the processing, such as screen drawing and network communications; it may or may not be a dedicated system. A PC is an example of an intelligent terminal when it's connected via a specialized peripheral board to a mainframe.

third generation language (3GL)   A general-purpose computer programming language used to create any type of application. Examples of 3GLs include BASIC, COBOL, C, and Pascal.

third-party add-on   A hardware or software product developed by one vendor to work with and enhance another vendor's product.

thread   A process within an application that carries out a particular operation or task. Single-threaded applications can only do one task at a time. Multithreaded applications can do multiple tasks at the same time, such as sorting a database while printing a report. The ability to perform multiple threads within an application is usually provided by the operating system.

transaction recovery logs   Log files maintained by a DBMS that keep a record of every recent transaction performed on a database. Provides data integrity services when a transaction fails or the system crashes by helping the DBMS return the database to a consistent state. Often, simply referred to as the *transaction logs*.

triggers   A particular type of stored procedure that is automatically executed when certain SQL commands (usually those that modify the data) are issued. Called *rules* by some vendors, triggers usually implement referential integrity (RI) in systems that don't support declarative RI.

twisted-pair cable   Electrical network cable consisting of two or more pieces of insulated wire twisted together and covered with one or more insulation layers. Round telephone wire is a familiar example.

two-phase commit   A form of transaction processing on multiple databases (or multiple tables within a database) that ensures that modifications made to every database involved in a transaction are successful before the transaction itself is considered successful.

upsizing   Moving an application from a smaller system to a larger one as the need for disk storage space and processing power grows. Usually refers to moving a PC-based database to a UNIX-based superserver.

user-transparent   A characteristic of systems in which data processing actions are taken without the user either being aware of them or manually performing them. For example, a user sends a query to a local database server, and the server automatically passes the query on to another server where the data actually resides but the user is unaware of the transfer.

virtual memory (VM)   A method whereby an operating system swaps inactive data and code to available disk space, freeing up working RAM for active applications. The data and code is swapped to the disk in *pages* (the size of the page is dependent on the CPU), so the process is sometimes referred to as virtual memory paging, or simply paging. OS/2 and UNIX are examples of operating systems that use virtual memory.

wide area network (WAN)   A network that connects computer systems from more than one building. A WAN generally consists of one or more LANs in separate locations that are interconnected with each other directly or through a central host.

■ Index

Make Your Best Connection with the Database Server Decision Tree

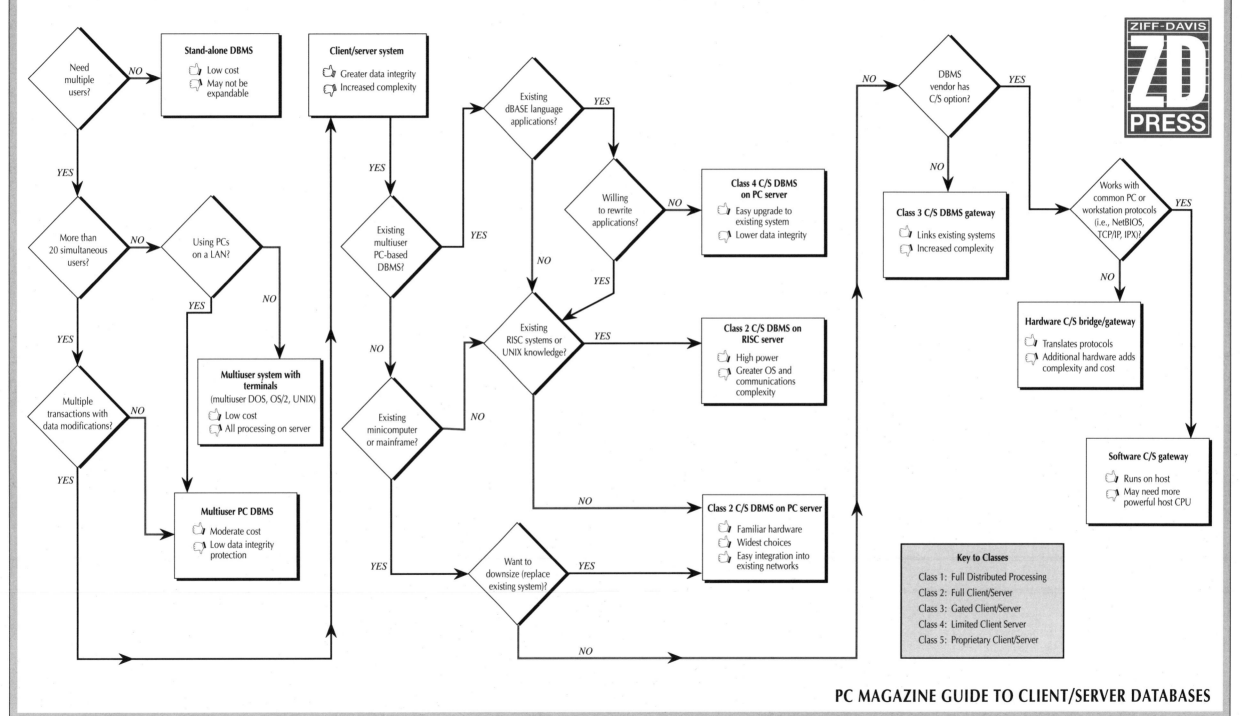

ZIFF-DAVIS ZD PRESS

Stand-alone DBMS
- 👍 Low cost
- 👎 May not be expandable

Client/server system
- 👍 Greater data integrity
- 👎 Increased complexity

Need multiple users?

More than 20 simultaneous users?

Multiple transactions with data modifications?

Using PCs on a LAN?

Multiuser system with terminals
(multiuser DOS, OS/2, UNIX)
- 👍 Low cost
- 👎 All processing on server

Multiuser PC DBMS
- 👍 Moderate cost
- 👎 Low data integrity protection

Existing multiuser PC-based DBMS?

Existing minicomputer or mainframe?

Existing dBASE language applications?

Willing to rewrite applications?

Existing RISC systems or UNIX knowledge?

Want to downsize (replace existing system)?

Class 4 C/S DBMS on PC server
- 👍 Easy upgrade to existing system
- 👎 Lower data integrity

Class 2 C/S DBMS on RISC server
- 👍 High power
- 👎 Greater OS and communications complexity

Class 2 C/S DBMS on PC server
- 👍 Familiar hardware
- 👍 Widest choices
- 👍 Easy integration into existing networks

DBMS vendor has C/S option?

Class 3 C/S DBMS gateway
- 👍 Links existing systems
- 👎 Increased complexity

Works with common PC or workstation protocols (i.e., NetBIOS, TCP/IP, IPX)?

Hardware C/S bridge/gateway
- 👍 Translates protocols
- 👎 Additional hardware adds complexity and cost

Software C/S gateway
- 👍 Runs on host
- 👎 May need more powerful host CPU

Key to Classes

Class 1: Full Distributed Processing
Class 2: Full Client/Server
Class 3: Gated Client/Server
Class 4: Limited Client Server
Class 5: Proprietary Client/Server

PC MAGAZINE GUIDE TO CLIENT/SERVER DATABASES